LINCOLN
AND THE
SIOUX
UPRISING
OF 1862

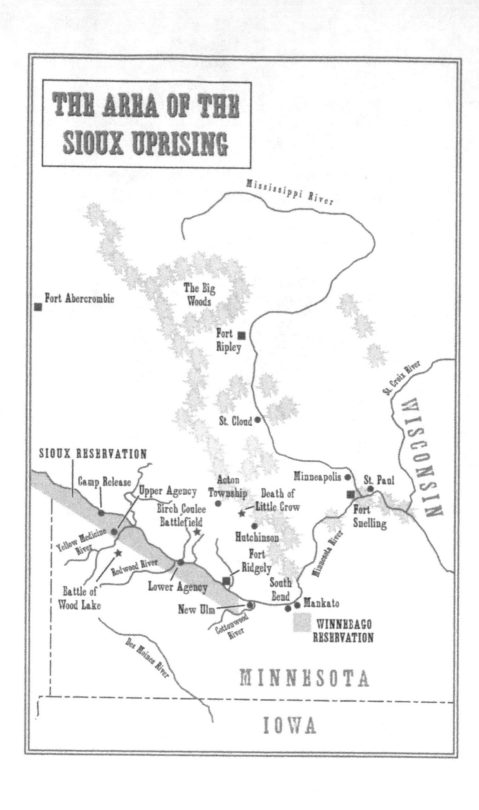

LINCOLN
AND THE
SIOUX
UPRISING
OF 1862

HANK H. COX

CUMBERLAND HOUSE
NASHVILLE, TENNESSEE

LINCOLN AND THE SIOUX UPRISING OF 1862
PUBLISHED BY CUMBERLAND HOUSE PUBLISHING, INC.
431 Harding Industrial Drive
Nashville, Tennessee 37211

Cover design by Gore Studio, Nashville, Tennessee

Library of Congress Cataloging-in-Publication Data

Cox, Hank H., 1945–
  Lincoln and the Sioux uprising of 1862 / Hank H. Cox.
       p.   cm.
  Includes bibliographical references and index.
  ISBN 1-58182-457-2 (pbk. : alk. paper)
  1. Lincoln, Abraham, 1809–1865—Relations with Dakota Indians. 2. Dakota Indians—Wars, 1862–1865. 3. Dakota Indians—Government relations. 4. United States—Politics and government—1861–1865. I. Title.
E83.86.C78 2005
973.7—dc22   2005008478

1 2 3 4 5 6 7 8 9 10—09 08 07 06 05

To
PROFESSOR SIMON D. PERRY
Marshall University
A great teacher

CONTENTS

INTRODUCTION

T HE GREAT FIRE IN Peshtigo, Wisconsin, of October 8, 1871, was one of the most deadly and destructive disasters in U.S. history. At least fifteen hundred people were killed—probably many more—and tens of thousands injured and left homeless. But few Americans know of this event because it happened on the same day as a lesser conflagration in Chicago in which perhaps three hundred people lost their lives, and that event has since become a staple of American folklore. Why everyone knows about the Chicago fire but not the much bigger one in Peshtigo is an accident of location and timing. Chicago was a major rail hub and economic center; Peshtigo was well off the beaten path and not a familiar name to most Americans. And in the nineteenth century, as in the present time, the news media could only handle one big story at a time. Thus the story of our nation's greatest fire calamity has been largely lost to history (if not to the people of Peshtigo).

Similarly, the great Sioux uprising of August 1862 in southwest Minnesota was the bloodiest event in the long and bloody history of warfare between white immigrants and Native Americans. It led to the largest public execution in the history of North America. The uprising marked the beginning of twenty-eight years of intermittent warfare with the Sioux, culminating in the massacre at Wounded Knee in 1890. Also, as I suggest in this work, it likely featured the largest and most prolonged gang rape in the history of this continent.

But like the Peshtigo fire, this seminal event of American history is largely unknown to the great majority of citizens because of location and timing. The events took place on what was then a remote frontier and against the backdrop of the Civil War. From the time of the first outbreak of violence in mid-August until the mass execution carried out the day after Christmas, the nation's news outlets struggled to keep tabs on the battles of Second Bull Run (Manassas) and Antietam, the Emancipation Proclamation, President Lincoln's suspension of habeas corpus, and the battle of Fredericksburg—not to mention a host of other less prominent crises attending the war between the states. The Sioux uprising was simply lost amid that news. I have found that even among people who take an avid interest in American history there is scant knowledge of this great upheaval.

My own attention to this story was kindled by a short passage in David Herbert Donald's *Lincoln,* a superb one-volume biography of the sixteenth president published in 1995. Donald is a prominent Lincoln scholar and a gifted writer. I and many others have come to a greater understanding of Lincoln and his era through his inspired work. In his 1995 book Donald devoted perhaps three pages to Lincoln's intervention in the Sioux war, and it was this brief reference that caught my interest. I thought it embarrassing that over a lifetime I could have read so many books devoted to American history in general, and to Lincoln and the Civil War in particular, and never encountered this remarkable story.

I retraced some of my steps to see if the fault lay in my cognitive powers, but though I perceive a very real erosion of my mental capacity that attends the aging process, in this case the fault was not mine, or at least not wholly mine. For example, James M. McPherson's wonderful one-volume history of the Civil War, *Battle Cry of Freedom: The Civil War Era* (1988), includes no specific reference to the Sioux war, only a throwaway comment that after the battle of Second Bull Run, Gen. John Pope was sent off to the frontier to fight Indians. I dug out Gore Vidal's *Lincoln* (1976), which was one of the first modern semihistorical works to debunk some of the more hagiographical myths that had grown up around Lincoln. Vidal knows history intimately, and in that book he did a masterful job portraying Lincoln as a wily political operative. I have drawn some of my understanding of Lincoln from Vidal's work, particularly with regard to his personal life, but nothing at all about Lincoln's solicitude for the Sioux. Vidal is a great writer but not always forthright. He did not even mention the Sioux in passing, presumably because the story did not abet his effort to debunk the great man in Washington.

After extensive research, I concluded that the Sioux uprising is an important story that has slipped past our collective memory. To be sure, there have been books about the uprising, but I had to root them out of musty corners of the Library of Congress or track them down via the Internet. In each case the author treated the Sioux war as a discrete event, mentioning the Civil War only as a backdrop. There are, of course, thousands of books about Lincoln, but few of them refer to the Sioux uprising as anything other than a sideshow, that is, if they mention it at all.

It would be absurd to claim I have reviewed all of the books and articles written about Abraham Lincoln. I may well have missed some that offered in-depth treatment of this subject, and to those authors, I apologize. However, I believe I can safely assert that most of the Civil War and Lincoln books I have read, and I have read many over my three score years, either ignore the Sioux war or mention it only in passing.

One excellent exception is *Lincoln and the Indians* by David Nichols (2000) that examines in detail Lincoln's policies toward the various tribes and devotes a full chapter to the president's handling of the Sioux uprising. But even here I felt that Nichols, while acknowledging that Lincoln had other matters on his mind, did not quite grasp the weight that was on the president's shoulders and did not put the Sioux story in its context. Nichols does offer a compelling description of the corrupt Indian system that Lincoln inherited and the ruthless pressure he was under, after the uprising was suppressed, to authorize wholesale executions of Sioux. I am indebted to Nichols for much of my understanding of the events described herein, but his story is not mine.

This work is a study of what I consider Abraham Lincoln's finest hour. At a time when he seemed to be physically bending under the weight of his responsibility, and he confessed to his cabinet that he was almost ready to hang himself, he took a terrible political risk on behalf of a despised people, knowing it would bring him no advantage, indeed knowing it could cause him and his cause irreparable harm. I believe this incident, more than any other, defines the character of our most remarkable president.

LINCOLN
AND THE
SIOUX
UPRISING
OF 1862

1

THE DOGS
OF WAR

On the bright Sunday morning of August 17, 1862, four Indians emerged from the Big Woods area northwest of St. Paul, Minnesota, trudging toward their homes some forty miles to the southwest. The Big Woods was primeval forest where Indians had hunted game since time immemorial, but game was increasingly hard to come by. These four Indians were young men in their prime, none more than thirty years of age. They had been hunting for ducks but were returning empty-handed, footsore, and hungry. They were all related to each other as brothers, half brothers, or cousins and belonged to a village in the vicinity of Rice Creek led by a minor Sioux chief, Red Middle Voice. Two of them were dressed in pants and shirts like white men, the others in loincloths and blankets like Indians, reflecting the bifurcated culture in which they lived. One of them wore two feathers in his headdress and another wore one. The feathers denoted prowess in battle and could have been won by killing an enemy, taking a scalp, or some other deed deemed worthy by Sioux culture. By all accounts the four young men were not looking for trouble that day, merely making their way home from an unsuccessful hunt.

In 1862 Minnesota *was* the western frontier. It was a sparsely settled country of rolling hills and lush green forests interspersed with a few farms and villages, some consisting of log cabins and clapboard houses of white settlers, others of tepees made from animal hides by indigenous peoples. Here and there houses and tepees existed side by side. The few roads were little more than dirt tracks, and telegraph lines had only recently reached the capital city of St. Paul on the shore of the Mississippi River. But there was no telegraph service in the southwest quadrant of the state.

To the west of the Minnesota frontier lay the rolling prairies of the Dakotas—endless grasslands stretching all the way to the Rocky Mountains. Few white people had visited there. To most Americans it was terra incognita, a vast wilderness where herds of countless buffalo darkened the plains as far as the eye could see, where wildly painted savages roamed with impunity, and the sky and the land reached tentatively for the horizon in a lazy embrace.

Scarcely four years before, Minnesota had entered the Union as a free state in an era of bitter debates about the delicate balance between free and slave states. The state was still raw country in the early stages of transition from wilderness to civilization, its deep, rich soil and ample rain beckoning landless farmers to put down roots where any man, no matter how humble his belongings, could aspire to independence and worldly wealth. The area represented for many the pot of gold at the end of the rainbow. For pennies an acre, anyone could claim a substantial block of promising farmland more than sufficient to feed a growing family and foster dreams of a more prosperous future. People were coming by the thousands to seize the opportunity that seemed almost unimaginable. The vast majority of settlers were zealous pioneers eager to get to work. They soon fell to building cabins and barns, erecting fences, and raising crops and livestock.

Some were people from eastern states, people who for one reason or another had been unable to establish themselves and, like their fathers before them, looked to the west for fresh opportunities. Others were from the vast cacophony of baronies and duchies of Northern Europe that would soon be known as Germany. They had mortgaged their meager possessions to fund a scary trip across the ocean on a creaky sailing vessel to a mystical place where arable land was said to be free for the taking and no man need bend his knee to arrogant aristocrats. These emigrants were struggling to learn a new language as they worked dawn to dusk, clearing trees and plowing the rich loam that had lain undisturbed for countless millennia. It did not take them long to realize what they had. The land was bountiful and replete with rivers and creeks unafflicted by drought. Winter came early, and the growing season was short, but that was nothing new to people from Northern Europe. It was immediately clear to them that any farmer with a bent for hard work could expect to prosper in Minnesota, and so they went to work with a vengeance. And they wrote letters home encouraging others to come.

In short order the trickle of pioneers quickened and became a flood. In 1850, when Minnesota had been a territory for a year, it had a white population of about six thousand and more than twice as many Indians, but even then the ratio was beginning to turn. St. Paul—then known as the hamlet of Pig's Eye—grew from a population of ten whites in 1846 to more than ten thousand by 1856. Across the river the new town of Minneapolis grew from nothing to a town of several hundred.

Where incoming settlers saw rich land inhabited by a few primitive savages, the resident tribes saw an invasion by an alien race that affronted their cultures at every turn. The conquest of North America by European transients had begun three centuries before, but only recently had they come in force to the Minnesota country of the scattered bands of Winnebagos, Chippewa, Ojibwas, and Sioux. The dominant tribe was the Sioux, sometimes called Dakotas, who for centuries had controlled the area between the Great Lakes and the Rocky Mountains north of the Platte River. Like countless eastern tribes before them, they were at once mesmerized by the wealth and power of the newcomers and abased by countless humiliations that became their daily fare as the whites established farms and villages on ancestral land the tribes had always assumed was their own. Government agents and traders routinely cheated the Indians and tempted them to vices while earnest missionaries pleaded with them to convert to Christianity, become farmers, and adopt the white man's way of life.

The native peoples were slow to recognize the shift in their fortunes because it was such a gradual process. Previous generations of Sioux had known white men, when they knew them at all, as trappers and traders who came and went, swapping guns and pots for animal skins, introducing liquor and syphilis to the tribes. The trappers and traders sometimes lived among the Indians, learned the Indians' languages, married Indian women, and adopted Indian ways. Sometimes the trappers and traders and the Indians came to deadly blows, but the whites did not fundamentally challenge the Indians' way of life. And by

1862 there was a substantial population of bilingual half-breeds who were both Indian and white and of uncertain loyalty to either.

Unlike the traders and trappers, however, the new settlers did not come and go, nor did they assimilate into Indian culture. They came in a steady flood that pushed the Indians ever backward, squeezing them into narrow confines. When the tribes protested this uprooting and threatened armed resistance, the government of the white settlers sent negotiators to buy them off. In July 1851 the northern Sioux bands ceded to the United States their lands in southern and western Minnesota (which was then a territory) for the seemingly munificent sum of $1,665,000 in cash and annuities. Two weeks later the southern Sioux signed away most of the southeast quarter of the Minnesota Territory for $1,410,000 in cash and annuities, which the treaty stipulated was to be paid out over fifty years.

All in all, the Sioux signed over almost 24 million acres of rich land that was opened to white settlement in 1854. The Indians were assigned a reservation along the upper Minnesota River some 150 miles long and 20 miles wide, extending 10 miles on each side of the river. For the some 7,000 resident Sioux who had always regarded the world as their domain and who relied upon wild game for most of their protein, it was a narrow confine that had no historical or cultural context. The U.S. government set up two administrative centers to handle the Indians' affairs, the Upper Agency (or Yellow Medicine) and the Lower Agency (Redwood).

In 1858 the Sioux were conned into selling the northern half of their remaining territory for thirty cents an acre, adding $266,880 to their total recompense but limiting their range even further. After all that they were still left with about a million acres of prime farmland that would have been sufficient had the Indians been inclined to agriculture. And the treaties of 1851 and 1858 included provisions intended to encourage the Indians to become farmers like their new white neighbors. Any Indian willing to make a go of farming would inherit eighty acres of arable bottom land and the basic tools of farming at government expense. But despite many years of entreaties and persuasion by government agents and missionaries, few Indians—perhaps one in ten—endeavored to do so. The majority of Indians remained what were called "Blanket Indians" wedded to the old ways of hunting and fishing. They derided the few farmer Indians as "Cut Hairs" and "Breeches Indians." Not surprisingly, many of the Blanket Indians, such as the four young warriors on their way back from the Big Woods on that sunny August morning, continued to come and go as they pleased, oblivious to any alien notion of property rights.

The English translation of the names of the four Indians making their way homeward that day were Brown Wing, Breaking Up, Killing Ghost, and Runs Against Something When Crawling. Around midday they came to the homestead of Robinson Jones in Acton Township of western Meeker County, about three miles from the present Grove City. The Indians were familiar with Jones, who, with his wife, managed a small enterprise embracing post office, inn, and store—a not uncommon enterprise on the frontier. On Jones's property near the road the four espied a hen's nest with eggs. One of the young men scooped them up greedily. Another Indian warned him to leave the eggs alone, that they belonged to the white man, who would make trouble. As recounted later by Chief Big Eagle, this made the first Indian angry.

"You are a coward," he allegedly retorted. "You are afraid of the white man. You are afraid to take even an egg from him though you are half-starved."

Such words are provocative to any young man of any culture. "I am not a coward," said the one. "I am not afraid of the white man, and to show you I am not, I will go to the house and shoot him. Are you brave enough to go with me?" The other accepted the challenge, and the four approached the house.

Jones was home with his two adopted children, fifteen-year-old Clara Wilson and her infant half brother. Jones's wife was away, visiting her son by a previous marriage, Howard Baker, who lived about half a mile away. At the Baker homestead Viranus Webster, a young man from Wisconsin, and his wife were visiting, living out of a covered wagon while they looked for promising farmland in the area.

The young Sioux reportedly demanded liquor from Jones, which he refused to provide. For some reason he left the two young children at the store and set out for the Baker homestead. The Indians followed Jones to the Baker farm, engaging him in more or less friendly conversation. When all were assembled at the Baker farm, still engaging in apparently friendly banter, the young Sioux challenged the white men to a shooting contest. After firing at a designated target in a nearby tree, the Sioux reloaded their guns, an act the white men neglected to emulate. Suddenly the young Sioux opened fire on the settlers, killing Jones, his wife, Webster, and Baker. Webster's wife remained in the covered wagon and was not harmed. Baker's wife took shelter in the house cellar with a child and avoided injury. The Sioux then left. When they passed by the Jones place as they were leaving, they shot and killed Clara Wilson. There is no evidence the attack was premeditated. None of the victims was mutilated, and neither of the homes was ransacked. The Indians stole horses from the farm and rode toward their village near Rice Creek.

Those living in the small Rice Creek village led by Red Middle Voice were generally regarded by other Lower Sioux as lowlife troublemakers in part because they had separated from the larger band led by Chief Shakopee, Red Middle Voice's nephew. The four young Sioux warriors who initiated the troubles bore an additional burden of being outsiders; they were Upper Sioux who had married Lower Sioux women. They knew their standing in the community was questionable and there was a chance they would be turned over to the whites, but the die was cast and they had no place else to go. Excitedly they recounted the events of a few hours before at the Jones and Brown properties. Their description of their deeds was taken as daring business by many of their fellows, including Red Middle Voice. Subsequent events suggest the chief was a murderous thug enthralled by violence. Yet Red Middle Voice did not possess sufficient clout to launch an all-out war on the whites, and he knew it. He immediately set out with the four killers and several others to Shakopee's village, about eight miles distant and near the mouth of the Redwood River.

The story of the attack on the white people excited Shakopee's warriors as it had those of the village of Red Middle Voice. Shakopee's young warriors joined those of Red Middle Voice, demanding an all-out attack on the whites, but Shakopee would not be stampeded. Though his band was one of the larger ones, Shakopee had just become chief following the death of his father and had yet to prove himself. He was the youngest of the Sioux chiefs in the area and had little prestige. Like his uncle, Red Middle Voice, he despised the whites but knew he lacked sufficient standing to launch a general uprising. He and Red Middle Voice decided they needed the support of other villages if an attack on the whites were to be successful. They considered several possibilities but in the end concluded there was only one viable option. The sun was setting as they led a growing band of eager combatants farther down the Minnesota River toward the Lower Agency and the village of Chief Little Crow, who they believed was the only Sioux leader with sufficient prestige to lead a real challenge to the whites.

At first blush, Little Crow did not seem a likely candidate for the job because he had signed the bargains that had ceded Indian lands to the whites. He lived in a two-story wooden house and often wore white man's clothes. To many Indians, especially the Blanket Indians, he was more white than Indian.

Little Crow had been born in 1820 in Kaposia, a village not far from the mouth of the Minnesota River, the present site of St. Paul. He was the second son of the first wife of Chief Cetanwakuwa ("Charging Hawk"). His older brother, who would have become chief, was killed in a fight with the Chippewa. Little Crow had four half brothers, two each by his father's second and third wives. Through a mistranslation of his father's name, white people called him Little Crow. His real name, Taoyateduta, means His People Are Red.

As a young man, Little Crow was reputed to have dissolute morals and was obliged to leave Kaposia because of threats from men who believed he had compromised their wives. He married and discarded two wives in succession and later acquired four more or less permanent mates, all sisters. Sharing a tepee with four sisters seemed to suit him, and he acquired a better reputation based on his glib speech and pleasant manners. He eventually took two more wives, six in all, and fathered twenty-two children, seven of whom were still alive in 1862.

When Little Crow was twenty-five, his father, Cetanwakuwa, died, and Little Crow returned to Kaposia to assume the role of chief. His father had told others that Little Crow "had very little good sense" and supposedly passed the patrimony to him only because "this is now the best I can do." But if Little Crow was deterred by this equivocal tribute, he showed no sign of it. Not everyone, however, looked forward to the Little Crow regime. Upon Little Crow's return, his two half brothers by his father's third wife conspired with some of the wronged husbands to put an end to Little Crow to prevent him from becoming their chief.

A big ceremony was planned to mark the transition from the old chief to the new. Two kegs of whiskey were purchased, and all the men were invited to the celebration. The basic plan of the conspirators was to start a quarrel and take advantage of the ensuing confusion to kill Little Crow. At the last instant a young brave knocked aside the rifle that was aimed at Little Crow's chest. The shot struck his right arm instead, and the arm remained crooked for the remainder of his life. Little Crow's friends quickly removed him from the scene, and a medicine man treated his wound with traditional remedies. Later the council of Karposias condemned the two half brothers, and they were executed. Little Crow emerged as the undisputed chief, albeit slightly damaged physically.

Over the ensuing years Little Crow undertook to remake his reputation, discouraging immoral behavior and drinking. When his own past was invoked in criticism, he dismissed it as the folly of youth. Little Crow was not handsome, but he had presence. A white admirer called him "the greatest man among the chiefs" of the Sioux and described his oratory as "bold, impassioned and persuasive." Another white said, "He was a man of greater parts than any Indian in the tribe." Little Crow exercised tremendous influence over both Indians and whites and acquired a reputation for negotiating deals between both parties.

As was mentioned earlier, Little Crow played a key role in negotiating the treaties of 1851 and 1858 and persevered over the objections of more cautious chiefs. On the latter occasion he was among a group of Indian leaders invited to Washington to meet with senior government officials to sign the appropriate documents selling the northern part of their land. On such occasions, Little Crow eschewed native Sioux dress for a black frock coat with a velvet collar. His party met with President James Buchanan, and later they were feted by a gathering of senators and congressmen, along with Supreme Court justices, cabinet officers, and other distinguished personages. There Little Crow addressed the group: "Warriors and friends: I am informed that the great white war chief, who of his generosity and comradeship has given us this feast, has expressed the wish that we may follow tonight the usages and customs of my people. In other words, this is a warriors' feast, a braves' meal. I call upon the Ojibway chief, Hole-in-the-Day, to give the lone wolf's hunger call, after which we will join him in our usual manner."

Hole-in-the-Day was a tall, ruggedly handsome character who got along well with whites and advocated the gradual adoption of white ways. The Ojibways lived north of the Sioux, with whom they warred intermittently, and had cut their own deals with the whites, swapping land for money. Hole-in-the-Day rose from his chair, straightened, and emitted a shrieking wolf howl, closing with a burst of war whoops that left an indelible memory with the guests.

During one of his many visits to Washington, while leaving the White House and walking past the Treasury Department, Hole-in-the-Day was besieged by a throng of admirers, one of whom was an attractive woman who begged an interview for purposes of a paper she intended to write. Hole-in-the-Day spoke enough English to invite her to his hotel room, and they quickly formed a romantic attachment. She followed him back as far as Minneapolis, where he bade her come no farther for fear his other wives would resent her. She bore him a son and died soon after. Their son was adopted by a white family named Woodbury.

After signing the treaties and accepting a new wagon in partial compensation for his role in the deal, Little Crow announced he would become a farmer, thus accruing the additional benefits promised any Indian who would accept a white lifestyle. He had his hair cut and took ownership of a two-story frame house two miles above the Lower Agency. It was modern for the time—plaster boards on the inside, a separate cooking shed, and two small rooms on the second floor. Tepees provided additional space nearby for Little Crow's large family of wives and children. He did not actually become a Christian but was known to attend worship services and in fact had attended church the same day the four warriors killed the four settlers near Acton Township.

Little Crow's collaboration with the whites was resented by many of his tribesmen, and they had let him know it two weeks before, when the Sioux bands met to elect a chief speaker—the equivalent of a chairman of the chiefs. The two other candidates, Chief Traveling Hail and Chief Big Eagle, did not possess standing anywhere near that of Little Crow. The election council proceeded as usual, with partisans of each candidate singing his praises while hurling exaggerated vitriol at the challengers. Little Crow reportedly took it all in stride until the vote was held and the speakership went to Traveling Hail.

The rebuff did not threaten Little Crow's leadership of his own tribe, but it tarnished his name and clearly struck a nerve. He was fretting about it on the night of August 17 when Red Middle Voice,

Shakopee, and about one hundred high-spirited warriors came to call at his house. Awakened in the main room on the ground floor of his home, Little Crow listened to the excited tales of his visitors. As recounted by Big Eagle later, Little Crow was skeptical.

"Why do you come to me for advice?" he asked. "Go to the man you elected speaker and let him tell you what to do."

"Little Crow is the greatest among the chiefs," answered Red Middle Voice. "Where he leads, all others will follow."

Only a few of the Indians, including the chiefs, could fit into Little Crow's house. Outside the hundred warriors emitted occasional war whoops, conveying a sense of excitement and determination.

"What do you want?" Little Crow asked.

"They want to kill all the whites," Red Middle Voice said. "They want to drive the Americans from the valley and get back our country."

"Red Middle Voice is a fool," Little Crow snapped.

Some of the chiefs nodded in agreement; others mumbled in disapproval. One by one they began to recount the abuses and humiliations they had been subjected to by the whites. One chief recounted an incident of some years before when Scarlet Point, an outlaw chief, led a band of renegade Lower Sioux into Iowa, where they killed some thirty white people in the Spirit Lake Massacre. The Department of Indian Affairs had ordered Little Crow to round up the renegades or face a cutoff of payments due in the land deal. Little Crow was obliged to track down Scarlet Point's band, but he eventually gave up the search. There were no consequences, a fact that made a strong impression on the Sioux: the white men seemed weak and indecisive.

Red Middle Voice pointed out that most of the young white men were away fighting. "All the white soldiers are in the south fighting other white soldiers," he said. "The Americans are so hard pressed, the agent must take half-breeds and traders' clerks from the reservation to help them." So it went in a prolonged debate, some of the chiefs demanding war while others warned against the consequences, none more vehemently than Little Crow.

"We have no choice," Red Middle Voice said. "Our hands are already bloody."

"Those are the words of a child," said Traveling Hail, who had arrived late at the council. "Red Middle Voice well knows blood will not wash off blood."

"Does Red Middle Voice want hundreds of Dakotas to die so four will be saved?" demanded Chief Wacouta.

"Dakotas who were not killed would be driven from such land as they have," said Big Eagle. "When the messenger came with word of the council and the reason for it, thirty-two of my warriors painted themselves and asked if I would lead them. I said, 'Yes, and you will have all the war you want. We will almost surely be defeated at last, but we are brave Dakotas and will do the best we can.' My braves are outside, painted and carrying guns. They want war, and I have promised to lead them. But I think war would be the act of a foolish child, and am opposed to it."

"We should not talk about war with the Americans," warned Traveling Hail. "Dakotas are brave and proud; they are not fools. Red Middle Voice and Shakopee talk, but what comes from their mouths is like the babble of children, as empty as the wind. We have no cannon and little ammunition. There are few Dakotas and many Americans. The Americans are as many as the leaves on the trees in the Big Woods. Count your fingers all day long, and white men with guns will come faster than you can count."

The argument seemed to be going against him, but Red Middle Voice wasn't done. He exhorted the chiefs to listen to the growing murmur of the braves outside, itching for war. "Listen to the voice of the young men," he said. "They want to kill. If the chiefs stand in the way, they will be the first to die."

Little Crow held his ground. "Dakota chiefs do not fear to die," he said. "They will do what is best for their people, and not what will please children and fools. What Red Middle Voice proposes is madness."

Red Middle Voice played his trump card, invoking the same school-yard logic that had prompted the killings at Acton Township earlier in the day. He stood over Little Crow, glaring down at him. "Little Crow is afraid of the white man," he said. "Little Crow is a coward." Little Crow rose and stood cheek to jowl with Red Middle Voice.

"Little Crow is no coward," he said, "but he is not a fool. When did Little Crow run from his enemies? Is he without scalps? Look at his war feathers! Behold the scalp locks of his enemies hanging on his lodge poles. Braves, you are like little children; you know not what you are doing. You are full of the white man's devil water. You are like dogs in the hot moon, when they run mad and snap at their own shadows.

We are only little herds of buffaloes left scattered; the great herds that once covered the prairies are no more. See! The white men are like the locusts; when they fly so thick that the whole sky is a snowstorm. You may kill one, two, ten, yes, as many as the leaves in the forest yonder, and their brothers will not miss them. Kill one, two, ten, and ten times ten will come to kill you."

Little Crow's oratory was his most impassioned, and even Red Middle Voice seemed temporarily intimidated. "Yes, the whites fight among themselves," Little Crow continued. "Do you hear the thunder of their big guns? No! It would take you two moons to run down to where they are fighting. All the way you would be among white soldiers as thick as the tamaracks in the swamps of the Chippewas. Yes, they fight among themselves, but if you strike one of them, they will all turn upon you and devour you."

The peace party thought for a moment they had carried the day, but Little Crow had more to say. "Fools," he blurted. "You will die like rabbits when the hungry wolves hunt them. Little Crow is no coward. He will die with you!"

There were no more questions or speeches, just a flurry of activity as the chiefs left the room and word spread among the surrounding braves. Though his conclusion did not seem to reflect his arguments, Little Crow had issued a general mandate for war. "He gave orders to attack the agency and kill all the traders," Big Eagle recalled. Indians left the house of Little Crow convinced they were being led into battle by Little Crow. In later years some would debate whether Little Crow actually intended to launch a war, but there was no question that he did. He himself never expressed reservations about it, and in succeeding days he would attempt to the best of his ability to wield the disparate Indian groups into a cohesive force. By morning the previous day's atrocities would seem tame stuff.

2

A DIVIDED HOUSE

SOME ONE THOUSAND MILES to the east, as the crow flies, the great white chief was thinking, not about red people, but about black people. Two years before, Abraham Lincoln, a relatively obscure lawyer from the frontier state of Illinois, had won the presidency with 40 percent of the popular vote. This was possible because the political structure had fragmented into four major parties—northern Democrats, southern Democrats, an odd assortment of political castoffs called the Constitutional Union Party, and the relatively new Republican Party, comprised primarily of former Whigs and Democrats. The Republicans had fielded their first presidential candidate in 1856 without success, but this time they made it with Lincoln, a former Whig, and his running mate, Hannibal Hamlin of Maine, a former Democrat. The 40 percent of the vote Lincoln and Hamlin received gave them a decisive edge in the Electoral College, and they brought with them a new Republican majority to Congress.

Their victory celebration was short-lived. Almost immediately after the magnitude of Lincoln's victory became known, southern states began to secede from the Union. South Carolina went first on December 20, followed in January 1861 by Mississippi, Florida, Alabama, Georgia, Louisiana, and Texas. Not long after that, Virginia, Arkansas, North Carolina, and Tennessee followed suit. By the time Lincoln arrived in Washington to be sworn into office as the sixteenth president in March, almost half the country had withdrawn or made clear its intention to withdraw from the Union with the intent to form a new country—the Confederate States of America. The possible secession of four Border States, Delaware, Kentucky, Maryland, and Missouri, which were slave states with strong ties to the Southern bloc, threatened to isolate the nation's capital within enemy territory. It was not an auspicious beginning for the Lincoln presidency.

In this dispute there was little ground for neutrality. All across the country, men were declaring allegiance either to North or South. Federal military facilities and arsenals in the South were quickly confiscated by Rebel partisans. An exception was Fort Sumter in the harbor of Charleston, South Carolina, where a Southern-born officer, Maj. Robert Anderson, refused to surrender his post to the fledgling Confederacy. The new president wrestled with deciding whether to attempt to resupply Anderson's small garrison, a prospect his military advisers assured him was hopeless. Lincoln feared such a move might precipitate open warfare with the South, which he was determined to avoid, if possible, but then the decision was made for him. The Southerners opened fire on April 12. Undermanned and cut off from support, Sumter soon surrendered. The Civil War was under way.

By August 1862 Lincoln had been leading his country through an increasingly bloody and destructive civil conflict for sixteen months, and he had precious little to show for it. People on both sides were increasingly restive that the matter remained unresolved. At the outset, North and South had assumed the conflict would be short and decisive. When Union Gen. William T. Sherman predicted the conflict would last years and involve huge personnel losses, he was derided as crazy.

It was a measure of this lighthearted attitude that at the first major clash of arms, near Manassas Junction, Virginia (called Bull Run by the Northerners and Manassas by the Southerners), in July 1861, cheerful groups of Washingtonians packed picnic lunches and drove their carriages out to watch the show, certain their army would prevail and put a quick end to the rebellion. At the end of the day, however, the Union forces were driven from the field in disarray, ruining the picnic.

The fight at Bull Run, which at the time was considered a major battle, resulted in fewer than five hundred deaths on each side. Afterward there was much marching back and forth by the opposing armies and lots of posturing by political leaders on both sides, but most Americans watched events unfold in the first few months of the war with relative equanimity. Many reputable political leaders believed a division of the country was preferable to all-out war, and certainly that was the prevailing view south of the Mason-Dixon Line. Minor clashes here and there throughout 1861 and early 1862 filled the news and kept everyone guessing which side had the upper hand, but thus far the war didn't seem to amount to much.

But in April 1862, near a rural church called Shiloh, on the Tennessee River, Union and Confederate troops clashed in a bloody two-day fight that left almost four thousand dead and another sixteen thousand wounded, many of whom died later. Shiloh (called Pittsburg Landing by the Confederates) had a sobering effect on both sides. The outcome was deemed a victory for the Union because the Rebels abandoned the field after the second day of fighting. Casualties were relatively equal on both sides, and the battle did not settle anything—except that it was going to be a long war and a bloody one. Sherman distinguished himself in that fight, commanded by Gen. Ulysses S. Grant, and there were no more questions about Sherman's sanity.

Public attention was focused primarily on the eastern theater of combat, where Confederate Gens. Robert E. Lee and Thomas J. "Stonewall" Jackson were earning formidable reputations as wily and resourceful commanders who, time and again, outwitted their Union counterparts. The Union enjoyed a substantial edge in numbers and equipment, but the story in Virginia was one of almost continuous Southern successes. By the summer of 1862 the Northern people were becoming disillusioned, questioning the ability of their leadership in Washington. The Republican Party was new and untested, its ideology a work in progress, its agenda suspect. More than a few members of Congress in the president's own party, and even some in his own cabinet, believed he was a country bumpkin out of his depth. There were conspiracies afoot to replace him with Secretary of State William H. Seward, who had come within a whisker of winning the Republican presidential nomination two years before. Crises were multiplying for the lanky western lawyer whose credibility, never conspicuously strong, seemed to weaken by the hour.

In August 1862, while the Sioux of Minnesota were launching their own rebellion, Lincoln was studying military textbooks, pondering the leadership of the Union armies, and trying to identify a general who could bring him victory. At the same time, he was wrestling with the more fundamental question of what the war was about.

When the Southern states had first made clear their intent to secede, Lincoln had thrown down the gauntlet that secession was not an option. At the outset, he made several serious efforts to downplay the divisions in the country and mollify the angry Southerners. Once it was clear that war was inevitable, he made it abundantly clear to all in his public statements that the purpose of the war was to preserve the Union. Hundreds of thousands of Union men flocked to the flag in response to that stand.

But somehow, in the face of mounting casualty lists, preserving the Union seemed an increasingly slender reed to sustain what was proving to be a lengthy and costly undertaking. Everyone knew what was really at stake. The threat of disunion was not the cause of the conflict, but rather a symptom of the real cause—slavery.

THE NATION Lincoln aspired to lead had been built largely by uncompensated labor. When the first Europeans washed up on the shore of North America, they found a vast wilderness overgrown with dense forests and inhabited by primitive tribes. It was an intimidating specter to people a long way from home. More than a few of the invaders were stricken down by a host of unfamiliar viruses against which they had no immunity. But others kept coming in an increasing tide, the excess population from a continent strangling in economic lethargy, afflicted with religious grievances, and innervated by an ancient class system that stifled initiative. Across the forbidding ocean lay a wild and untamed wilderness that offered freedom and opportunity.

The first and most conspicuous challenge faced by the European colonists was the need for Herculean labor. The land was rich and would sustain abundant crops, but first it had to be cleared of trees— millions of hardwood giants that had grown unchecked in the New World for millennia. And the settlers were armed with the most primitive of tools—axes, saws, shovels, picks—and had no power beyond that of human muscle and a few draft animals. The first people who came to the New World were looking for freedom and opportunity, but the investors who put up the money to send them were looking to make a profit. They wanted whatever the land had to offer—gold, crops, hides—harvested and sent back to Europe.

The settlers soon figured out there was little gold to be found in the wilds of North America, nor other precious jewels, such as had rewarded the Spanish conquerors of Mexico and Peru a few decades before. But there were agricultural products of value, including many new ones unfamiliar to the world they had left behind: potatoes, tomatoes, corn, and tobacco. The latter meant nothing to the Europeans until the Indians taught them to smoke, but it didn't take long to catch on. By the time of the American Revolution, tobacco was a major export for the colonies and fostered many great fortunes on both sides of the Atlantic.

But between the first colonial settlements along the coast and the prosperous colonies that challenged Great Britain in 1776 was an ocean of human sweat. It takes a long time to chop down a huge hardwood tree with an ax or crosscut saw, take it apart, and pull the stump from the ground. And that had to be done over and over many times to clear a block of land for planting crops. At the same time, the trees had to be hacked into logs and boards for houses and barns. And someone had to find food to eat and create shelter while the land was being cleared. The entire undertaking demanded astronomical hours of backbreaking work.

The early colonists addressed this challenge at first with contract labor in the form of indentured servants—in effect swapping passage to the New World to willing penniless European young people in exchange for fixed terms of uncompensated labor, usually seven years. It worked for a while, but indentured servants had a way of working off their obligations and striking out on their own. Another source of labor was required. African slaves fit the bill.

It was not a new idea. As early as the seventh century, Arab inroads into North Africa were bringing black slaves into the Islamic world. The Arabs also enslaved whites, including many from areas north of the Black Sea, and in fact the very word *slave* probably derives from the same root source as *Slav.* But Africans eventually emerged as the slaves of choice simply because they were readily available from established slave traders who had been doing business in Africa for centuries. By the time of Columbus's discoveries, slavery was common practice in the eastern Atlantic islands of Madeira and Cape Verde, where slaves were being used to cultivate crops on organized plantations. This became the prototype for slavery in the New World.

Slavery in North America during the late 1600s and early 1700s was generally a more benign enterprise than it would later become, if only because everyone was engaged in a struggle for survival. Slaves often worked alongside indentured servants and in many cases were brought to the New World on the same terms. In a time when everyone was working from early morning until nightfall to wrest a living from the wilderness, every hand was needed and appreciated, if not necessarily compensated. The records of early colonial times tell many stories of blacks working overtime to buy their freedom, setting up households of their own, participating in public and economic life, and sometimes even acquiring slaves of their own.

But there was always something about the Negroid features that differentiated the African slaves from the white indentured servants, a subtle distinction of class that mitigated against evolution of a substantial free-black population. A white indentured servant could change his status and blend in with the overall population. An African slave was always black and instantly recognizable.

The import of African slaves into the New World began as a trickle and gradually became a flood. North America was a vast continent, and there was much work to be done. The ensuing period of almost three centuries witnessed the greatest shift of population the world has ever seen, almost all of it from Africa to the New World. Most of the slaves taken to America were from West Africa, and most of them went first to the West Indies, where they were acclimated to slave life before being sent on to North America. By 1820 at least ten million blacks had been brought to the New World compared with some two million whites who came voluntarily. The fact that the ten million blacks had been reduced to only six million, while the two million whites had become twelve million, speaks volumes about the relative fortunes of the two groups.

The generally benign treatment of slaves in North America in the early colonial period soon gave way to the era of large plantations where slavery was a mass enterprise managed by professional overseers. The always marginal status of slaves degraded to that of commodities.

In the early colonial period, slavery was also legal in the northern colonies but for a variety of reasons did not catch on as it had in the South. Northern geography lent itself to small firms instead of huge plantations, and the mills and factories of New England were not amenable to slave labor. The brutality of slavery was abundantly clear to everyone who witnessed it firsthand, and a reaction set in among people with little economic investment in it. Religious leaders in the northern colonies inveighed against slavery, and the first abolitionist societies were born. By the time of the American Revolution, the new nation was already evolving into two societies, one slave and one free. About 97 percent of the black population lived in the southern colonies, and almost all of them were slaves.

Many of the drafters of the Constitution of the United States, the same men who waxed so eloquently about freedom and independence, were themselves slaveholders. It was an irony not lost on the British, whose alleged tyranny was the cause of such profound indignation in Philadelphia. "How is it that we hear the loudest yelps for liberty among the drivers of Negroes?" huffed the witty lexicographer Dr. Samuel Johnson.

The slaveholders who convened in Philadelphia to forge the first democracy the world had seen since the days of ancient Greece were for the most part unapologetic about slavery and indignant that anyone would suggest they should be. Slavery was ordained by Scripture and handed down to them from their ancestors in time-honored fashion. Their ministers reassured them that slavery was ordained by God's Word, and in fact there is little in the Old or New Testaments to suggest otherwise. Certainly no public person of any standing, north or south, thought blacks were the equal of whites or that they should enjoy full citizenship. The degraded lot of the slaves seemed to be the natural order of things, the system they were born and raised in. The slaves, despised because they were ignorant and uncultured, were ignorant and uncultured because they were despised.

And yet it was equally clear to many, if not most, that the slaves were human and that slavery itself presented troubling moral and ethical issues. More than a few of the Founding Fathers who convened in Philadelphia to draft the Constitution were acutely aware of the conspicuous contradiction between their lofty rhetoric about freedom and the base reality of the world in which they lived. Boston's John Adams, who would later serve as president, was stridently antislavery. Benjamin Franklin, who had once owned a slave, had by the time of the Constitutional Convention become an outspoken critic of slavery. An antislavery bias was becoming well entrenched among religious leaders in the

North, and there were more than a few at the meetings in Philadelphia who pressed for a long-term plan to abolish the institution.

But to condemn slavery in the abstract was one thing; to advocate a practical solution was another. The fortunes of many of the men at the table were built upon slavery, and even the antislavery contingent offered no practical solution for what should be done with millions of illiterate Africans who it seemed were conspicuously unqualified to participate in public life or even take care of themselves. There was an elephant in the room at Philadelphia but no consensus to recognize it. The constitutional conspirators in Philadelphia knew, if a new nation was to be born, the question of slavery had to be set aside for a later day.

Like many of the Founding Fathers, George Washington had built his personal fortune on slave labor. But as he got older, he began to have misgivings about it. The year before he died, he came to regard slavery as a blight upon the country and its abolition a highly desirable goal. "Not only do I pray for it, on the score of human dignity," he said, "but I can clearly foresee that nothing but the rooting out of slavery can perpetuate the existence of our union, by consolidating it in a common bond of principle." Washington made provision in his will to free all of his slaves upon his death, and before he died he made certain that a similar provision was in the will of his wife, Martha. She reportedly objected to this provision because it would deny her children from a previous marriage a substantial part of their inheritance, but his bequest was honored. It was fairly common for slaveholders, after their deaths, to free their slaves, suggesting a growing recognition that slavery was incompatible with the values of civilized society.

The great wordsmith of the revolution, Thomas Jefferson, also condemned slavery in the abstract. The "momentous question" of slavery, he said in 1820, near the end of his life, "like a fire bell in the night, awakened and filled me with terror." But Jefferson continued to hold slaves until the end of his life, and he made no provision for them beyond the grave. In any event, he died destitute because of a lifetime of fiscal irresponsibility and was in no position to grant them freedom.

There is considerable evidence Jefferson fathered several children by a slave, Sally Hemmings, which was a common enough occurrence among slaveholding families in the Old South. Virtually every plantation included its share of relatively fair-skinned blacks whose peculiar origins somehow escaped the notice of the fine ladies in the manor house. Slavery had an insidious way of degrading both slave and slave owner, undermining morality and inducing callousness to human suffering.

There had been some fleeting hope among thoughtful political, civic, and spiritual leaders that slavery might somehow wither away over time, but that proved to be wishful thinking. Instead, slavery became steadily more entrenched. Cotton supplanted tobacco as the primary cash crop of the southern states, and Eli Whitney's cotton gin made it a mass-production item dependent upon unpaid labor. As the soil of the Atlantic states became depleted, the cotton growers moved toward Alabama, Mississippi, Louisiana, and Texas. Great agricultural empires evolved. The import of slaves from Africa was outlawed in 1807, but natural reproduction replenished their ranks. Instead of ships bearing slaves across the Atlantic, there were endless "cobbles" of slaves chained together and wending their way under the watchful eyes of slave drivers from Maryland, Virginia, and the Carolinas toward the Deep South. Slaves were bought and sold by ones, twos, and threes without regard to affections or family ties. To be "sold down the river" was the ultimate degradation of a slave, but there was no recourse. A slave was property, not humanity.

By the time Lincoln was elected president, cotton was the nation's leading export. It provided raw material for the textile miles of New England as well as Old England. Slaves were big business, representing more capital than any other asset, except land. In 1860 the value of slaves was roughly triple the value of the country's capital stock in manufacturing and railroads. While Washington and Jefferson may have understood the basic contradictions of slavery and longed for its demise, their direct descendants did not. As the writer Upton Sinclair observed, it is difficult to make people understand something when their livelihood depends upon them not understanding it.

Unfortunately for the South, the allocation of most available capital to investment in slaves mitigated against other investments, such as railroads and manufacturing, in which the South badly lagged the North. It also seemed to impede investment in education in the South, where illiteracy was rampant. By the 1850s the North was outpacing the South in population, commerce, and industry.

Constant hectoring by northern critics about the evils of slavery aggravated the South's sense of inferiority and persecution, evoking ever more bitter confrontations that political leaders were constantly challenged to defuse. The issue never lay dormant for long primarily because the young nation was constantly expanding toward the west, adding new territories and states, each of which raised anew the question whether the new addition would be slave or free. Every American had an opinion on the subject, and it was almost invariably strongly held. Popular books, such as Harriet Beecher Stowe's *Uncle Tom's Cabin* (1852), fanned the flames of sectional rivalry and resentment. Her overwrought portrayal of the brutality of slavery made it an instant best seller and drove the defenders of southern values to distraction. Southern writers tried to reply with equally bad prose in a series of books that attempted to glamorize slavery, but nothing evoked the response of *Uncle Tom's Cabin* with its images of decent black folk abused by the cruel overseer Simon Legree.

In 1859, when abolitionist John Brown led a motley band of would-be liberators in a raid on the federal arsenal at Harpers Ferry, Virginia, the battle lines were drawn. A contingent of marines, led by Col. Robert E. Lee, quickly put an end to the mini-insurrection, and Brown was hanged, but the issue continued to seethe. Lincoln's election was the spark that lit the fuse. There was no question at all in the minds of southerners that Lincoln was the enemy come to destroy their way of life.

LINCOLN HIMSELF had antislavery roots. His father, Thomas Lincoln, was adamantly opposed to slavery, and it was one of the reasons he uprooted his family from Kentucky and moved across the Ohio River into Indiana in 1816, when his son was seven years old. Thomas opposed slavery in part because he belonged to a religious sect, the Separate Baptist Church, that condemned it, and also because he regarded it as an economic threat. Kentucky had entered the Union in 1792 as a slave state and was rapidly evolving into the plantation economy that characterized slave states. Small individual farmers like Thomas Lincoln believed they were being squeezed out by the big landholders with their uncompensated labor.

Like most youngsters, Abraham inherited his parents' biases, in this case a bias against slavery that he carried with him all his life. Remarking that he had always been "naturally antislavery" in 1864, he said, "I cannot remember when I did not so think and feel."

By the mid-1850s many people shared that sentiment while an apparently equal number resented it, with increasing fervor on both sides. An open conflict for the soul of the new state of Kansas brought matters to a boil. Kansas was in theory free to determine for itself whether to be slave or free, but antislavery and proslavery partisans poured into the territory and began positioning themselves to influence the elections. Tempers flared and guns were drawn. Soon the territory was known as "Bleeding Kansas."

The turmoil in Kansas prompted Senator Charles Sumner, a strident abolitionist from Massachusetts, to take the floor of the Senate for two days and denounce "the shameful imbecility of slavery" and condemn in purple prose the southern politicians who defended it. It was an inflammatory oration that enraged the proslavery faction and elicited criticism even from Sumner's allies because of its intemperate tone. Two days later a congressman from South Carolina, Preston Brooks, attacked Sumner at his desk, beating him senseless with a gold-headed cane. It was a measure of the temper of the times that the House was unable to summon the required two-thirds majority to expel Brooks. He resigned anyway and went home, whereupon he was quickly reelected and returned to Washington. People all over the South sent him canes in tribute to his deed.

Northerners could not fathom the mentality that would encourage southern people to openly approve such a grievous crime. For their part, southerners could not fathom northerners who openly interfered with agents seeking to return runaway slaves to their rightful owners. In attempting to bridge the moral chasm between slavery and free, the law became untenable.

As the nation stumbled awkwardly toward open conflict, politicians north and south were staking out their positions on the great debate. Few made their stands known more clearly or forcefully than Abraham Lincoln of Illinois, who had one two-year stint in the House of Representatives to commend him for higher office. By 1858 Lincoln was locked in a battle for a Senate seat against Stephen A. Douglas, the leading Democrat in Illinois and widely known for his oratorical skills. In a series of public debates both candidates had ample time to stake out their positions on the key issues of the day, the main one being slavery. A crucial point of debate was the recent Dred Scott decision by the Supreme Court, which had ruled that a slave taken into a free state by his master did not automatically become free but rather had to be remanded to his status in his home state.

Douglas sought to take advantage of racial prejudice, accusing the new Republican Party of wanting "to vote and eat and sleep and marry with negroes." Lincoln rejected "the counterfeit logic which concludes that, because I do not want a black woman for a slave, I must necessarily have her for a wife. My understanding is that I can just leave her alone." The authors of the Constitution, he said, never intended to say that all people were equal in all respects, but they were equal in certain inalienable rights "among which are life, liberty, and the pursuit of happiness."

Revisionist historians challenge Lincoln's commitment to emancipation in part because of the equivocal way he danced around the issue during the debates with Douglas. But Lincoln was campaigning for office in Illinois, and there was little question that the voters in that state in those days harbored a virulent bias toward blacks. Only ten years before they had voted by overwhelming margins for a constitutional amendment to bar free blacks from entering their state. The overall support for this measure was 70 percent, and in some sections it was 90 percent. Given the sway of the voters he was seeking to influence, the significant fact is not that he muted his opposition to slavery but that he expounded it at all.

Douglas made the obvious point that slavery was enshrined in the Constitution, put there by the drafters, many of whom were slaveholders. But Lincoln refused to accept the obvious. He pointed out that the term *slavery* does not appear in the Constitution but rather "person held to service or labor," and that it foreordained the elimination of the slave trade in twenty years. "Thus, the thing is hid away," Lincoln said, "in the Constitution, just as an afflicted man hides away a wen or a cancer, which he dares not cut out all at once, lest he bleed to death; with the promise, nevertheless, that the cutting may begin at the end of a given time." He went on to point out how those same Founding Fathers took steadily more aggressive actions against slavery: prohibiting slave commerce in 1794, prohibiting the import of slaves into Mississippi in 1798, prohibiting Americans from engaging in the slave trade among foreign countries in 1800, restraining internal slave trading in 1803, and in 1807 prohibiting the import of any more slaves—which was made a capital offense in 1820.

In one of his most famous perorations, Lincoln said: "A house divided against itself cannot stand. I believe this government cannot endure permanently half slave and half free. I do not expect the government to be dissolved—I do not expect the house to fall—but I do expect it will cease to be divided. It will become all one thing or all the other."

It is generally said that Lincoln lost this round to Douglas, for the Democrats carried the state legislature and Douglas went to the Senate. But in the debates Lincoln established himself in the public mind as a "thoughtful" critic of slavery, setting himself apart from the firebrand abolitionists who demanded outright emancipation.

By August 1862 Lincoln was struggling to decide whether to make the Civil War a crusade against slavery. There was widespread concern that such a declaration would alienate many in the North who had little interest in the welfare of slaves, and that many Union soldiers would refuse to fight for such a cause. There was also the delicate matter of Delaware, Kentucky, Maryland, and Missouri, four key slave states that were still in the Union and would likely take offense at such a move. And there was the even more fundamental question of what would be done with four million slaves if and when, by dint of Union arms, they actually were set free. On August 14, three days before the Sioux outbreak in Minnesota, Lincoln summoned to the White House a delegation of African American leaders to discuss their future.

"You and we are of different races," he said to them. "We have between us a broader difference than exists between almost any other two races." After pointing out that blacks and whites were equal nowhere in America, he asked them to work with him on a plan to colonize former slaves in Central America. Not surprisingly, this gambit was turned down by the black leaders and later harshly criticized by abolitionist leaders of both races when they learned of it.

But as historian David Herbert Donald observed, Lincoln had another purpose—to set the stage for emancipation by suggesting he had a plan to deal with the slaves once they were free. He followed it up with a reply to abolitionist Horace Greeley, who, in an editorial published in the *New York Tribune* called "The Prayer of Twenty Millions," demanded immediate emancipation of all the slaves. "My paramount objective in this struggle *is* to save the Union, and is *not* either to save or destroy slavery," Lincoln said. "If I could save the union without freeing *any* slave, I would do it, and if I could save it by freeing *all* the slaves, I would do it; and if I could save it by freeing some and leaving others alone, I would also do that. What I do about slavery, and the colored race, I do because I believe it helps to save the Union; and what I forbear, I forbear because I do *not* believe it would help save the Union."

At the time he wrote these words, Lincoln's Emancipation Proclamation lay locked in a drawer, awaiting a propitious moment when a military victory might give him sufficient cover to embark on such a bold course.

3

ONE CAN KILL TEN

O N AUGUST 18, JUDGE Abner C. Smith of Meeker County conducted an inquest into the deaths of five whites near Acton Township. The victims were buried in a single grave in the Ness Norwegian Lutheran Cemetery, not far from present-day Litchfield, where a state monument now marks the site.

While Judge Smith was doing his duty, probably concluding the attack had been an isolated act by a few outlaws, around him all hell was breaking loose. At first light the braves who had gathered at Little Crow's house the night before were now adorned with war paint and raring for blood. They surrounded the buildings of the Lower Agency that consisted of traders' stores, barns, and other buildings overlooking the Minnesota River. Moving forward in groups of four or five, they targeted specific structures. At a prearranged signal, they opened fire on the unsuspecting whites.

The first target was the trading post of Nathan and Andrew Myrick, two of the most hated traders in the region. James W. Lynd, a thirty-two-year-old former state senator and an Indian scholar, was working as a clerk at the Myrick store. Lynd was the father of two daughters by one Indian woman and the father of an as-yet-unborn child by another. He spoke the Sioux language and had written a book, not yet published, about Sioux customs, history, and traditions. As he stood in the door, wondering what the Indians wanted at such an early hour, Plenty of Hail, a young brave, shot him down. Inside the store another clerk, George W. Divoll, heard the shot and was killed when he went to see what was going on.

Nathan Myrick was not at home, but Andrew was upstairs in his room. He heard the commotion, surmised something bad was afoot, and attempted to escape out a back window, sliding down a lightning rod to the ground. He was shot down before he reached the cover of the nearby woods.

All around the agency compound whites were taken unawares and made easy targets. Another trader, Francois La Bathe, was killed in his store along with one of his clerks. At the store of Louis Robert, two clerks—Patrick McClennan and Henry Belland—were shot to death, as were two more, Joe Belland and Antoine Young, at the store of William H. Forbes. Another man at the Forbes store, George H. Spencer, was wounded and sought refuge in an upstairs bedroom.

"Not expecting to live a great while, I threw myself upon a bed and while lying there could hear them opening cases of goods and carrying them out, and threatening to burn the building," Spencer recounted. "I did not relish the idea of being burned to death very well. I had been upstairs probably an hour when I heard the voice of an Indian inquiring for me."

The inquisitive Indian was a Sioux named Wakinyatawa, who intervened on Spencer's behalf. "If you had killed him before I saw him," Wakinyatawa said to the other Indians, "it would have been all right, but we have been friends and comrades for years, and now that I have seen him I will protect him or die with him." Wakinyatawa took Spencer to his tepee and tended his wounds with traditional remedies.

The superintendent of farms at the agency, A. H. Wagner, and two of his employees were trying to prevent the Indians from stealing horses when Little Crow came upon the scene. "What are you doing?" Little Crow asked his warriors. "Why don't you shoot these men?" The Sioux fired, wounding Wagner and killing the other two men. Wagner died soon after.

By then it was clear to all the whites at the agency that they were under attack. Everyone tried to escape, most of them by taking the Redwood Ferry across the river while the Indians looted and burned the agency compound. Sanctuary for the whites was Fort Ridgely, thirteen miles to the southeast. The operator of the ferry—whose name was Hubert Millier, Charlie Martel, Oliver or Peter Martel, or Jacob Mauley—kept working the ferry until most of the surviving whites had passed across. The Sioux eventually figured out what was going on and killed and disemboweled the ferryman. A small and unobtrusive marker at the site of the ferry on the north side of the river honors his courage and identifies him as Charlie Martel.

J. C. Dickinson operated a government boardinghouse at the agency and escaped across the river with the girls who worked in his establishment. Another survivor was the Reverend Samuel Hinman, an Episcopal missionary who had preached a sermon of brotherly love the previous day to several of the Sioux, including Little Crow. Hinman's group also made it to safety.

Dr. Philander Humphrey, the Lower Agency physician, was not so fortunate. He crossed over on the ferry with his wife and three children and headed toward the fort. Stopping at an abandoned home, Humphrey sent one of his sons to a nearby spring to fetch water. While the boy did so, Indians surrounded the family, killed the doctor, and set fire to the house, burning to death the doctor's wife and the other children. Humphrey's son watched helplessly from a hiding place as the Sioux decapitated his father.

John Nairn, a government carpenter, stayed on the south side of the river with his wife and four children and moved through the woods along the prairie. They did not cross the river until they were nearly to Fort Ridgely, and they arrived there safely. Nairn's assistant, Alexander Hunter, and his wife fell behind because Hunter was lame; they were later caught and killed by the Sioux.

Mrs. Joseph DeCamp, wife of the government sawmill operator, was with her three sons in their home, which was a distance away from the agency and hidden behind some trees. Her husband was in St. Paul on business. Some Indians not involved in the uprising warned her of what was going on and led her to a safe haven in the Sioux village led by Chief Wacouta. While there she overheard a conversation among some young warriors whom she had earlier spent time with, teaching them English. They were boasting of their bloody work that day and looking forward to more. She inquired what had provoked them to commit such deeds. She reported that they laughed and said, "It is fun to kill white men. They are such cowards. They all run away and leave their squaws to be killed. One Indian can kill ten white men without trying."

While the Sioux were killing and plundering at the agency, other warriors were moving farther afield, committing atrocities in their wake. Joseph Reynolds and his wife, Valencia, were instructors at a government school near the village of Chief Shakopee. Their home was on the road between the Upper and Lower Agencies and was a "public house" where passersby could obtain meals. The Reynoldses lived with two hired girls, Mary Anderson and Mary Schwandt, and a niece, Mattie Williams. On Monday morning they were visited by a trader from the Upper Agency, Francis Patoile. While sharing breakfast, someone brought word of the attack on the Lower Agency. The entire group set out for the town of New Ulm, the largest settlement near the reservation, about sixteen miles south of Fort Ridgely on the Minnesota River. Reynolds and his wife were in a buggy, working their way along the bluff adjacent to the river, while Patoile with the girls in his wagon swung west toward the prairie. The Reynoldses stayed far enough away from the Lower Agency to avoid detection but paused to check out the scene. "We crawled up to the crest of the ridge on our hands and knees," Valencia Reynolds reported later. "The doors of the stores were open and Indians were all about."

They passed by the agency undetected. A bit farther on they saw sixty Indians about half a mile away, and then later encountered "a naked savage on foot." The lone warrior had a double-barreled weapon and attempted to fire at the whites, but the gun misfired. Joseph and his wife decided to head for Fort Ridgely, which was closer than New Ulm.

Meanwhile, Patoile and the girls also managed to bypass the agency sight unseen, but when they were within ten miles of the fort, they encountered fifty "very noisy and perfectly naked" Indians who were returning from an afternoon of looting and killing at nearby hamlets along the Cottonwood and Minnesota Rivers. Patoile was shot four times and fell out of the wagon dead. Mary Anderson was shot through the abdomen and died four days later. She and the girls were taken to Wacouta's village where Mrs. DeCamp and her children were being held. Mary Schwandt, who was fourteen years old, said her captors took her to an unoccupied tepee where they "perpetrated the most horrible and nameless outrages upon my person." Mary Anderson also was raped repeatedly until she died from her wounds.

All told, thirteen people were killed in the attack on the Lower Agency, and seven more were killed trying to flee. About ten women and children were captured by the Indians, and as many as forty-seven escaped to Fort Ridgely while the Indians were preoccupied with plunder.

The Lower Agency was now a smoldering ruin. Behind the embers of what had been the Myrick trading post, the body of Andrew Myrick lay sprawled on the ground, a wad of grass stuffed in his mouth.

THE TREATMENT of Myrick's body was a message by angry Sioux that their actions were not occurring in a vacuum. Many of the Sioux were starving, watching their wives and children die for lack of food and shelter because of a corrupt system that seemed designed to deprive them of their scant means of livelihood. For many of the Sioux at the Lower Agency, Andrew Myrick was a symbol of their oppression.

The treaties by which the Sioux ceded their land to the whites should have provided them with more than enough for their basic needs, even for those who declined to become farmers and adopt the ways of the whites. As a practical matter, however, very little of the annuity funds set aside for the Sioux in payment for their land actually reached them. The bureaucratic apparatus created to adjudicate the issues related to the Indian treaties, as well as the payment of annuities as prescribed by the treaties, was riddled with graft and corruption on a scale that beggars description.

The first Office of Indian Affairs had been set up in 1824, and the president was charged to name a commissioner of Indian affairs who reported to the secretary of war. That seemed a reasonable home for the Indian office at the time, because the relations with the tribes were often characterized by open conflict. The Office of Indian Affairs was moved to the Department of the Interior in 1849, and by the time Lincoln became president, it had become a veritable fountain of federal largesse that enabled the party in power to reward its supporters. Most of the opportunity lay with the White House, which appointed the secretary of the interior and the commissioner of Indian affairs, but as a practical matter, Indian affairs were also a keen congressional interest. The chairmen of the committees supervising Indian matters tended to be from the western states where the tribes lived, and the officeholders were careful to respect the wishes and interests of the chairmen of important committees in Congress.

Essentially all the treaties signed with the Indian tribes—the Sioux and others—required the Indians to cede land to the whites in exchange for money that was supposed to provide the Indians with their basic needs plus appropriate incentives to encourage them to become farmers and otherwise adopt white customs and lifestyles. On every Indian reservation were government employees designated to ensure the treaty obligations were fulfilled. Working hand in hand with the agents were traders who were more or less quasi-government employees in that they usually enjoyed the backing of the government and an effective monopoly over their captive customer base. The traders sold the Indians food and basic goods at inflated prices. Working in tandem, the agents and traders generally conspired to make off with most, if not all, of the Indians' annuity payments long before they reached their lawful destination. There was some debate whether the agents or traders were the most corrupt, but it was mostly an irrelevant discussion because, in the words of one Minnesota observer, "It is believed that the trader is, in all cases, a partner of the Agent. He is usually a near relative."

The situation did not invite honesty. The agents were generally paid fifteen hundred dollars a year or less, and their immediate supervisors only a little more. That was not much even in those days, but as one investigator reported to Lincoln, clever agents could "in four years lay up a fortune more than the President's salary."

The basic method of defrauding the Indians of their money was to simply present a claim to the agent in charge of disbursement that the intended recipients owed the trader, or any other white, a given amount. Of the $475,000 that the Sioux were to be paid when they moved to their new reservation, an employee of the American Fur Company, Henry Hastings Sibley, filed a claim for $145,000. Hugh Tyler, a lawyer representing traders and half-breeds, demanded $55,000. The trading firm of Bailly and Dousman claimed it was owed $43,000. And so it went. No doubt some of the claims had some basis, but the Indians were not allowed to challenge the claims, and the Indians could not vote. The only limit on the fraud was whatever limit the individual claimants admitted to their greed, and their greed was almost limitless. Of the $266,880 the Sioux were supposed to receive for the north half of their reservation, more than $12,000 went to Sibley and $155,000 to thirty-four other "certified" claimants. Almost $90,000 was allowed on the claims of three groups of traders—the Myricks, Roberts, and Browns. Very few dollars actually reached the Indians.

The fraud was widespread and brazen, and little if any effort was made to conceal it. The records overflow with well-documented cases of outright theft that almost never brought punishment of any kind. One agent lived miles away from the Indians he was supposed to serve, paying a clerk to keep the requisite accounts, and on one occasion he somehow managed to have his quarterly salary paid twice. Another built himself a large house and other structures with the Indians' money, leaving them destitute. An audit conducted in 1859 found that $265,000 had been spent in violation of Indian Office regulations, and that one agent, who had been working for $1,000 a year, had retired after two years with $17,000. Yet another agent somehow rang up $41,000 in three years.

The White House was ostensibly responsible for this chicanery, but Congress was not without blame. "I have been told on very good authority that very little of the large appropriations we generally make to negotiate a treaty goes to the Indians," said Senator William Pitt Fessenden of Maine on the Senate floor. "It goes to a lot of people who get together and have a good time and divide the spoils and make a treaty."

One of the most articulate critics of the Indian system was a respected religious leader in Minnesota who saw it close up and was appalled. Reverend Henry Benjamin Whipple was the first Episcopal bishop of Minnesota, appointed to that position in 1859 at the age of thirty-seven. He brought to his job a youthful energy and religious fervor that thrust him into the center of the vortex erupting among the Sioux of Minnesota. He had traveled to Richmond to be ordained a bishop, and there he might have met a young Virginia colonel, Robert E. Lee, who was a delegate to the General Convention of the Episcopal Church. But Lee was away at the time, suppressing John Brown's rebellion at Harpers Ferry.

In his first year as bishop of Minnesota, Whipple logged more than three thousand miles in his horse-drawn buggy, holding services and preaching sermons in churches, schools, and the occasional saloon. By the time of the Sioux uprising, Whipple seemed to know virtually everyone of note in the young state, including Frederick Weyerhauser, an enterprising young sawmill operator on the Chippea River; he would later found the great pulp and paper products company of the same name.

Whipple became an early advocate of the church's missions among the Indians, an interest his white congregations sought to discourage. Minnesota was a free state, and most of the inhabitants had at least some sympathy for the Negroes held in bondage in the southern states, but few of them extended similar concern for the Indians. "Minnesota was anti-slavery regarding the Negroes," recorded one contemporary observer, "but locally it was more anti-Indian."

Whipple was unmoved by such considerations. "God being my helper," he said, "it shall never be said that the first bishop of Minnesota turned his back on the heathen at his door." The more time he spent on the reservations, the most incensed Whipple became about the treatment afforded the Sioux and other tribes. In the spring of 1860 he wrote an impassioned letter to President Buchanan, demanding a wholesale restructuring of the Indian system that would treat the indigenous peoples as wards, not independent nations. He recommended honest administration of the Indians' legacies, an effort to curb alcohol abuse, and that the Indians be encouraged to take up farming. Buchanan did not respond.

That autumn Whipple followed up with a visit to Washington, where he called upon an unidentified southern politician to press his concerns. The politician then and there informed the bishop that Lincoln was likely to be elected president, and if he was, the South would leave the Union. Whipple was shocked. "Is it possible," he asked, "that I hear a representative of the government admit that even its trusted servants are plotting its destruction?"

Whipple returned to Minnesota and devoted even more attention to the various Indian tribes, looking for opportunities to help them improve their lot since it seemed unlikely any help would be coming from the government. In response to his deeply held concern and unceasing advocacy of their cause, the Indians called him "Straight Tongue" reflecting his penchant, unusual for a white man, for telling them the truth. His efforts on their behalf became a steady irritant to his white constituents long before the outbreak of August 1862.

In March 1862, six months before the uprising, Whipple wrote another letter to the president, this time to Lincoln. "The Indian agents who are placed in trust of the honor and faith of the government are generally selected without any reference to their fitness for the place," he charged, and they accept the jobs "because there is a tradition on the border that an Indian agent with fifteen hundred dollars a year can retire upon an ample fortune in four years.

"The Indian agent appoints his subordinates from the same motive," Whipple continued, "either to reward his friend's service, or to fulfill the bidding of his Congressional patron. They are often men without any fitness, sometimes a disgrace to the Christian nation; whiskey-sellers, bar-room loungers, debauchers, selected to guide a heathen people. Then follows all the evils of bad example, of inefficiency, and of dishonesty, the school a sham, the supplies wasted, the improvement fund curtailed by fraudulent contracts. The Indian, bewildered, conscious of wrong, but helpless, has no refuge but to sink into a depth of brutishness."

From this depth of their brutishness, the Minnesota Sioux found more than sufficient provocation to rise against their persecutors. The winter of 1861–62 had been unusually hard because of a crop failure the season before. The Sioux were desperately in need of their annuity payment, which by tradition was due when "the prairie grass was high enough for pasture," which had always meant the end of June for the Lower Sioux and two weeks later for those at the Upper Agency. But June came and went and then July with no money. Many of the Sioux concluded reasonably enough that the agents and traders were once again conspiring to make off with their money.

In reality, Congress was tardy that year in appropriating the Indians' money, probably because of other business attending the war. Also, there was some discussion within the Treasury Department whether to pay the Indians with gold, as was customary, or to issue them the new paper currency that the Lincoln administration had begun printing to finance the war. Gold was in short supply, but the Indian treaties specified they be paid in gold, and it seemed a sure bet that substituting paper for gold would cause trouble. But not until August 16 did the customary payment of seventy-one thousand dollars in gold reach St. Paul, still a long way from the Sioux.

At the Upper Agency a large crowd of several hundred angry Sioux demanded the local agent release some of the food stores in advance of the payment because the people were starving. There were about one hundred soldiers on hand to keep order, but the officers in command were hesitant to take on that many Indians. They persuaded the agent, Thomas Galbraith, to release enough food to mollify the Indians, at least for the time being. The crisis subsided.

At the Lower Agency, Little Crow obtained a pledge from the Indian agent that food would be issued to his people, but then the traders refused to cooperate. Complicating the picture was an informal "soldiers' lodge," a group of young warriors who convened on their own and sought to take matters into their own hands. Many of them believed Little Crow had sold out to the white men and could not be trusted to represent their interests. This group insisted that no claims of the whites should be permitted against the annuities until the claims of the Sioux were heard in open council. This proposal the traders dismissed out of hand, no doubt because they would have had a bit of explaining to do. "If they are hungry," said trader Andrew Myrick, "let them eat grass or their own shit."

THERE MAY have been more than grass in the mouth of Andrew Myrick's corpse that fateful August Monday, but the Sioux were out to settle scores with more than one surly trader. They spread out in small groups to attack individual farms along the roads to Fort Ridgely and New Ulm and places in between. The basic modus operandi was to call out greetings, shake hands all around, and then commence the butchery of settlers, few of whom had time to consider what was happening to them. The Sioux warriors split the skulls of men; clubbed children to death; raped daughters; chopped off heads, breasts, and genitals from the corpses; and then looted whatever goods could be taken, setting fire to what remained.

The settlers were largely defenseless because most of the young men were off to the war, and those who remained were poorly armed, if at all, with shotguns or obsolete muskets. Many of the German immigrants had just come from lands where poor farmers like them were not allowed to own weapons. Thus no Indians were killed during the early massacres.

The settlers were also compromised by an air of disbelief that such things were actually happening. The Edward Magner family lived along the road between Fort Ridgely and New Ulm. Escapees from the Lower Agency came fleeing past them toward the fort, warning of the horror under way. Magner and his family left for the fort, but Magner somehow became convinced that the danger was overblown. He turned back to water his livestock and was hacked to death by Indians.

Not far from the Magner home lived Ole Sampson with his wife and three children. Sampson was shot dead by Indians. His wife hid with her children in a wagon near their home, but they were found by the Indians, who wrested her baby from her, threw it in the grass, and then lit a fire under the wagon. Badly burned, the mother escaped to retrieve the baby, but the two older children died in the flames.

One party of twenty-eight settlers, including four men, assembled and headed out for the fort. Helen Carrothers survived the ordeal and described their encounter with seventy Sioux warriors. She stood up in her wagon and pleaded with them for mercy. "You must not kill us," she said. "Many of you are my friends, and have often been kind to me. We are your friends, also. When have you ever come to our homes, wanting food, and been turned away hungry? The Great Spirit would be very angry with you if you killed your friends."

"We would like to spare you," said one warrior slowly in English, "but all whites must die."

Further negotiations, including an agreement by the settlers to relinquish their horses, brought momentary respite, but soon the carnage began. One Indian, Carrothers reported, seized "a sweet and pretty child of two, and beat her savagely over the head with a violin case, smashing her head horribly out of shape. Then he took her by her feet and dashed her brains out against the wheel of the wagon, spattering her mother with blood and brains. Another fiend took the nine-months-old boy, hacked off his limbs with a tomahawk, and threw the pieces at the mother. Then they made a big fire and tossed featherbed, woman and mangled children into the flames."

Some of the worst atrocities were committed by followers of Red Middle Voice who appears to have been something of a maniac. His warriors took perverse pleasure in hacking off the limbs of victims before they died. They nailed children to doors, running spikes through their arms and legs and swinging them back and forth until they expired. At one cabin they killed a homesteader and his two sons in a field and murdered his wife and two youngest children in their house. Their thirteen-year-old daughter was stripped naked and raped by twelve Indians.

At another cabin the Sioux led by Red Middle Voice set upon homesteader John Schwandt, shot him to death, killed his wife, Christina; his pregnant daughter, Caroline; his two sons, Christian and Frederick; Caroline's husband, John Waltz; and a hired man. Schwandt's twelve-year-old son August was tomahawked and left for dead, but he remained conscious and later recalled watching the savages rip his sister open, remove her unborn baby, and nail it to a tree. August eventually made it to

Fort Ridgely along with his sister Mary, who had been working as a hired girl at another homestead.

One of the scariest of the Sioux warriors in the eyes of his victims was a character named Cut-Nose, so-called because he had lost part of his proboscis in a fight. In the first two days of the outbreak he devoted his attentions to the Beaver Creek settlement on the north side of the Minnesota River. Several women and children had gathered there to flee, huddled in their wagons, when Cut-Nose and others approached. While other Sioux held the wagon's horses, Cut-Nose leaped inside and systematically tomahawked eleven women and children. Wresting a baby from its mother, he and the others riveted the child to a fence with a bolt from one of the wagons. They made the mother watch while the child died and then chopped off her arms and legs, leaving her to bleed to death. They then murdered some twenty-five more people, tossing their bodies from their wagons, which they then filled with plunder and headed off to their villages.

Upon returning to their homes, covered with blood and bearing the scalps of their victims, the warriors were generally greeted with disdain by their elders and women. To kill the enemy Chippewas was regarded as bold business, but the slaughter of helpless white farmers and their women and children was viewed as shameful. "Soldiers and young men," Little Crow said to them the day after the killings at the Lower Agency. "You ought not to kill women and children. Your consciences will reproach you for it and make you weak in battle. You were too hasty in going into the country. You should have killed only those who have been robbing us so long. Hereafter, make war after the manner of white men."

But Little Crow accepted the goods pillaged from the trading posts and the settlers' homes and distributed them among his followers. He took custody of several white captives brought to him, mainly women and children, and permitted some to escape. He sent word to other Sioux villages to urge them to rise up against the whites, especially among the bands of the Upper Agency. Some of the chiefs allied with Little Crow, such as Big Eagle and Mandato, tried to prevent their young men from joining in the raids, working for a consensus for concerted military action against Fort Ridgely instead. But Red Middle Voice and Shakopee smiled on the butchery of the settlers and urged their young men toward further atrocities.

4

GOD WILLS
THIS CONTEST

O N AUGUST 21, 1862, Secretary of War Edwin M. Stanton received a telegram from Minnesota Governor Alexander Ramsey: "The Sioux Indians of our western border have risen, and are murdering men, women and children." He conveyed a message from Minnesota's secretary of state, John H. Baker, who described a fearful scene. "A most frightful insurrection of Indians has broken out along our whole frontier. Men, women and children are indiscriminately murdered, evidently the result of a deep-laid plan, the attacks being simultaneous along our whole border."

There was no doubt in Washington who would have conceived such a "deep-laid plan." Early in the war the Confederate government had made efforts to recruit Native Americans to the Southern cause. Senior members of Lincoln's cabinet, including Interior Secretary Caleb Smith, had no doubt the Rebels were behind the Sioux uprising. "I am satisfied the chief cause is to be found in the insurrection of the southern states," he reported to Lincoln, asserting that "southern emissaries" were known to be agitating among the Sioux. Thomas Galbraith, the Indian agent at the Upper Agency who had been forced to relinquish some food to his starving charges, also claimed that "southern sympathizers" were responsible for instigating the violence. It either never occurred to him that the starvation he had done so much to augment might have been the root cause of the turmoil—or he was trying to divert blame to outside sources.

Lincoln was not prone to rash conclusions, but even he was suspicious of a link between the Confederacy and the Sioux uprising. "Information was received," he reported to Congress, "that a simultaneous attack was to be made upon the white settlements by all the tribes between the Mississippi River and the Rocky Mountains."

There can be little doubt that the government of Jefferson Davis was doing all in its power to foster such activity by the western Indians, but these efforts produced only marginal results. Not long before the firing on Fort Sumter, thousands of Cherokees and Choctaws had been forcefully evicted from their ancestral lands in the Southern states and moved west into unfamiliar country west of Arkansas. The eastern Indians, many of whom spoke English and wore white men's clothes, came into almost immediate conflict with the Apache, Arapaho, and Cheyenne tribes of the west. Their exile was a story of relentless deprivation, humiliation, and violence. It is difficult to fathom why the Confederates believed these aggrieved Indians would make common cause with the South, but in 1861 Richmond sent emissaries to the Cherokees, Seminoles, and Creeks to seek their active collaboration.

For reasons of their own, some of them took the bait. Cherokee Chief John Ross owned slaves, wore a frock coat and a stovepipe hat, and lived in a large plantation house. Possibly because of his standing as a slave owner, and also because he feared losing his status as Cherokee leader to his rival, Stand Watie, Ross agreed to fight with the South. Both he and Watie soon had a chance to show their usefulness to the South at the battle of Pea Ridge in Arkansas in early March 1862.

At Pea Ridge, Union troops under Gen. Samuel R. Curtis, a veteran of the Mexican War, were opposed by a Rebel force led by the dashing Gen. Earl Van Dorn of Mississippi, a distant relative of former President Andrew Jackson. Van Dorn would later be shot to death by one of several men whose wives the amorous general had romanced. At Pea Ridge, Curtis led a relatively small army of ten thousand men. To meet him, Van Dorn had a force of between sixteen thousand and twenty-five thousand—the indeterminate number reflecting the presence or absence of large clusters of Indians who tended to come and go as they pleased. But most of Van Dorn's troops were white, and they had sixty pieces of artillery.

Curtis entrenched his troops on an elevated ridge, his artillery dug in behind log bunkers. Van Dorn decided the position was too formidable to assault frontally. He left his campfires burning at night and stealthily moved his troops under cover of darkness around each end of the Union line. Given his advantage in numbers, this should have worked out well—and it almost did. At first light the Rebels moved on the Union positions and made early gains. Curtis's cavalry on his right collapsed, and their commander called for help. The forces on his left lost their cannon to enemy fire and were hard-pressed by Southern infantry. At that moment the Rebels launched a huge frontal assault on the Union center. A major Confederate victory, at least by the standards of the conflict thus far in 1862, seemed in the offing.

But almost immediately the Confederates began to have difficulty controlling their Indian allies. One group of Indians captured a Union cannon, built a stack of straw under it, and set it on fire, commencing a great victory dance well before the battle was fully joined. The Indians refused to emulate the tactics of the white men in the face of artillery fire—lying down until it passed harmlessly overhead. Many were shot down unnecessarily because they had no sense of discipline. They preferred to fight as individuals, climbing trees and hiding behind rocks. The notion of movement within orderly units was too foreign to their own ideas of combat. Gradually, the disciplined Northerners began to chop holes in the Southern lines where the war-painted braves behaved erratically. At a propitious moment, Curtis ordered a massive charge toward the heart of the Rebel line and promptly collapsed it. By the time Van Dorn withdrew from the field, he counted fewer than 3,000 men left from his original force, though most of the absentees, including most of the Indians, had likely scampered off in different directions. The Union side lost 1,384 killed, wounded, or missing. And the battle ended a Confederate effort to invade Missouri.

In the South overall—and to a lesser extent in the North—efforts to use Indians in the Civil War varied between calamitous and pathetic. As the braves had demonstrated at Pea Ridge, they could be a liability in a pitched battle against disciplined troops. At other times they were simply nuisances who potentially committed atrocities against prisoners, slaves, and—in the case of southwest Minnesota—civilians.

A Union captain recounted receiving a detail of Indians from the Fifth Wisconsin to help him destroy Confederate stores in Jackson, Mississippi. "No sooner had they comprehended the nature of the work we had to do," he wrote, "than they put their war paint on and with demoniac yells . . . began putting the torch to every house they came to. The fire engines were summoned to put out the flames, but the Indians blocked the firemen's efforts by jabbing their bayonets into the hoses." Other Federal troops had to be called in to control the Indians.

Nevertheless, several Indians served with distinction as officers in both the Northern and Southern armies. Col. Ely S. Parker was a Seneca serving on the staff of Ulysses S. Grant. But overall the Indians as a group made scant contributions to the war effort on either side.

Of course none of this was abundantly clear to Union leaders in 1862, and in any case there was no question of the Indians' ability to create havoc where there were no white troops to impose order. On August 25 Minnesota Governor Ramsey wired Washington that the Sioux war was getting worse. "The panic among the people has depopulated whole counties," he said, demanding an extension of the draft deadline by which Minnesota was expected to contribute another 5,360 men to the Union cause. Mr. Lincoln's army at the time was facing a severe shortage of troops at a critical juncture when the Rebel army seemed to be in the ascendancy. War Secretary Stanton denied the request, but Lincoln overruled him, telling Ramsey, "Attend to the Indians. If the draft can not proceed, of course it will not proceed. Necessity knows no law. The government cannot extend the time."

John Nicolay, one of Lincoln's personal secretaries, was in Minnesota at the time of the Sioux uprising. Nicolay was a gaunt creature of uncertain health who had been straining under the workload attending management of the president's personal communications. He had gone west with Indian Commissioner William P. Dole to observe negotiations with the Chippewas when the Sioux uprising broke out. If there was anyone who enjoyed Lincoln's attention and confidence, it was Nicolay. He, Dole, and Minnesota Senator Morton S. Wilkinson, wired Lincoln: "We are in the midst of a most terrible and exciting Indian war. Thus far the massacre of innocent white settlers has been fearful. A wild panic prevails in nearly one-half of the state."

Lincoln responded to the news of Sioux depredations by doing something he had sworn he would never do only three weeks before: recruit blacks into the Union army. The president had avoided such a move for a variety of reasons, not the least of which was the general presumption North and South that blacks were incapable of standing up to whites in battle. (That is, conventional wisdom assumed Native

Americans were formidable warriors but did not infer the same qualities in African Americans.) There were also questions whether Union soldiers would accept black soldiers as allies and how extreme the reaction of Southerners would be. But the Sioux uprising underscored the dramatic need for more men in blue, and August 25 was the day that Secretary of War Stanton authorized Gen. Rufus Saxton to organize black soldiers into fighting units.

This decision received little attention at the time, but it was to have far-reaching implications. At first, blacks taken into the army were used for menial tasks, but there was too much fighting to be done, too many gaps in the ranks, for that to last long. Meanwhile, Southerners reacted badly. Black soldiers taken prisoner at Fort Pillow in Tennessee were massacred by troops under the command of Gen. Nathan Bedford Forrest. Other blacks taken captive were enslaved. Soon the system employed by both sides of paroling captives who promised to fight no more until formally exchanged was abandoned because the South refused to treat black soldiers as prisoners of war. Both North and South were soon inundated with huge numbers of prisoners, and both seemed unable or unwilling to provide decent living conditions for the POWs. The death toll in prisoner of war camps, North and South, was deplorable.

To virtually everyone's surprise, blacks proved to be effective combat troops. The celebrated attack of black infantry on Fort Wagner by the Fifty-fourth Massachusetts Infantry depicted in the film *Glory* is a case in point. By the end of the war, one out of four Union soldiers was black. In 1935 the influential black historian and social commentator W. E. B. DuBois attributed much black progress directly to the participation of blacks in the Civil War. "He [the black man] might labor for the nation's wealth, and the nation took the results without thanks and handed him as near as nothing in return as would keep him alive," DuBois wrote. "But when he rose and fought and killed, the whole nation with one voice declared him a man and a brother. Nothing else made emancipation possible. Nothing else made Negro citizenship possible, but the record of the Negro soldier as a fighter."

THOUGH LINCOLN offered no specific reason for his sudden about-face on the delicate question of black soldiers, the apparent cause for the reversal of policy was the Sioux uprising. The following day,

August 26, Governor Ramsey called for creation of a new military department in the Northwest (meaning Minnesota) to deal with the Indian insurrection.

That August, Lincoln had other things on his mind. The Union army in Virginia was at the time divided between the commands of George B. McClellan and John Pope. This situation galled McClellan, who a few weeks before had been in sole command, but his reluctance to commit his troops to battle had prompted Lincoln to put much of the Union army under Pope. As reports of Sioux atrocities poured into Washington, Pope was in Virginia, near Manassas, getting ready for a showdown with Robert E. Lee. McClellan was in the eastern Virginia Peninsula area, where he had allowed himself to get boxed in by inferior Rebel forces. The president wired McClellan to move quickly to Pope's support, but McClellan, to virtually no one's surprise, dragged his heels.

"McClellan to me is one of the mysteries of the war," Grant later commented in his memoirs. A native of Philadelphia, McClellan graduated second in his class as West Point in 1846. He served with distinction in the Mexican War and was later sent overseas to study strategy and tactics of the Crimean War. In 1857 he resigned his army commission for a job as chief engineer for the Illinois Central Railroad. McClellan was later promoted to vice president and moved to the Ohio & Mississippi Railroad, where he was a division president until he reentered the army in 1861 after the outbreak of the war.

McClellan won a couple of minor victories in western Virginia, what is now West Virginia, which prompted a summons to Washington in July after the disastrous defeat of the Union army at Bull Run. A dapper little man with a knack for dramatic gestures, McClellan was hailed as the "Little Napoleon" due to the way he mimicked the French emperor in his theatrical poses, and he was given carte blanche to command virtually all Union troops in the eastern theater of the war. Only thirty-four years old, he was boyishly handsome with blue eyes and reddish brown hair. He had an imperious air that inspired confidence and enabled him to step quickly into a leadership vacuum that existed in part because so many of the army's top officers had defected to the South. Even McClellan was dazzled by the red-carpet treatment he received. "I seem to have become the power of the land," he wrote to his wife.

McClellan proved masterful at administration and organization as well as public relations. He soon had the army in order, its units coherent, its supply lines intact, and most important, its morale in fine fettle. There was never a question that the ordinary soldiers in his command worshiped "Little Mac" to a degree that few other Civil War commanders ever experienced—with the possible exception of Lee.

But by the summer of 1862 McClellan's star was losing some of its luster. For all of his considerable abilities and star power, McClellan had a deficiency that loomed conspicuously in a military leader: he did not like to fight. He demonstrated a seemingly endless supply of excuses and rationales for avoiding battle that, after a while, began to undermine his standing with Washington officials. When he did engage the enemy, it was usually with poor results, as at Ball's Bluff on October 21, 1861, when Union troops suffered heavy losses. McClellan responded to this disaster by demanding the removal of his nominal commander, the ancient Gen. Winfield Scott, who was sent into overdue retirement. This left McClellan with even more power, including control of the Union armies in Ohio and Missouri. "Draw on me for all the sense I have, and all the information," Lincoln said to him. "In addition to your present command, the supreme command of the Army will entail a vast labor upon you." Replied McClellan with characteristic arrogance, "I can do it all."

All of it, that is, except fight. He came up with an ambitious scheme to transport the bulk of his army down the coast to the Virginia Peninsula, where he could assault Richmond from the east. Lincoln was reluctant to let him leave Washington undefended and did not see how attacking Richmond from the east would convey any advantage over attacking it from the north, but he acquiesced. In was in the ensuing Peninsula campaign that McClellan demonstrated the crucial shortcomings that would short-circuit his career. His movements were inordinately slow in part because he insisted on overestimating the strength of the enemy forces arrayed against him, usually by huge margins.

Admittedly, intelligence gathering in the war was a hit-and-miss affair with emphasis on the latter. Even so, McClellan's penchant for assuming the role of underdog was conspicuous to Lincoln and most of official Washington. His primary source of information was Allan Pinkerton, founder of the security service that bears his name today. Pinkerton and company demonstrated some ability in managing internal security issues for the Lincoln administration in the early months of the war, but his aptitude for enemy intelligence was woefully lacking.

He repeatedly assured McClellan that Lee had 120,000 troops or more at a time when Lee was fortunate to field half that many. Thus McClellan spent much of his time nagging Lincoln for more men and equipment to enable him to contend with a vast Rebel army that existed only in McClellan's cautious imagination.

"If by some magic I could reinforce McClellan with one hundred thousand men today," Lincoln told a friend, "he would be in ecstasy over it, thank me for it, and tell me that he would go to Richmond tomorrow, but when tomorrow came he would telegraph that he had certain information that the enemy had 400,000 men, and that he could not advance without reinforcements."

If Lincoln gradually soured on McClellan, there can be no doubt that the general returned the president's contempt with interest. Having assumed high command, McClellan grew weary of the president's meddling and needling him to action. He consorted frequently with Democratic leaders in Congress and wrote to his wife that Lincoln was "nothing more than a well meaning baboon." Lincoln's late-night visits to McClellan's home to discuss strategy were a special irritant to the general. One night in late 1861 Lincoln stopped by the McClellan household with Secretary of State William H. Seward and personal secretary John Hay. The general was out, so they decided to wait until he came back. After a while, McClellan came home and, being informed the president was waiting for him, went straight to bed. About a half hour later, Lincoln sent word upstairs that he was still waiting. McClellan sent word back that he had gone to bed and did not wish to be disturbed.

Hay expressed astonishment that anyone would demonstrate such disrespect to the president, but Lincoln did not protest. He paid no more late visits to the general's house. He did remark to aides that he would gladly "hold McClellan's horse" if he would only win a victory.

McClellan did fight a few battles with Confederates in the Peninsula campaign, and not always poorly. At Malvern Hill, during the Seven Days' battles, he positioned his troops and artillery well enough to give Lee's forces a severe licking, throwing them back with heavy losses. But even there he had no notion to follow up the victory by moving against the retreating Rebels, though his senior generals urged him to do so. As was his custom, McClellan blamed his lack of success on Lincoln, the War Department, and of course, superior enemy numbers.

Prior to any fighting of the Peninsula campaign, on March 11, 1862, Lincoln suspended McClellan from command of all the armies. Again separate armies were commanded by separate generals with only fledgling coordination coming from Washington. McClellan now commanded the Army of the Potomac, which had already launched the Peninsula campaign. In late June another Union army was formed out of three separate commands—the Mountain Department, the Department of the Shenandoah, and the Department of the Rappahannock— and dubbed the Army of Virginia. John Pope, fresh from victories in the western theater at New Madrid, Missouri, and Island Number 10 on the Mississippi, was named to command this newly constituted force of about fifty thousand men. Meanwhile, McClellan still commanded almost twice that many on the peninsula, but he had long ago lost the initiative and camped on the James River. In late August, when it became clear that Pope was headed for a major showdown with Lee, Lincoln ordered McClellan to move quickly to Pope's aid. It came as a surprise to no one that McClellan took his time to respond.

POPE HAD a reputation for braggadocio that rivaled McClellan's arrogance. His first act as commander of the new Army of Virginia was to issue a formal address to his men that many of them found insulting in the extreme. "I come to you out of the west where we have always seen the backs of our enemies," Pope proclaimed. Denigrating the use of phrases like "lines of retreat" and "bases of supply" that he said occurred with too much frequency among the correspondence of Union officers, he said, "Let us study the probable lines of retreat of our opponents and leave our own to take care of themselves. Let us look before us and not behind. Success and glory are in the advance, disaster and shame lurk in the rear."

Not surprisingly, McClellan and Pope despised each other, and this animosity carried over to McClellan's subordinates and argued against any close and effective coordination of Union efforts against Lee's army. At times it seemed that Union generals in the East reserved their most intense enmity for each other and regarded the Confederate leaders with purely professional respect.

On August 24 Lee's Rebels were facing Pope's Yankees across the Rappahannock River in a standoff. The Southern commander probed for an advantage while Pope slowly gathered more troops, however grudgingly culled from McClellan's command. On this occasion Lee concocted a daring plan, which quickly became a distinctive hallmark of his command. He would send Stonewall Jackson with about half the Army of Northern Virginia plus Jeb Stuart's cavalry around the Union right with the idea of crossing the Rappahannock and getting behind the Federals, cutting off their communications and supplies along the Orange & Alexandria Railroad. The other half of Lee's army would be commanded by James Longstreet in some diversionary actions against Pope and would follow Jackson later. To divide one's forces in the face of superior numbers is generally regarded as the height of foolishness by professional soldiers, but Lee seemed to sense the disarray among his adversaries, and he had a way of making such daring schemes pay off.

Jackson moved north on August 25 and reached Salem, Virginia, that night. At dawn he sent Stuart's cavalry and some infantry to capture the Union supply depot at Manassas Junction. By this time several of McClellan's units had finally linked up with Pope, raising his aggregate strength to as much as seventy-five thousand men. Despite his many quarrels with Lincoln and the creation of Pope's command, McClellan still believed that he would be in command when the two armies were united. Pope assumed that McClellan and he were equals under the command of Washington-based General in Chief Henry W. Halleck. Thus on the eve of battle there was confusion on the Union side about who was in charge.

Even so, the Union army's prospects brightened as Pope gradually realized that Lee had divided his army, leaving both halves vulnerable to destruction. On the morning of August 27 Pope moved aggressively away from the Rappahannock to interpose his forces between the Rebel forces led by Jackson and Longstreet and to defeat them separately. Meanwhile, Jackson's troops were busy plundering the supplies at Manassas Junction with such intensity that even the irascible Stonewall had difficulty getting them refocused on battle. Southern soldiers were accustomed to going days without food and marching miles without shoes. To be loosed among tons of food and supplies temporarily deranged men otherwise noted for iron discipline. Late in the day Jackson ordered his command to pack everything they could into their wagons and to torch the remainder. Pope ordered his forces to concentrate on the scene as quickly as they could. "We shall bag the whole crowd," he chortled.

In his haste to get at Jackson, Pope forgot about Longstreet, the stolid warrior Lee called "my old war horse," and assumed he was still west of the mountains. By the time the first units of Pope's command reached Manassas Junction, the Southerners had gone. The Union commander was reduced to probing for Jackson's corps without the aid of cavalry directly under his control—another casualty of the confused command structure.

But while Pope was looking for Jackson, Jackson was looking for Pope. Stonewall assumed Pope was planning to unite his command with McClellan's and wanted to engage him before that happened— much as Pope wanted to have at Jackson before he combined with Longstreet. In the late afternoon of August 29, units of Jackson's and Pope's commands came into contact near the old Manassas battlefield of the preceding summer. There was heavy but indecisive fighting. Meanwhile, Longstreet was coming up from the west, trying to fight his way through scattered Union forces so he could join Jackson. To the east McClellan was holding two corps near Alexandria in defiance of an order from Halleck to send them to Pope. As was his custom, McClellan was convinced Lee had one hundred thousand men and paid no attention to an accurate report from Pope that he had engaged only twenty-five thousand under Jackson's command. When directly urged by the White House to move, McClellan countered with a suggestion that all available troops be placed under his command to defend Washington, leaving Pope "to get out of this scrape by himself."

The night before the fighting, Pope had issued battle orders based on an inadequate understanding of the disposition of Jackson's men as well as his own. His most telling mistake was an assumption that Longstreet had been driven back. In reality, Longstreet was less than ten miles from Jackson, and the only force between the two Rebel armies was a small Union cavalry detachment. Further breakdowns in communication among senior Union commanders, some of whom were deliberately subverting Pope, aggravated an already dangerous situation. The following morning Pope hurled his men piecemeal against Jackson's lines in fierce fighting. The Federals demonstrated extraordinary courage, as they often did, and they almost broke Jackson's line on several occasions. But they could not quite force the day.

The best efforts of the Union infantry were compromised in part because Pope only managed to get a relatively small number of his troops actually into the fight and because some of his senior commanders were either still loyal to McClellan or hostile to Pope or both. The most conspicuous of these was Gen. Fitz John Porter, who made no secret of his disdain for Pope and could not bring himself to accept orders from him. For this blatant dereliction of duty at Second Bull Run, Porter was later court-martialed and expelled from the army.

Strangely enough, on this occasion while the Union army fought with only part of its available forces, Lee's troops did the same. Lee repeatedly urged Longstreet to press an attack to relieve Jackson's forces, but Longstreet demurred because he knew other large Union forces, including McClellan's, were in the area. He had no way of knowing the Federal commanders were sitting on their hands, and he doubtless would not have believed it if someone had told him. As a general principle, then and later, Longstreet preferred to fight on the defensive, luring his enemy into attacking his entrenched positions.

Lincoln's great frustration was judging military leaders for senior command. Although he had served in the Black Hawk War, he had no combat experience to draw on, and as a self-educated backwoodsman he had no military training. He had placed the aging Halleck in supreme command because Halleck was reputed to be highly intelligent and experienced in military affairs. But Halleck lacked the will to make difficult decisions and impose them on his subordinates. Thus McClellan routinely ignored Halleck's orders, and Halleck had no response. "I am almost broken down," he said at the time of Second Bull Run. "I can't get General McClellan to do what I wish."

There were many senators and more than a few congressmen who were eager to substitute their judgment for Lincoln's. But though many of them held the president in contempt, they were mice nibbling at his shoes. Their best advice served only as petty annoyance. Ill-equipped as he was by experience and education, Lincoln had to make the tough calls on his own.

The night before Second Bull Run, Lincoln was at the War Department, the rococo building across from the White House that is now the Old Executive Office Building, staying near the telegraph for news from the front. Throughout most of the battle, Pope's dispatches were optimistic, reflecting both the fluid conditions on the field and his aggressive state of mind. On the evening of August 30 Lincoln was relaxed enough to take dinner at the home of War Secretary Stanton, who assured him that "nothing but foul play could lose us this battle." Later, back at the War Department, Halleck was equally upbeat. For a while Lincoln believed he was on the verge of a great victory that would turn the tide of the war and enable him to issue his emancipation proclamation.

But as so often happened in those troubled days, Lee intervened to spoil the occasion. The night before, Rebel forces had pulled back to adjust their lines and attend to routine support functions. Mistaking that move as a withdrawal, Pope sent a victory note to Washington and ordered his men to pursue the fleeing enemy. But the enemy troops weren't fleeing. They were dug in and ready to meet the onslaught. The two armies once again locked in a deadly embrace, and again the Federals went forward with incredible dash and resolve. The Southerners almost broke. Many of them ran out of ammunition and were reduced to throwing rocks at the Yankees. But at the critical moment, Longstreet came up, hit the advancing Union troops from the flank with heavy artillery, and then threw all five of his divisions at them in an all-out attack. The Union ranks broke and fled. After three days of heavy fighting, Lee left about fourteen hundred dead on the field and some seven thousand wounded. Union losses were on the order of two thousand killed and ten thousand wounded.

On Monday, September 1, the ragged elements of the beaten Union army were pouring into Washington, where they besieged the saloons and bordellos, relating tales of yet another disastrous defeat at the hands of Lee. And Lincoln's gaunt frame was beginning to stoop as if weighted down with an invisible load. "Well, John," he said to Hay, "we are whipped again." Pope pulled back to Centreville, where, he reported to Washington, he would be able to hold his men. "I don't like that expression," Lincoln said. "I don't like to hear him admit that his men need 'holding.'"

THE NEXT day, despite adamant opposition from his cabinet, Lincoln relieved Pope of command and ordered McClellan to retake command of the defense of Washington. In one of his darkest hours, Lincoln kept a steady hand. Whatever the Little Napoleon lacked as a fighting general, the president realized his general was a superb organizer. "If he can't fight himself," Lincoln said, "he excels in making others ready to fight."

It was perhaps a measure of the desperation of the Union soldiers that they greeted McClellan's return with shouts of joy and raucous cheers, but then he had always been popular among the frontline troops if only because he was so reluctant to see them bloodied in battle. Within a matter of days McClellan had the army reorganized and back in the field, ready to fight again. It was fortunate that he did, because Lee had taken his army, not south toward Richmond, but north into Maryland. Lincoln saw this move as an excellent opportunity to isolate the Rebel army far from its base and destroy it. Lee and Confederate President Jefferson Davis knew they were playing a dangerous game, but they hoped a dramatic invasion of the North would afford their own people some relief from the constant fighting on their home ground and just possibly encourage the Northern people to support peace candidates in the November midterm elections. By September 4 Lee's fifty-five thousand veterans splashed across the Potomac River thirty-five miles north of Washington. They were spoiling for another fight, one they hoped would be decisive.

During these dark days Lincoln jotted down some of his thoughts. Prior to the war he had never articulated a clear religious vision and had steered clear of membership in any particular sect. But the weight of office drew him to spiritual musings. Noting that both Northerners and Southerners believed their cause was in harmony with Providence, he wrote: "I am almost ready to say this is probably true—that God wills this contest, and wills that it shall not end yet. By His mere quiet power, on the minds of the now contestants, He could have either saved or destroyed the Union without a human contest. Yet the contest began. And having begun, He could give the final victory to either side any day. Yet the contest proceeds."

5

GOD LED AND
WATCHED OVER US

FORT RIDGELY WAS NOT a fort as the term is generally understood. There was no stockade or defensive entrenchment, just a bunch of buildings around a parade ground. Probably named for Capt. Randolph Ridgely, an artillery hero who died in the Mexican War, it had been established in 1853 in the northwest corner of Nicollet County so soldiers could keep an eye on the Sioux. Two-story framed buildings served as officers' quarters on the east and west sides of the parade ground. There were also two stone structures, a large two-story troop barracks, and a one-story commissary building that offered the only defensible positions from which to withstand a siege. The fort was about thirteen miles southeast of the Lower Agency on a spur of high prairie tableland about 150 feet above the Minnesota River. Deep ravines to the east, north, and southwest offered attackers safe approach to within rifle range.

On August 18, 1862, when the first refugees from the massacres began to appear, there were seventy-six men and two officers of Company B of the Fifth Minnesota Infantry on hand to deal with three thousand unruly Sioux at the Lower Agency and four thousand at the Upper Agency. The commander was Capt. John Marsh from Filmore County in southeast Minnesota. He had served with a Wisconsin regiment for ten months in the East and had fought at First Bull Run, but he had no experience in fighting Indians. As refugees poured into the fort area, each with a horror story more extreme than the previous, Marsh realized he had a serious situation on his hands and few resources at his disposal. By sundown his fort bulged with more than two hundred fugitives, most of them women and children.

The captain's first action was to dispatch young Cpl. James McLean to ride after a troop of fifty men that had passed through the fort the day before. Led by Lt. Timothy J. Sheehan, the unit was bound for Fort Ripley on the Mississippi River. Marsh reasoned the lieutenant should be close enough to return to his aid. "It is absolutely necessary that you should return with your command immediately to this post," he wrote to Sheehan. "The Indians are raising hell at the Lower Agency."

Marsh then set out for the Lower Agency with forty-six men plus an interpreter, Peter Quinn. He left twenty-nine troops plus the sutler, the surgeon, and the ordnance officer at the fort under the command of nineteen-year-old Lt. Thomas Gere. Marsh and Quinn rode mules while most of the men rode in wagons. Along the way they passed more refugees moving toward the fort. These included Reverend Samuel Hinman, the Episcopal missionary who only the day before had preached a sermon attended by Little Crow. Hinman and others warned Marsh that he would be heavily outnumbered if he continued, but the young officer was undeterred.

Marsh led his men up the north side of the river, which was swollen by summer rains. There were only a few places where the Minnesota could be safely crossed in high water, and Marsh had no idea where they were. He headed toward the Redwood Ferry, the only known crossing of the river to the Lower Agency. The Union soldiers passed mutilated bodies and burning houses, confirming the severity of the situation they faced.

The Sioux, meanwhile, had anticipated the arrival of troops from the fort and assumed correctly they would come by way of the ferry. More than a hundred warriors crossed to the north side and hid amid the heavy growth of willow grass and hazel that offered excellent cover; an equal number took cover on the south side where the ferry landed. The Sioux plan was to wait until the soldiers were on the ferry at mid-stream and then open fire. When Marsh's troops were within about a mile of the ferry, they abandoned the wagons and approached on foot in single file. At the ferry they saw a familiar face on the other side.

White Dog, whose Indian name was Shoonkaska, was a young Sioux of splendid physique reputed to be an amorous sort whose attentions were enjoyed by many maidens, both Indian and white. He was a farmer who had been employed as a farming teacher at the agency. He was also fond of the white man's firewater and was often in the Lower Agency jail, sleeping off his excessive consumption. Communicating with the interpreter Quinn, White Dog urged the soldiers to cross on the ferry to attend a council with the Sioux.

Marsh was reluctant to take the bait, but as he wavered a shot rang out prematurely and the battle was on. Taking fire from three directions, at least twelve of Marsh's men were cut down almost immediately. The captain rallied the survivors well enough to fire a return volley at the Sioux behind them, but he realized his situation was desperate. He led his surviving soldiers south, along the river, through some thick underbrush that extended for about two miles. The underbrush provided good cover, but when the troops had worked their way into it, they found themselves facing yet more Indians waiting for them to emerge onto open ground.

Marsh's only remaining option was to lead his men into the river, hoping to reach the south side and return to the fort. The captain was a strong swimmer, but he developed a cramp and sank out of sight. His men tried to save him, but they failed. It was left to nineteen-year-old Sgt. John Bishop to salvage what was left of Marsh's command. The sergeant led fifteen survivors, including five wounded, safely back to Fort Ridgely. Eight stragglers showed up later. A total of twenty-four men were lost, including the commander.

While Marsh and his men were being ambushed, a wagon carrying two boxes loaded with seventy-one thousand dollars in gold—the long-overdue annuity money—arrived at Fort Ridgely from St. Paul. The money was escorted by a supervisor from the Indian office and four guards. The supervisor proposed to take the money to the Lower Agency, but Lieutenant Gere wisely persuaded him to stay at the fort. Gere, the supervisor, and the guards were the only ones who knew about the gold.

Gere was feeling the heat. He hurriedly wrote messages dated 8:00 p.m. August 18 to the commanding officer at distant Fort Snelling and to Governor Ramsey: "Capt. Marsh left this post at 10½ this morning to prevent Indian depredations at the Lower Agency. Some of the men have returned and from them I have learned that Capt. Marsh is killed and only 13 of the company are remaining. The Indians are killing the settlers and plundering the country. Send reinforcements without delay." Apparently as an afterthought, he added at the bottom. "Please hand this to Gov. Ramsey immediately."

Pvt. William Sturgis, riding the best horse Fort Ridgely had to offer, set out with the message by way of St. Peter, where he was to notify the Renville Rangers, a company of Civil War volunteers on their way to Fort Snelling. The two forts were 165 miles apart, and the route between the two was over rough country. Sturgis arrived after eighteen hours in the saddle, having ridden all night and half the following day.

DURING MARSH'S ill-fated mission, Sioux messengers were carrying reports of the action to the Upper Agency with a call from Little Crow that others join in the battle to drive the white men from their land and avenge years of abuses and humiliations. The northern Sioux leaders were at first in disbelief. A council was called among the chiefs who were available plus a smattering of aggressive young warriors who were elated by the news and eager to lead a similar uprising on their own turf. Some of the most militant among these were a group of young Yanktonais Sioux from the Dakota Territory to the west who were not part of the Upper Agency, were not entitled to annuity payments, and had no business in the discussion. Two important chiefs who should have been present, Standing Buffalo and Red Iron, lived too far away to be summoned in time for the council. They were represented by members of their bands who were on the scene, but they had little influence in the outcome.

The council quickly polarized between a war party and a peace party, with a clear majority in the former. Many of the younger braves, including the Yanktonais, were eager to join forces with the Lower Sioux to kill the whites and loot the storehouses. Like most Indians, they carried festering resentments against the whites who treated the Sioux and their culture with undisguised contempt. But not everyone in the council was of the same mind. Some of the older chiefs resented that the Lower Sioux had embarked upon such a fateful course without discussing it with the northern tribes. They warned it would bring retribution from the whites, who would surely drive the Sioux to the west, leaving them destitute. Others counseled that, despite their distaste for the whites, the whites were a necessary evil—the source of weapons and ammunition without which the Sioux would be at the mercy of their traditional enemies, the Chippewas. Still others reasoned that, like it or not, the Lower Agency Sioux were past the point of no return—the actions of the Lower tribes would surely bring down the wrath of the whites on all the Sioux regardless of who participated.

Among the chiefs debating the situation were several Christian converts who spoke against an attack on the whites. The most outspoken and credible of these was John Otherday, a forty-two-year-old full-blooded Sioux who had become a Christian four years before. Otherday was a man who did not do things by halves. He adopted the white man's dress, married a white woman, and endeavored to take up farming like a white man. But while other Indians who adopted the white man's ways were often insulted or worse, no one dared denigrate Otherday in such a way. Prior to his conversion, he had earned the reputation of a ruffian who could more than hold his own in a fight. In fact, it was Otherday who had given Cut-Nose the wound that became his name.

Otherday sent a protest via messenger to the rampaging warriors at the Lower Agency. "Some of you say you have horses and can escape to the plains, but what, I ask you, will become of those who have no horses?"

"I hear some of you talking very loud and boasting you have killed so many women and children," added the Christian Chief Little Paul. "That is not brave; it is cowardly. Go and fight the soldiers! You dare not! When you see their army coming on the plains, you will throw down your arms and fly in one direction and your women in another, and this winter you will all starve."

But Otherday and Little Paul could not control the meeting. Toward midnight it became clear the council would not reach a consensus. Otherday stealthily gathered most of the local whites from the Upper Agency in the brick warehouse where much of the Indian agency's food and other supplies were kept, and he personally stood guard over them through the night. In the meantime, he dispatched two other Christian chiefs to warn the missionaries at two nearby settlements of what was afoot. Dr. Thomas Williamson operated a mission about three miles north of the Upper Agency, and the Reverend Stephen Riggs managed an outpost about two or three miles northwest of Williamson's. They and their wives and other missionaries in their charge were reluctant to accept what they were told by Otherday's emissaries. Many of them had been working with the Sioux for twenty-five years or more, attempting to impart their religious faith and encourage the Indians to abandon their traditional lifestyles and cultural values. It was a tough slog, and the missionaries were subject to incessant criticism from both Indians—who resented the power and arrogance of the whites—and other whites who believed the Indians were intractable savages beyond the reach of civilization. Now the missionaries were watching their life's work dissipate before their eyes, and they did not accept it gladly.

Nevertheless, it was difficult to dispute the witness of the Christian chiefs who warned them in explicit terms what would happen if they did not flee. Of particular concern were their young daughters who, the Christian chiefs said, were especially vulnerable to the depravity of the Sioux warriors. Reverend Riggs, his wife Martha, and the others at their mission joined the Christian chiefs in prayer and sang a favorite hymn, "God Is the Refuge of His Saints." By midnight the people of the Riggs mission had taken refuge on an island in the Minnesota River.

During the night the Sioux attacked trading stores at the Upper Agency and began looting. The Myrick brothers owned a second store at the Upper Agency, and not surprisingly, it was attacked first. The attackers shot and wounded Stewart Garvie; he lived above the Myrick store. Trailing blood, Garvie found his way to the warehouse where many of the whites were hidden under the watchful eye of Otherday. Another trader employee, Peter Patoile, who worked at the store of his kinsman Francis Patoile, was also seriously wounded but not killed.

That left four trading stores at the Upper Agency unattended by anyone. By dawn the Sioux were deeply engrossed in plundering everything they could find from the hated traders, loading it onto wagons, and helping themselves to whiskey. Amid the confusion, Otherday quietly led sixty-two men, women, and children to the nearest river crossing about half a mile away. Many were on foot. Some, like the wounded Garvie, rode in wagons. Among them were Indian agent Galbraith's wife and three children, subagent Nelson Givens and his family, Otherday's family, the agency physician Dr. J. L. Wakefield, and several other white residents of the trading post. Otherday took the fugitives on a three-day trip north of the river to the Abercrombie road and then eastward to a trail leading to Cedar City in McLeod County, where Garvie died of his wounds. The group then continued on to Hutchinson, from where they scattered out to settlements in Glencoe, Carver, Shakopee, and St. Paul.

Peter Patoile had been too badly wounded to reach the warehouse. Spitting blood, he hid in the forest for days and observed the looting of the agency stores. Living on roots and berries, he wandered across the prairie for almost two weeks. Somehow his wounds healed of their own accord, and he eventually appeared at a settlement some forty miles north of the present-day city of St. Cloud, about one hundred miles as the crow flies from where he started. He had covered about two hundred miles on foot in a meandering course to get there and was almost hanged when he arrived because the locals were anxious about the massacres they were hearing about and thought he might be an Indian. Cooler heads prevailed, and he was sent to explain himself to the authorities in St. Paul.

Congress later awarded Otherday twenty-five hundred dollars for his heroism, which he needed because his Sioux neighbors burned his house to the ground and trashed his fields. He used the money to buy farmland near Hutchinson, where he and his family made another start at farming.

While Otherday was leading his group away from the Upper Agency, Reverend Riggs waded ashore from the island and went to the agency to see what was going on. He observed the looting under way and learned of Otherday's escape. He returned to his people on the island, stopping on the way to warn the Williamson mission and urge them to evacuate. The Williamsons, however, insisted they were in no danger and would remain.

Riggs now led a party that had grown to more than thirty people on a route along the north side of the Minnesota River south toward Fort Ridgely. The route chosen by Otherday was safer, but Otherday knew the way through swamps and forest and the Riggs party did not. Also, Fort Ridgely was much closer than Cedar City.

Unknown to Riggs, the Williamsons had learned of the killing of teacher Amos Huggins, who had lived among the Sioux all his life. That changed their minds about leaving. Several people from the Williamson mission now moved separately in the same general direction as the Riggs party toward the fort.

The Riggs party, moving slowly on foot and with ox-drawn wagons, proceeded warily through Sioux territory and expected to be attacked at any moment. At night they slept without fires, and they soon exhausted their food. On Wednesday they were joined by four whites armed with "guns of not much account" on their way to New Ulm, which was sixteen miles southeast of the fort. On Thursday night—cold, wet, and hungry—the pilgrims killed a cow and feasted. By noon the next day, Friday, August 22, they reached the mouth of Birch Coulee Creek, thirteen miles northwest of Fort Ridgely and just across the river from the Lower Agency. As they paused, the Williamson party came into view, along with three others. Including the four partially armed men who joined them, the Riggs party now numbered forty-two, including thirty women and children.

During their pause, they heard cannon fire from the fort, indicating it was under attack. They had no way of knowing what the situation was there or whether the fort offered sanctuary. Dr. Williamson's son-in-law, Andrew Hunter, volunteered to scout the situation. He crawled into the fort, through the besieging Sioux, and learned that it was swamped with more refugees than it could handle. The soldiers advised him that his group would be received but, because of the overcrowding, the livestock would have to be left to the Indians. Hunter returned to the Riggs party, carefully avoiding the Sioux a second time.

Riggs and Williamson decided to circumvent the fort and head for Henderson, several miles distant. The four men going to New Ulm tried to leave at this point, but they were dissuaded by the cocked pistol of a man named Moore. By dawn they were well beyond the fort, and the men bound for New Ulm were allowed to leave. The four rode away from the missionary party, entered a ravine, and were promptly killed by Sioux warriors who apparently were stalking the Riggs party.

The missionaries arrived safely at Henderson the following Monday. They were greeted with wonder by friends who had heard they were all dead. "Surely, God led us and watched over us," said Martha Riggs.

It isn't clear how the Riggs and Williamson parties managed to escape the Sioux during their painfully slow flight unless the landscape was filled with thousands of refugees and there weren't enough Sioux to kill them all. Across southwest Minnesota the entire white population was uprooted and set in motion.

FORT RIDGELY would likely have fallen quickly had the Sioux moved upon it immediately while Lieutenant Gere had only a handful of men. Little Crow had intended to do precisely that, but he first had to persuade his obstreperous young warriors to do his bidding. The warriors were full of fight, having taken confidence from their victory over Marsh's detachment at Redwood Ferry. Little Crow convened a council from among the chiefs who were available. This assembly did not include Red Middle Voice, Cut-Nose, and certain other thugs who were elsewhere engaged in attacking homesteads, pouncing on refugees, killing men, raping women, nailing children to trees, and looting whatever goods were transportable. Little Crow, Big Eagle, and other chiefs objected to these atrocities and attempted to shame the warriors into restraint. But the warriors, as brutal as they were, were fighting in traditional fashion. The atrocities against whites were essentially the same as those committed against the Chippewas and other tribal enemies who did the same to the Sioux when they could.

Little Crow at least understood the need to hit the enemy's strongpoint when it was vulnerable. He reported to the council that his scouts had spotted approximately fifty soldiers on the way to the fort (Sheehan's troops) but said they were still hours away. The fort had "wagon guns" (cannon), he acknowledged, but only a handful of soldiers to operate them. It would be a simple operation, he said, to overrun the fort, seize the guns, and deprive the enemy of their only base in the area.

But Little Crow immediately encountered opposition from the young warriors who had set their sights on New Ulm as their next target. In 1862 New Ulm was by far the largest settlement near the reservation. Founded by German colonization societies in Chicago and Cincinnati in 1854–55, New Ulm had by this time a population of about nine hundred. The settlement was on the north side of the river a few miles southeast of the Lower Agency, almost due south of Fort Ridgely. Most of the houses were scattered on low ground near the river, with a smaller cluster of homes higher up and separated by a slough that offered attackers ample cover. The town was even less suited for defense than Fort Ridgely.

Various chiefs and braves took turns expressing their opinions, some advocating a move against the fort, others against New Ulm, and still others indicating a willingness to attack either. The debate consumed the better part of two hours. In the end about two hundred voted to attack the settlement; the remaining hundred preferred an attack on the fort. The decision was yet another blow to Little Crow's prestige and did not augur well for the future of his enterprise.

LITTLE CROW'S dilemma was the same that had vexed other tribal leaders over the past three centuries in their mostly futile efforts to resist the encroaching white man. The Sioux were the equal of their enemies in bravery and ability to withstand the hardship of campaigning in the field. They were generally as well armed in terms of individual weaponry, and they were clearly superior in their knowledge of the country and ability to launch surprise attacks from deep cover. That they depended on the white men for their arms should not have compromised their effectiveness in a pitched battle, because they had the equipment they needed to fight, at least in terms of the limited engagements they were fighting in Minnesota.

What they lacked was organization and discipline. Chiefs like Little Crow had no authority to compel obedience other than suasion, and that was insufficient to sustain coordinated actions during a campaign. Every effort to forge unified action was subject to long-winded debates that rarely reached consensus. Those who disagreed with the final decision could, and often did, walk away. Once a battle was engaged, the chiefs could not rely on their troops to maintain formation and continue fighting in the face of tough opposition. Even during the fight at Redwood Ferry, a premature shot from the Sioux side compromised the surprise and enabled half the soldiers to escape.

Some of the most outspoken advocates of the uprising, such as Red Middle Voice and Cut-Nose, were absent and thus could neither voice their unqualified support for the fighting nor intimidate the half-hearted. Little Crow was acutely aware that these firebrands were thus undermining the war effort, but there was nothing he could do about it except use what forces he had at his disposal.

All available evidence suggests that a leader like Red Middle Voice, who in fact was banished from his own village and forced to find refuge elsewhere long before the 1862 uprising, was a homicidal killer. In a civilized society he would have been locked up or, more likely, hanged. But the Sioux had, at best, limited means for suppressing violent characters in their midst. Red Middle Voice was not only on the loose, he was perhaps the most influential individual in unleashing the violence of the uprising. Having helped set anarchy in motion, he seized the opportunity to commit unspeakable depredations that invoke shudders more than a century later. But he contributed nothing to the decisive battles against the soldiers and did not await the inevitable retribution.

While the Sioux debated among themselves, Lieutenant Sheehan and his 50 men reached Fort Ridgely. They had been camping for the night when Marsh's messenger found them. A twenty-five-year-old officer with a keen sense of the need for speed in dealing with Indians, Sheehan wasted no time. He double-timed his soldiers forty-two miles in nine and a half hours. Soon after their arrival, the Renville Rangers—consisting of 50 half-breed volunteers that Indian agent Galbraith had recruited for Civil War duty—also arrived at the fort, plus another group of volunteers from St. Peter. Sheehan assumed command from the nineteen-year-old Gere, who was no doubt relieved to be relieved. The fort's defense had quickly grown from 22 armed men to about 180, and they guarded 300 refugees and two boxes of gold.

When the one hundred or so Sioux who had sided with Little Crow in the vote learned of the fort's reinforcements, they went back to their villages. The remaining Sioux set out to besiege New Ulm.

THE PEOPLE of New Ulm anticipated the assault by the Sioux and were busy mustering such defenses as they could. Brown County sheriff Charles Roos and German immigrant Jacob Nix, who had military experience, took charge, organizing forty or so men into militia units. Others were put to work erecting barricades around a section of town that included some brick buildings, which offered the best prospects of defense. Couriers were sent to nearby settlements to request assistance while others went into the countryside to find farmers who might be hiding or unaware of the danger. One group of sixteen men sent out along the Cottonwood River southwest of the town was ambushed on its way back; eleven were killed.

The first assault came in the afternoon of August 19 when about one hundred warriors, roughly half of those who had voted for the attack, emerged from the woods above the town and opened fire. The other half had gone down the Cottonwood to raid homesteads, murder, and loot. Apparently no chiefs were present to give instructions to the attackers. The few defenders fought back as best they could and managed to keep the Sioux at bay. A few whites made a small attack beyond the barricades and put the Indians in that section to flight. The Sioux managed to set fire to a few houses, and one thirteen-year-old girl caught in the crossfire was killed. By midafternoon a sudden rain doused

the fires, and sixteen mounted men from St. Peter rode into town to assist in the defense. The Sioux departed without booty or prisoners.

THE SIOUX then turned their attention to Fort Ridgely, which was still
in a precarious position despite the arrival of reinforcements. A key to
the fort's defense was provided by Sgt. John Jones, an ordnance expert
in charge of the cannon and ammunition. He quickly taught the men
of Company B to load and fire the cannon and formed them into three
artillery units. Jones himself and Dennis O'Shea, an experienced ar-
tilleryman, had at their disposal five field pieces—a 6-pounder, three
12-pounders, and one 24-pounder.

On Wednesday afternoon, August 20, Little Crow appeared with
between three hundred and four hundred warriors. He led a diversionary attack on the west side of the compound while the main force attacked from a ravine on the northeast corner, gaining control of some of
the fort's buildings. Combined rifle and cannon fire drove the Indians
back into the woods. At the same time Sergeant Jones focused cannon
fire on other Sioux coming from the south and west. At one critical
juncture a group of soldiers moved under cover provided by the cannon
to retrieve ammunition and powder from an exposed magazine building
on the outskirts of the compound. The fighting lasted about five hours,
and then the Sioux withdrew.

The Sioux had never before encountered artillery and found it dis-
quieting. One witness said they were "mortally afraid" of what they
called the "rotten balls" being fired at them. A heavy rain fell overnight
and through much of the next day, giving the defenders a respite to secure more water and beef up their defenses.

6

THE TOOLS
WE HAVE

THE UNION DEFEAT AT Second Bull Run marked Lincoln's low
point of the war—at least to that point. The president had ac-
corded great confidence in John Pope, the son of an old associate
from Illinois who had accompanied the president's party on its 1861
inaugural trip to Washington. Pope was a strident antislavery Republican, unlike the Democrat McClellan who was maddeningly ambivalent
on the subject. Also, Pope was a fiery advocate of aggressive action in
the field, which also contrasted sharply with McClellan's affinity for
strategy and maneuver. During the Seven Days' battles on the Virginia
Peninsula the previous June, while McClellan was being roughly han-
dled by Lee's troops, Pope was in Washington at Lincoln's side at the
War Department, explaining the meaning of reports from the field.
Pope made no effort to conceal his scorn for McClellan's dilatory tactics. Yet Pope became restive in the role of presidential adviser and
made clear his desire for a field command. The result was Second Bull
Run, which was, if possible, an even greater disappointment to Lincoln than it was for Pope.

Like many political leaders before and since, Lincoln struggled
with his responsibility to oversee military action. He had little military
training or experience to guide him. It is simple enough to say that a
president should leave the fighting to his military leaders, but what
criteria is he to use to decide which military leaders are competent
and which are not? McClellan had certainly proved himself adept at
organization and defense, but the South could not be conquered by

defensive measures, a reality that McClellan either refused to grasp or was not concerned about. Pope had refreshingly demonstrated the aggressiveness Lincoln sought in his generals, but it had led to a resounding defeat. The president was at the end of his tether.

There is an old saying attributed to various French statesmen that war is much too serious a matter to be left to generals. During these troubled days, Lincoln was stealing what free moments he could to hurriedly read books on military strategy, struggling for an understanding that would enable him to raise the right men to positions of power in the Union command structure.

Lincoln's priority at the moment was how to deal with his defeated favorite general. He summoned Pope for a personal meeting on September 4. There the general blamed the battle's outcome on everyone but himself, reserving particular venom for McClellan for not moving to his support and for Fitz John Porter for openly subverting Pope's efforts. There was substance to Pope's complaints, but it was equally clear that he was generally despised by his subordinates, and given the general's irascible temperament and eagerness to fault others, it wasn't hard to see why that might be. Given a choice between Pope and virtually the entire Union officer corps, Lincoln decided to sacrifice Pope. The following day he ordered the fallen general to Minnesota to deal with the Sioux outbreak.

This was not merely a guise to get Pope out of town. Minnesota Governor Ramsey had requested that a new command be created to deal with the Sioux, and in response Lincoln created the Department of the Northwest, comprised of Minnesota, Nebraska, Wisconsin, Iowa, and the Dakota Territory, with Pope in command. Pope deemed this mission a significant comedown, which it surely was, and true to his nature, he was not a little shy about sharing this opinion with others. He said Lincoln's failure to defend him from critics was "feeble, cowardly and shameful." Pope demanded that War Secretary Stanton tell him "the meaning of the order" and asked if it was the result of "treachery of McClellan and his tools."

Stanton replied, "The Indian hostilities require the attention of some military officer of high rank, in whose ability and vigor the Government has confidence." He added, "You cannot too highly estimate the importance of the duty now intrusted to you." Stanton said he was certain Pope would be able to "meet the emergency."

Pope was to spend a good bit of his time in exile in Minnesota writing angry letters to friends and legislators in which he blamed his defeat at Second Bull Run on the "praetorian system" of McClellan and his cronies. But he was still an army officer and accepted the mission given him by the president. Pope was soon in Minnesota, sending inflammatory reports about the extent and implications of the Indian uprising back to Washington.

By then Lincoln's primary attention was no longer on Pope or the Sioux uprising in Minnesota; it was on Lee's army in Maryland. This was a calculated gamble by Lee and Confederate President Jefferson Davis to take the battle to the enemy. Except for a few rather minor clashes in Kentucky, the Civil War thus far had been fought exclusively on Southern territory. Confederate leaders believed it would be a good experience for the Yankees to have their own country fought over for a change. They did not really believe they had the power to subdue the North or overrun Washington, but they had reason to believe that a large-scale invasion, attended by a few successful battles, might erode Northern support for the war. The Confederacy did not need to defeat the North but merely survive. Also, Southern leaders perceived a realistic chance they could sow discord among Marylanders who were widely reputed to be ambivalent about the conflict. Maryland was a slave state that had come close to seceding in 1861, discouraged at the last moment by the presence of Union troops in and around Annapolis when the crucial vote was cast. Lee hoped his troops might yet persuade Maryland to join the South, and if not, at least he might recruit fresh troops for the Southern cause.

The prospect of Maryland soldiers wearing gray was enough to cause any Union stalwart nightmares. Had Maryland declared for the South, the Union capital would have been an isolated enclave in enemy territory. The Rebel invasion of Maryland was also causing great consternation in nearby Pennsylvania, where Governor Andrew Curtin demanded that the president send eighty thousand trained troops immediately to the state's defense. "We have not eighty thousand disciplined troops, properly so called, this side of the mountains," Lincoln replied.

As if Lincoln did not have enough to worry about, his cabinet was in an uproar over McClellan's imminent return to command. Lincoln made the decision without consulting them, no doubt mindful of how hostile their reaction would be. Secretary of War Edwin M. Stanton in particular was perturbed by the news. He had no confidence in McClellan. Working with Treasury Secretary Salmon P. Chase, Stanton drew up a bill of particulars for the president, asserting that McClellan was at a minimum incompetent and probably a traitor to boot. Attorney General Edward Bates persuaded them to tone it down a little bit. The final draft asserted it was "not safe to entrust to Major General McClellan the command of the armies of the United States." Interior Secretary Caleb Smith agreed to sign it. Seward was absent that day, and Postmaster General Montgomery Blair took a pass on it. Navy Secretary Gideon Welles agreed that McClellan's removal would be prudent, but he declined to sign because he believed it would be "discourteous and disrespectful to the President."

This petition from his cabinet hit Lincoln at an extremely difficult time when he needed their support. It was indeed "discourteous and disrespectful to the President" and came close to insubordination, but Lincoln curbed whatever anger he may have felt, as he did when he suffered McClellan's rudeness the night he called on him at home. The president was more sad than angry. He told his cabinet that at times he felt almost ready to hang himself. Acknowledging McClellan's shortcomings, which were nothing new to him, Lincoln still insisted, "We must use what tools we have."

Other critics in and out of government took Lincoln to task for recalling McClellan because it seemed to telegraph confusion and indecision at a critical time when the nation's will was being sorely tested. Senator Garrett Davis of Kentucky called on Lincoln to cashier Stanton and Chase, whom he described as "the most sinister of the cabinet." Meanwhile, Massachusetts Governor John A. Andrew announced a meeting of his fellow governors to be held in Altoona, Pennsylvania, later in the month to consider ways of saving the president "from the infamy of ruining his country."

Amid all this politicking, a group of activist Christian abolitionists from Chicago, representing several denominations, called upon Lincoln to issue an executive order to free all the slaves. Lincoln was no better disposed to take that action than he had been a month before, when he was encouraged to reply to *New York Tribune* editor Horace Greeley's "Prayer of Twenty Millions." Noting that the recent Confiscation Act, intended to allow the seizure of slaves being used for Confederate military purposes, had produced scant result, he said, "What good would a proclamation of emancipation from me do, especially as we are now situated? I do not want to issue a document that the whole world will see must necessarily be inoperative, like the Pope's bull against the comet."

To further compound his anxieties, Lincoln's latest call for volunteers for the army was getting a tepid response. (Not until the following March would the government resort to conscription to bolster Union ranks in a move that sparked bloody riots in New York.) The president scanned the horizon for a whiff of good news, but at this dark turn, little was to be seen.

AT SUCH a time the president should have been able to draw strength from his family, especially his wife of almost twenty years, Mary Todd Lincoln, who had over their lifetime together worked zealously to promote his political career. But Mary Lincoln had already commenced a descent into madness that would years later land her in an insane asylum for four months, after which she would flee the country. By autumn of 1862 his marriage had probably become to the president as big or greater burden than that of his office.

The proximate cause for Mary's decline was the death of their eleven-year-old son, Willie, the previous February, apparently from typhoid fever. The boy's demise had hit both mother and father with profound force. It was not unusual for young people, and especially children, to die of fevers and infections in those days, and Willie was not the first child they had lost. Twelve years before, four-year-old Edward had died of pulmonary tuberculosis. At the time Mary was pregnant with Willie, who was born twenty days later, while his parents were still in mourning for Edward. Death was a frequent visitor to people of the nineteenth century, and the Lincolns saw their share of it. Even so, Willie's death was a cruel blow that snapped something in Mary Lincoln's fragile psyche.

Mary Todd had been born to an aristocratic Kentucky family in 1813, one of sixteen children. She was seven years old when her mother died, and her father soon remarried. Mary attended the Shelby Female Academy in Lexington and later Madame Mentelle's School for Girls. She was well educated by the standards of the time and certainly more cultured than her future husband. She supposedly spoke French fluently, though it is unclear who on the frontier of the mid-nineteenth century would have made that judgment.

In 1832 Mary went to live with a sister married to an up-and-coming politician in Springfield, Illinois, which is where she met the lanky young lawyer named Lincoln. It was a chaotic courtship, interrupted by a broken engagement, but they were married finally on November 4, 1842. Their first son, Robert, the only one of their four boys who would reach maturity, was born on August 1, 1843. Their last son, Theodore, called Tad, was born ten years later in 1853. Of the four, Willie was generally acknowledged as the most intelligent and attractive, and both parents doted on him.

Even in the early days of her marriage, Mary Lincoln showed signs of mental instability. She would go for weeks or months without incident—raising her young family, participating in community affairs, and hosting small social events. But she was subject to severe headaches that often left her immobile and sporadic fits of rage that could turn violent. Years later, neighbors recalled an incident of her chasing her husband down the street with a weapon in her hand—whether a broomstick or knife is unclear. Lincoln's response was generally to pick up one of the children and walk away. He clearly loved his wife, was generally supportive of her, and did what he could to help her work through her violent moods.

Perhaps her most conspicuous failing, and one that almost propelled her into the spotlight of a congressional investigation, was her propensity to spend vast sums of money she did not have. In January 1861, prior to her husband's inauguration, she went to New York and purchased on credit a new wardrobe and other fineries designed to show the Southern grand dames of Washington society that she was no frontier hick. Mary knew her husband would soon be earning twenty-five thousand dollars a year, a princely sum in those days and at least five times what he had been earning before. But her spending quickly raced ahead of even that bounty as eager merchants gladly extended credit to the new first lady. It soon became clear that Mary was unable to relate the significance of numbers on a page to her family's finite income. Nor did she see anything improper about accepting gifts from new friends and expectant officer seekers, which her extravagance rendered almost inevitable.

The previous occupant of the White House, James Buchanan, was a bachelor—the nation's only bachelor president—and the Executive Mansion's furnishings reflected the absence of a feminine hand. Mary set out to improve the ratty surroundings, securing from Congress an appropriation of twenty thousand dollars to be spent over four years to refurbish the president's house. It seemed like a lot of money to the legislators who approved it, but they had no idea what the president's wife was capable of. She set off for Philadelphia, where she immediately bought the most expensive drapes, carpets, china, and other furnishings—chairs, sofas, hassocks, and fine French wallpaper—regardless of price. On her return to the capital she personally supervised a complete cleaning and replastering of the entire mansion until it shone as it probably never had before.

By autumn she had overspent the entire four-year budget allocation by a considerable margin. She was acutely sensitive to the potential damage her irresponsible spending might cause her husband and went to extensive lengths to prevent him from learning about it. She tried to cover her tracks by selling old White House furniture and then by having the White House steward dismissed and pocketing his salary, a desperate move of questionable ethics. But none of that came close to covering the huge financial deficit she had created. When anyone tried to assist her in confronting the reality of her debt, she became enraged to the point that Lincoln's secretaries, John Nicolay and John Hay, who suffered the brunt of her acid tongue, took to calling her the "Hell-cat."

When creditors demanded payment, Mary finally had to prevail upon the commissioner of public buildings to inform the president about the situation and urge him to request a supplemental appropriation from Congress to cover the shortfall. Lincoln was outraged and made loud protests about the foolishness of spending so much money for fancy "flub dubs for that damned old house" when his soldiers slept without blankets. But in the end he had to protect his wife. Congress quietly approved two appropriations to pay her bills. It is an advantage to a president to have his party in control of both chambers of Congress.

Mary Lincoln's age and peculiar behavior patterns suggest she may have been undergoing a severe bout of menopause, but such things in those days were beyond the ken of medical practice. In any event, the death of Willie pushed her over a psychological precipice. She took to her bed for weeks, not bestirring herself even to attend Willie's funeral or to look after his brother Tad, who was recovering from the same fever that killed Willie. When she finally emerged from her chambers, she was so bedecked in mourning black that she was scarcely recognizable. All White House social functions were cancelled indefinitely, including the weekly concert of the Marine Band held on the Executive Mansion lawn. "When we are in deep sorrow," she said, "quiet is very necessary to us."

In a pathetic effort to communicate with Willie, Mary Lincoln began to confer with spiritualists. As many as eight séances were held in the White House, one of which the president attended. After a while Mary became convinced she could communicate with the dead without the aid of a medium. "Willie lives," she told a relative. "He comes to me every night and stands at the foot of the bed with the same sweet adorable smile he always has had." She added, "Little Eddie is sometimes with him."

By all accounts, the White House was a depressing place in those days. When Mary did consent to participate in public functions, it was clear to all that her heart was elsewhere. So obsessed was she in her personal grief that it seems never to have occurred to her that her husband was likewise suffering a trial of spirit—national as well as personal—and he might have needed her support. To the contrary, she entertained some extremely eccentric views about public issues and public men, including members of the cabinet, that she freely shared with the world, apparently unaware of the complications such statements created for her husband's administration.

As it seemed the world was closing in on him, the president spent what free time he could muster playing with Tad and helping him to raise a kitten and pet dog. Tad was affectionate but had a speech defect and apparently suffered from a learning disability. At the age of nine he was totally undisciplined and unable to dress himself. He could neither read nor write, despite the best efforts of private tutors brought in to deal with him. Yet Lincoln professed no great concern about Tad's development or lack of development. "Let him run," he said, "there's time enough yet for him to learn his letters and get pokey." So Tad interrupted cabinet meetings and frequently stayed with his father until late at night, often sleeping with him.

Lincoln's oldest son, Robert, was in Massachusetts, studying at Harvard. The president professed great respect and affection for his eldest son, but there was a distance between them. Robert was handsome, intelligent, and personable, and he got along famously with the president's secretaries, Nicolay and Hay. But Robert's visits to the White House were uncomfortable for all concerned. He and his father never seemed to find much to say to each other. Some historians wonder if the president, given his awkward appearance and humble origins, resented his son's dashing good looks and easy access to a formal education. Everyone in the Executive Mansion was relieved whenever Robert returned to school.

Mary Lincoln said it was the death of Willie that bestirred the president to ponder religious matters. "During this time, he increasingly turned to religion for solace," she said. "He first thought about this subject when Willie died, never before." It was true that Lincoln had never expressed much interest in religion prior to his election to the presidency. But he had begun addressing the deity with some conviction soon after he became president and the nation entrusted to his care began to fragment. In his letters and speeches he made frequent reference to God and implored his aid. In his first inaugural address, he said peace was still possible by "intelligence, patriotism, Christianity, and a firm reliance on Him, who has never yet forsaken this favored land." He and Mary leased a pew at the New York Avenue Presbyterian Church, and the president had several long conversations with its pastor about the afterlife.

Lincoln never experienced a "conversion" as the term was understood by Protestants in his time or ours, but he said later that during this period his religious views underwent a "process of crystallization." At heart, says historian David Herbert Donald, he remained a fatalist, taking more wisdom and inspiration from the writings of Shakespeare than the Bible.

LINCOLN ACHED for his dead son and fretted about his demented wife and listened for fresh reports about the Indian uprising, but his first concern was Robert E. Lee. The Confederate commander led a paper army of fifty-five thousand troops into Maryland, though his ranks were sorely depleted by stragglers who were exhausted, hungry, sick, and often barefoot. Most of them were gaunt and clothed in rags. One Marylander described them as "the filthiest set of men and officers I ever saw; with clothing that had not been changed for weeks. They could be smelt all over the entire inclosure." Another civilian recalled later, "They were the dirtiest men I ever saw, a most ragged, lean and hungry set of wolves." Despite their mean condition, however, they were in fine spirits. They were accustomed to whipping the Union forces sent against them, and victory can lift a soldier's sprit above mean conditions.

Lee moved north toward Frederick, Maryland, some forty miles north northwest of Washington. Somewhere between him and Washington, Lee knew, McClellan was maneuvering for a showdown. As always, McClellan vastly overestimated the size of Lee's force, but the reality on the ground was a Union army much larger than Lee's. And the men in the ranks were spoiling for a fight. Like two hungry tigers, the Blue and the Gray stalked each other through the Maryland countryside, looking for a chance to strike.

One of Lee's intentions—to induce and encourage a sympathetic response from the residents of Maryland—was coming to nothing. He had done his part to this end to the best of his ability. He had issued a statement to the people of Maryland, saying he had come "with the deepest of sympathy for the wrongs that have been inflicted upon the citizens of the commonwealth allied to the States of the South by the strongest social, political and commercial tics." But the Marylanders looked upon Lee's ragged host with pity and shut their doors against them. Still, there were isolated acts of kindness and charity. A few farmers welcomed the Rebels to their wells and provided what food they could spare, but such acts were not indicative of political sympathy or a will to collaborate against the Washington government. On September 7 Lee wrote to Davis, "I do not anticipate any general rising of the people in our behalf."

Lee's army invested Frederick for a five-day hiatus from their extended wanderings, and it proved to be something of a lark for both occupiers and occupied. The general consensus among the locals was that the raggedy Southern boys acted a lot better than they looked. No one was killed or "impressed" into the Southern army, and the women walked the streets unmolested. The only violence occurred when local residents in sympathy with secession trashed a local newspaper office, but the Rebels quickly restored order and put the rowdies in jail.

Lee's soldiers seized the first chance they had in a long time to eat a few square meals, clean their clothes, and—for many—obtain shoes. A local citizen, Dr. Lewis H. Steiner, who made no bones about his loyalty to the Union, took time to record some observations of the occupiers. "The movement they have now made is believed by them to be a desperate one, and they must 'see it through,'" he wrote. "They all believe in themselves, and are terribly in earnest. They assert that they have never been whipped, but have driven the Yankees before them whenever they could find them."

The occupation was almost comical in spots. Lee, Jackson, and Longstreet attended a local church where the minister, a loyal Union man, dressed down the invaders for their impertinence. True to form, Stonewall Jackson went to sleep, missed the sermon, and didn't awake until the final hymns.

Jeb Stuart took the lighthearted atmosphere a step further, organizing a ball at Urbana, a few miles from Frederick. Local ladies were invited to participate regardless of their political persuasion, and a band from Mississippi provided the music. During the dance, riders appeared, warning of the approach of Union cavalry. Stuart's horsemen dashed off to attend to the enemy and later returned to the dance, a few of them bloodied but unbowed. Their gallantry was rewarded as the young ladies tended their wounds.

On September 9 Lee convened his generals. He and Jackson hit upon a plan to send Stonewall with almost two-thirds of the army to capture the Federal arsenal at Harpers Ferry as well as its garrison of ten thousand soldiers. Lee's army was a long way from its supply base in Richmond, and in any event, the Confederate government was barely able to supply the army's most basic needs even when it was nearby. Lee was content that he could find sufficient food in the lush Maryland countryside—and his men meticulously paid shopkeepers and farmers with worthless Confederate money for anything they took—but Lee worried about his fragile supply line of arms and ammunition through the Shenandoah Valley. The Union garrison at Harpers Ferry threatened that lifeline.

It was not the first time Lee had divided his army in the face of superior forces, and Longstreet (as always) complained about this breach of military protocol. "Are you acquainted with General McClellan?" Lee replied. "He is an able general but a very cautious one."

Lee added also that the Union army was demoralized, but in this he was mistaken. He understood McClellan quite well and yet underestimated both McClellan's organizational skills and his popularity with the troops.

Lee's basic plan was to seize the Harpers Ferry arsenal, reunite his army, and move into Pennsylvania toward the capital of Harrisburg. The topography of western Maryland and northern Virginia seemed to abet his scheme, or more likely Lee sought to take advantage of what was there. A trio of mountain ranges, the most important being the thirteen-hundred-foot-high South Mountain, running north and south, made it easy for Confederate cavalry to fend off Union horsemen at a few key passes, leaving McClellan ignorant of Lee's whereabouts or intentions.

The daring plan that came to be known as Special Orders 191 envisioned three separate groups of Rebel troops converging on Harpers Ferry from different directions. In effect, Lee's army would be divided into four distinct parts in the presence of a superior enemy. No fewer than twenty-six of his forty brigades were committed to the Harpers Ferry mission, which was more than enough to ensure its success, but it left Lee with fourteen brigades alone against McClellan's host and a river between him and the main part of his army.

Seven copies of Special Orders 191 were made in the standard manner and dispersed to the appropriate commanders. At 4:00 a.m. on September 10 the ragged Confederate army began to march out of Frederick to the cheers of many young ladies who lined the streets to bid them good-bye. By nightfall the ragged Rebels were gone and Frederick little the worse for wear. By the next day Jackson's corps was across the Potomac and moving on Martinsburg. The twenty-five hundred Union soldiers there quickly retreated to Harpers Ferry, leaving the town to the Southerners, who were warmly received by their fellow Virginians. But other units encountered difficulty and resistance, and soon Lee's timetable began to erode. Then Lee received word that Union troops were moving down from Pennsylvania to Hagerstown. So he further fragmented his already dispersed troops by taking Longstreet and two divisions to Hagerstown to meet that alleged threat. Lee's army was now scattered across the countryside in five parts. When the Confederate commander entered Hagerstown he found no Union force there.

Meantime, McClellan had moved his headquarters to Rockville, about thirty miles south of Frederick, where he took stock and sent his cavalry to search out the Rebels. He had 85,000 men in his command while another 72,500 troops stood guard on Washington a few miles south. Amid the uncertainty, McClellan's imagination again took control of him. He peppered Washington with reports of huge Rebel forces, first Jackson with 80,000 and then Longstreet with 30,000 more. "All the evidence that has been accumulated from various sources since we left Washington goes to prove most conclusively that almost the entire rebel army in Virginia, amounting to not less than 120,000 men, is in the vicinity of Frederick City," he wrote.

By September 12, after a sharp cavalry fight in the middle of town, the last Rebels were driven from Frederick, and it became a Union city once again. When McClellan rode in, he was almost overwhelmed by well-wishers and admirers. People pushed babies to him to kiss and heaped garlands on his horse. Meanwhile, a reporter from the *New York Times* reported that certain members of McClellan's senior staff were encouraging him to turn the army around, march on Washington, remove Lincoln from office, and make a separate peace with the South.

The following day there occurred one of the accidents of war that can profoundly affect history. A group of Indiana soldiers was camped where some Rebel units had been camped a few days before. One of them spotted a clump in the tall grass nearby. It was a copy of Special Orders 191 wrapped around a bundle of cigars. A sergeant and a corporal were quick to recognize the names on the paper and grasp its significance. They took it to their company commander, a captain, who skipped several layers of military hierarchy to take it to corps headquarters. Gen. Alpheus Williams and one of his aides were stunned. They realized, if the paper were authentic, they had in their hands the enemy's disposition and battle orders. The orders were soon in McClellan's hands, verified by a staff officer who recognized the handwriting of Lee's chief of staff, Robert H. Chilton. Little Mac knew what he had in his hands. Even assuming his gross overestimate of the enemy numbers, he now knew the enemy force was scattered in pieces and waiting to be smashed one at a time. He knew Harpers Ferry still held out.

"Here is a paper," he told one of his generals, "with which if I cannot whip Bobbie Lee, I will be willing to go home."

Then he sent what was surely the most effusive message he had ever sent to Lincoln, and it must have brought a glimmer of hope to that sad face. "I have all the plans of the rebels, and will catch them in their own trap if my men are equal to the emergency. I now feel that I can count on them as of old. My respects to Mrs. Lincoln. Will send you trophies."

7

A TERRIFIC YELL

FORT RIDGELY WAS NOT only ill-designed for defense, it also lacked a well or cistern, relying for water on a spring-fed reservoir about a quarter mile away. Normally the soldiers kept an ample supply of water in the fort, but on Friday morning Lts. Timothy J. Sheehan and Thomas Gere discovered their containers were almost dry. They quickly dispatched men to the reservoir only to discover the Sioux had trashed it the day before, making it unusable. They assembled a work crew with shovels to dig the spring free and recreate the reservoir. Working feverishly, expecting to be attacked at any moment, they replenished the fort with enough water to last five days.

Work crews finished just in time. Little Crow returned with a significant force determined to take the fort, or as Big Eagle called it later, a "grand affair." He was there with Little Crow and Mankato and some chiefs who had opposed the uprising, including Wacouta and Traveling Hail. They had decided it was acceptable to join the uprising because it involved military action against a military foe, not the wanton murder of women and children. About five hundred warriors from the tribal groups associated with the Lower Agency were there, plus about three hundred from the Upper Agency, defying the Christian chiefs who wanted no part of it. Red Middle Voice was not there, but many of his warriors were. Altogether, eight hundred Sioux warriors were on hand, in the words of one historian, "either over dressed or not dressed at all." Both naked and dressed were smeared with war paint—black, red, blue, and yellow.

The Sioux were confident of success. Their scouts reported that the fort had received no major reinforcements and probably numbered no more than two hundred active combatants. That gave the Sioux a four-to-one advantage that they calculated was more than sufficient to assure them of victory. Leaving their horses in the care of squaws, they hid among the foliage around the fort from which they unleashed fire arrows in the hope of creating chaos. But recent rains made it hard to start fires, and those that did produce flames were quickly doused by the defenders. The opening round went to the defenders.

Little Crow and the other chiefs had been impressed by the noise and effect of the army's artillery, and they invested great effort in explaining to their warriors that the cannon were slow to shoot and move. The guns could be overrun and silenced easy enough, he said. The task was to rush the men at the guns quickly and put them out of action. Many of the Sioux had rifles as good or better than those carried by the soldiers; others were armed with bows and arrows and tomahawks. Little Crow and the other chiefs were so confident of success that they brought up a caravan of empty wagons, presumably stolen recently from settlers, and placed them across the river from the fort to transport the booty that would surely be theirs.

The next phase of the battle was a steady drumbeat of gunfire on the fort intended to keep the defenders on edge and force them to exhaust their ammunition. The Sioux briefly took control of the stables south of the fort, but they were driven back by cannon fire that set the stables on fire. A similar foray into the sutler's house was fended off in the same manner. During the preliminary action, an artillery shell exploded near Little Crow, injuring him. He was helped off the field.

The basic Sioux plan was for a concerted attack on the fort from all sides at the same time, intending to overwhelm the defenders. There was little effort to disguise this plan, and the soldiers in the fort understood what was coming. From every window and door, in every convenient nook and angle in their hastily erected barricades, the men of Companies B and C and the Renville Rangers waited with their rifles and the little ammunition at their disposal. Several women took part by producing cartridges from the powder and lead balls that were in stock, and at least one participated in the actual fighting by helping operate one of the field pieces.

Artillery proved to be a decisive factor. At every angle of the perimeter was one of the five guns that comprised the fort, and each was manned by gunners who now knew their task and were under excellent supervision. At about one o'clock, at a given signal, the Sioux erupted with raucous war whoops and converged on the fort. Charge after charge came from the surrounding ravines, but each onslaught was met with deadly accurate rifle fire from the soldiers. Dozens of Indians fell wounded or dead, and none ever penetrated the defensive perimeter. The Sioux pulled back in confusion but continued to shoot toward the fort's defenses. Answering fire from the fort abated because the soldiers were low on ammunition. From inside the fort the defenders could hear the Indian chiefs exhorting their warriors to greater effort.

The Sioux renewed their attack, briefly getting some fresh fires started. The soldiers answered with deadly effective artillery fire. With Little Crow out of action, Mankato led the main assault. The fighting continued for about six hours, but the continuous firing of the cannon disrupted the Sioux continuity, not to mention their state of mind. Mankato made one final attempt to rally his warriors for a decisive push, but as he was organizing his ranks, a volley from the fort's biggest cannon, a 24-pounder, tore into them with a huge roar, killing several Indians and scattering the rest. There was no further effort to take the fort. The Sioux withdrew. One white defender was killed and seven others wounded. Many of the buildings far from the fort's center were destroyed, and Sioux squaws made off with several cattle, mules, and oxen, but that was about all the Indians had to show for their work. The seventy-one thousand dollars in gold remained safe within the fort.

"We thought the fort was the door to the valley as far as St. Paul," Big Eagle said later. "And if we got through, nothing could stop us this side of the Mississippi. But the defenders of the fort were very brave and kept the door shut."

WHILE THE Sioux were attacking Fort Ridgely, elsewhere other warriors continued the massacres of civilians wherever they could be found. The white settlers living nearest the Upper and Lower Agencies were already dead or in flight, so the Sioux began to branch out farther in all directions, seeking settlers who had either not heard of the massacres or who for one reason or another had not sought safety in flight.

There was one more army installation, Fort Abercrombie, well to the northwest on the Dakota side of the Red River, that came under Sioux attack. A small garrison of fewer than a hundred men was assaulted on August 30 and again on September 6. Abercrombie's soldiers discovered to their dismay that most of their ammunition did not fit their weapons, and they spent many frantic hours cutting cannon canister apart to make rifle slugs that fit their barrels. But when they had to, they mounted a brisk defense. Cannon fire took a heavy toll on the Sioux, who withdrew but maintained a steady harassment of the fort for several weeks. A relief column arrived at the fort on September 23, effectively ending the siege though there were a few more skirmishes. Total casualties at the fort amounted to five dead and five wounded. Casualties among the Sioux, who probably came from the Upper Agency, were much higher.

Everywhere else the action was inconsistent. Acts of the most perverse brutality were relieved by occasional acts of courageous mercy in which Sioux defended whites from other Sioux. Some settlers were massacred while others were allowed to proceed unmolested. And a growing population of prisoners, almost all of them women and children, began to accumulate under Little Crow's protection near his village. They were generally treated poorly, and many of the women were raped repeatedly.

The fighting was almost totally one-sided. Most of the young white men of military age were off fighting the Confederacy. Many of the remaining settlers either had no weapons or were too befuddled to use them effectively. They generally regarded the local Indians as harmless beggars who posed no serious threat beyond that of occasional minor theft. They were taken by surprise and were ill-prepared to defend themselves.

About thirty German families living near what is now Sacred Heart, Minnesota, learned of the depredations going on around them and set out as a group in eleven ox-drawn wagons toward Fort Ridgely. By sunrise they had traveled about half the distance when they were overtaken by Sioux warriors, some of whom were known to the settlers. The Sioux persuaded them that the killing, which they had all by now heard about, was being done by Chippewas on the warpath and that they should return to their homes. But as soon as they had reached one of the houses, the Sioux turned on them and killed all the men and most of the women and children.

Milford Township, situated on the eastern edge of the Lower Agency just west of New Ulm, had the highest casualty rate. The residents were taken unaware on August 18 when the Sioux pounced, killing more than fifty people before the sun went down.

The story was the same all over the region. At the Scandinavian settlement of West Lake, forty miles or so north of the Upper Agency, the Sioux came to the home of Anders P. Broberg, a Norwegian immigrant. After shaking hands all around, the Sioux killed Anders, his eleven- and fifteen-year-old sons, and his brother John. They then turned on Broberg's wife, whose screams and struggles created enough diversion to enable her daughter, Ernestina, to escape. Mrs. Broberg was beaten to death.

Broberg's brother Daniel lived nearby with his family. They in turn were massacred by the Sioux. Of the two families, Ernestina was the only survivor.

On the western border of Minnesota at Big Stone Lake, near present-day Ortonville, the Sioux killed four traders' clerks and government employees at a local trading post and then looted the place.

Here and there a few settlers managed to escape. Guri Endreson lived with her husband, Lars, and their five children near Willmar in Kandiyohi County. The Sioux attacked, killing Lars and one son and badly wounding another boy. Guri and her youngest daughter escaped by hiding in the cellar. The Sioux left, taking the two older girls with them. Guri put her wounded son on a sled and set off with her daughter for the cabin of her son-in-law five miles away. There she found her son-in-law and another man, both severely wounded. She also discovered a wagon and team that the Sioux had overlooked, put the wounded people in it and set out for the nearest settlement, Forest City, some thirty miles away. The two abducted daughters somehow managed to escape their captors and joined their surviving family in Forest City.

Such stories were the exception. About forty-five miles southwest of the Minnesota River in Murray County lie several lakes, the largest being Lake Shetek, headwaters of the Des Moines River. Two Sioux chiefs, White Lodge and Lean Bear, had settled there to get as far away from the whites as they could. But eleven white families had settled nearby, and when the chiefs heard of Little Crow's insurrection, they sent word they wanted to join in. Their most immediate target, predictably, was the local white population.

One of the settlers who lived alone, Charlie Hatch, saw smoke rising from a nearby homestead. Sensing trouble, he went there to discover a haystack ablaze and the body of a neighbor nearby. Hatch mounted his horse and rode quickly from farm to farm to warn others that trouble was afoot. Soon the families had convened at John Wright's solid two-story log home, which was the most formidable structure in the area and an obvious refuge. About thirty people, mostly women and children, were assembled when a Sioux warrior they knew as Old Pawn rode up with several other Sioux. Old Pawn told them what had happened at the Lower Agency and that several hundred "bad Indians" were in the area looking for trouble. A woman named Koch arrived to report that Indians had killed her husband, Andrew. She had gone to warn other neighbors, seen Indians in the vicinity, and come instead to the Wright homestead. Upon hearing this, Old Pawn and the other Sioux returned to their tepees not far away. Straightaway they came back naked and adorned with war paint. Old Pawn offered the lame explanation that by adopting this guise, they could defuse tensions with the "bad Indians" and protect the settlers. "We will fight for you when the time comes," he said.

Six of the white men had guns. Old Pawn urged them to fire the weapons. "That will scare the bad Indians," he said. "They will be afraid to come near."

"Do you think we are fools?" demanded one settler. "We will keep our guns loaded and cocked."

Old Pawn said he would go to the Koch farm to retrieve Andrew's body if one of the whites would accompany him. No one volunteered. Another group of painted Sioux on horseback appeared in the distance. Old Pawn and one of his companions rode out to confer with them. He soon returned with a warning that three hundred "bad Indians" were getting closer. He urged the settlers to take refuge in the woods because the "bad Indians" would surely attack and burn the Wright house.

The settlers were about two miles from the forest bordering the lake. In between lay a great slough—about three hundred acres of swampy lowland usually flooded but relatively dry and passable in summer. Several of the settlers argued against leaving the cabin, which was

solid, fairly well stocked with powder and shot, and housed other implements that could be used as weapons. It offered a formidable defensive position from which to fight off Indian attacks.

But Old Pawn argued persuasively that they would be outnumbered ten to one and that most of them were women and children who
could contribute little to a fight. At least in the swampy area they could
seek out individual hiding places where some of them could escape detection. They agreed to go. A few of the women and the younger children climbed into the one wagon that was available; the others walked.
When they were about halfway to the lake, on the edge of the slough, a
group of about a dozen mounted Sioux—including Old Pawn—bore
down on them. There was a general panic as the settlers leaped from
the wagon and dashed helter-skelter toward the slough. They all made
it into a clump of high grass, though at least four of them received bullet wounds on the way. Near the edge of the grass, the armed men
stopped and turned to fire, taking aim at an Indian who was trying to
ride between them and the slough. They killed Chief Lean Bear, but
that did not deter the other Sioux.

Thus commenced what came to be known as Slaughter Slough.
The settlers found themselves in a relatively narrow band of tall grass
and brown rushes, about seven feet high in places, separated from the
main part of the slough by an open area. They were out of sight but effectively surrounded. The Indians rode around them emitting war
whoops. After a while, the Sioux, led by White Lodge and Old Pawn,
settled down on a nearby ridge to enjoy the spectacle. The high ground
gave them an excellent angle for shooting into the slough.

The ground in the slough was dry and covered with briars and
rough dried mud, which was uncomfortable to sit or lie on. Every time
a settler moved, it caused a ruffle of the tall vegetation that drew fire
from the surrounding Sioux. The settlers could not see each other or
their attackers, but the sporadic fire began to take a toll. The air was
filled with cries from people as they were hit by gunfire as well as pleas
for help. But families were separated and unable to help each other.
Some of the men had managed to reach the main part of the slough,
but they were isolated from their wives and children. Every effort to
move toward someone in need drew more fire from the Sioux. Sarah
Ireland screamed in pain when she was shot in the abdomen. Lavina
Eastlick had been hit in the heel during her flight to the tall grass, then

she was grazed in the side and a moment later in the head. She felt blood running across her face. She cried out for her husband.

"I'm coming, Vinnie," he replied, but she warned him off. "Don't. Stay where you are." She heard a groan and called out to him again. "John is dead," said Mrs. Koch.

Four of the five Eastlick children, all boys, were near their mother. The oldest was eleven and the youngest fifteen months. She called out to her missing boy, Giles, but got no answer. The other boys kept asking if their father was alive. She warned them to be quiet lest the Indians get them. Other women screamed out when they were hit by gunfire, and a chorus of agony filled the desolate foliage.

The day grew warm and the slight breeze tapered off, increasing the discomfort of the besieged. Old Pawn began calling out to the women and children to come out of the slough, assuring them they would not be hurt. By this time, Old Pawn's credibility was at low ebb, but then so were the options available to the surviving settlers in the slough. William Everett invited Old Pawn to come to him. Old Pawn demurred, "No, you must come out," he said.

"Somebody else talk to him," Everett said. "Tell him I'm dead."

Everett's wife, Almira, stood up and waved her hand from a high point in the slough. "Pawn," she called out, "that last shot killed Billy."

"Come out," Old Pawn called. "I want you and Julia Wright for my wives."

"Only if Lavina will go along," Almira said, trying to stay on her feet as blood dripped from her wound.

"He asked for Julia," Lavina said. "I don't think Julia has been shot, but I have."

Almira and Julia struggled out of the slough as best they could, Almira dripping blood, followed by their children. The Indians called to them to climb to the top of the ridge. They worked together in that direction, helping Almira move as best they could. Near the top of the ridge, Almira died.

Old Pawn stood among the refugees and called out to the others to see that they were unharmed. One of the remaining men urged the women to take the children and go. Lavina took the opportunity to find her husband, who was dead, before she went toward the Indians. Near the top of the ridge were several armed Sioux and their squaws. Lavina looked back toward the slough and saw her four-year-old

Freddy trying to make his way toward her. A squaw saw the boy also and ran in long strides down the slope toward him. Lavina thought for a moment the squaw would rescue her child, but the squaw picked up a heavy piece of wood and bashed the boy on the head. He stumbled bleeding past his mother, unseeing. Then she saw another squaw punishing her son Frank the same way. She tried to move toward him, but an Indian blocked her way, threatening her and her baby, Johnny. The Indian beckoned her to the ridgeline with Johnny and one of her little boys, Merton. Mrs. Koch and several other women were already there. Two of the mothers, Sophia Smith and Sophia Ireland were struggling to bring along their children, some of whom had been wounded. Two Sioux watched them, laughed, then shot them down.

Lavina Eastlick reached the crest with another woman, Laura Duley. An Indian executed Duley's son, Bill, in front of her eyes. "You said you would not kill women and children," Lavina screamed. Old Pawn gave her a bad look and raised his rifle to fire. As Lavina tried to move away, he shot her. The ball tore into her back, exited near her hip, and struck her arm on the way out. She fell and Old Pawn moved away. Lavina called out to Merton to take care of Johnny.

Julia Wright was prodded by an Indian to return to the slough and bring out the guns the men had used. She returned with one weapon that was obviously defective. The Indian hurled it to the ground near where Lavina lay.

It began to rain. Lavina heard the Indian ponies moving and was afraid they might step on her. She struggled to move out of the way. A Sioux saw her move, picked up the defective rifle, and clubbed her on the head and shoulders.

Late that night Lavina regained consciousness in the pouring rain. She struggled to reach the other women and children, including her own. They all lay dead on the ground around her. Throughout the next day she tried to move bit by bit but was unclear where she was going. She heard some people cry out, then some shots, then silence. She continued to struggle along. After three days she reached the rough dirt road that led to New Ulm—seventy miles away. A mail carrier in a one-horse sulky came along and picked her up. Farther on, they picked up Thomas Ireland, who had been wounded eight times but was still alive. The next day they added to their load Alomina Hurd and her one- and three-year-old sons. Alomina's husband was among those killed.

When they had traveled about fifty miles from Lake Shetek, they came upon a small figure moving along the road with a bundle. It was Lavina's son Merton still carrying his brother Johnny. More than two weeks after Slaughter Slough, they reached Mankato. Lavina recovered from her wounds and later returned to the Lake Shetek area, where she remarried.

Julia Wright and Laura Duley were taken captive, along with six children, by White Lodge and spent several weeks roaming the western plains. In November they were ransomed and returned to their families.

Having been severely bloodied at Fort Ridgely, the Sioux warriors decided to again attack New Ulm, which had no artillery. It seemed an easier conquest than the stubborn fort and its soldiers and heavy guns. The earlier attack on New Ulm had been a relatively small affair; this time the Sioux came back with 650 men, fewer than had attacked Fort Ridgely but enough to take a simple town—or so it seemed. Also, in the earlier attack, the Sioux had no leader. This time they were led by Chiefs Mandato, Wabasha, and Big Eagle. Little Crow was still out of action due to injury.

Since the earlier fight, volunteers had been pouring into New Ulm from all over the region. Most of them were poorly armed, using guns intended for hunting game, usually shotguns. Some were armed only with pitchforks or axes. But among the volunteers were some doctors, including Dr. William W. Mayo of LeSeur, who came with surgical supplies. (Mayo's sons, William and Charles, would later found the famous Mayo Clinic.) They set up a makeshift hospital at the Dakota Hotel, the most imposing structure in the town. Built in 1859, it was a fifty-foot square of raw timber and clapboards.

The citizen defenders of New Ulm chose Judge Charles E. Flandrau of St. Peter as their commander. Designated by the citizens as a colonel, Flandrau had arrived late on the night of the first attack with 125 Frontier Guards from St. Peter. Flandrau was an attorney who had served at one time as an Indian agent. Alert and athletic, he had helped organize the Frontier Guards and was comfortable with responsibility.

During the few days between the first and second Sioux attacks, the town's forces were replenished by a hundred men from Mankato, another group from La Sueur who called themselves La Sueur Tigers, and several other local units. By Friday, Flandrau had about three hundred men under his command, most of them poorly armed. He directed some to build fortifications while others combed the surrounding countryside for refugees and kept watch for the Sioux. They found many mutilated bodies and reported the sound of heavy artillery from the direction of Fort Ridgely. They had no way of knowing what was going on at the fort, but they could guess and wonder about the outcome. Altogether, there were about a thousand people crowded into New Ulm by Saturday, far overtaxing the little town's meager resources. Sanitation became an obvious problem, and with it the threat of disease.

On Saturday morning, Flandrau's scouts reported seeing fires apparently set by the Sioux to convey the impression the fort had fallen. Flandrau sent 75 men across the river to check it out. They were cut off by the Sioux, had to retreat to St. Peter, and did not get back to New Ulm until the following day. This reduced Flandrau's fighting strength temporarily to about 225 men.

At midmorning the Sioux emerged from the woods west of the town and formed a long curved line on the upper terrace. "Their advance upon the sloping prairie in the bright sunlight was a very fine spectacle," Flandrau recalled, "and to such inexperienced soldiers such as we all were, intensely exciting. When within about one mile and a half of us the mass began to expand like a fan, and increase in the velocity of its approach, and continued this movement until within about double rifle-shot, when it had covered our entire front. Then the savages uttered a terrific yell and came down upon us like the wind."

The yell had the desired effect on the defenders, many of whom scattered before the onslaught, abandoning houses that the Sioux immediately occupied. But the whites rallied and retook most of the houses. "The firing from both sides then became general, sharp and rapid," Flandrau recalled. "And it got to be a regular Indian skirmish, in which every man did his own work after his own fashion."

Some twenty of the La Sueur Tigers took possession of a large windmill a few blocks from the business district that gave them a commanding view of the area. Sharpshooters all, they took a toll on the Sioux and prevented them from overrunning the barricades in several locations.

For a while the superior numbers of the Sioux were beginning to tell as they advanced from structure to structure toward the defenders. While the action was concentrated in the upper part of town, some Sioux sneaked into the lower part and set fire to some buildings, which provided a cover of smoke that drifted into the main part of the business district, causing the defenders to choke and gasp. It was house-to-house fighting for most of the day, and no one had time to fight fires.

About midafternoon some sixty Sioux gathered near the ferry on the river behind the downtown buildings. Realizing an attack was imminent from that quarter, Flandrau sent an equal number of defenders to rush the Sioux in a charge that took the warriors by surprise and put them to flight. It was the pivotal moment that broke the back of the siege. Fighting continued intermittently but to no great effect. Toward sundown the Sioux retired from the field.

After dark, Flandrau ordered that 40 buildings outside the defensive perimeter be burned, making some 190 structures in all that were destroyed at New Ulm. The following morning a few Sioux returned and fired on the town, but they were at too great a distance to do any harm. Flandrau convened a council that decided to evacuate the town. They were short on ammunition and food and also fearful of an epidemic among the noncombatants who had huddled for five days "in cellars and close rooms like sheep in a cattle car."

Altogether, the defenders of New Ulm counted 34 dead and 60 wounded among their number, a shockingly high ratio from a force of only 225. No one knows how many Sioux were killed and injured. The following morning the citizens loaded what possessions they could into 153 wagons and set out on foot toward Mankato, about thirty miles away. "A more heart-rending procession was never witnessed in America," Flandrau observed. "It was a melancholy spectacle to see 2,000 people, who a few days before had been prosperous and happy, reduced to utter beggary, starting on a journey . . . through a hostile country, every inch of which we expected to be called upon to defend from an attack."

Flandrau accompanied the train, but security was aided by 150 fresh troops from Nicollet and Sibley who had arrived after the siege was lifted. Flandrau considered the journey a dangerous expedient, but they all reached Mankato safely that night. He had wanted to return to New Ulm with 150 men to guard what remained of the town, as well as the goods that had been left behind, but his men balked. They were bone weary and eager to return to their own homes. "I did not blame them," Flandrau said.

"This was no sham battle, no trivial affair," wrote Minnesota historian William F. Folwell, "but an heroic defense of a beleaguered town against a much superior force." There is little question the battle of New Ulm saved other nearby towns from being overrun, but it did not end the uprising.

8

THE WHOLE LANDSCAPE
WAS RED

NEWS OF THE MINNESOTA massacres reached Washington and points east weeks after the fact, a time gap attributable to the remoteness of the region and the absence of reliable, timely news delivery. Telegraph wires had only reached St. Paul two years before and had yet to penetrate the Minnesota River Valley. There were four daily newspapers in St. Paul, but they had no reporters or correspondents near the Sioux territory. Most news agencies had focused their resources on the Civil War, which was a large story taking place in many locations at the same time, demanding a lot of legwork from correspondents. To further muddy the waters, the first reports of the uprising were brought to St. Paul by displaced settlers seeking refuge, and their individual and sometimes conflicting reports presented a confusing picture of what was going on.

These stories were met with a degree of disbelief based upon long experience with the hysteria that generally attended reports of Indian violence. Early accounts of the Sioux uprising in the St. Paul papers were carefully phrased as "unconfirmed reports" and "possibly exaggerated rumors." If that weren't confusing enough, some of the early reports did in fact prove to be exaggerated. For example, it was widely reported that the missionaries from the Upper Agency had all been killed. Just as that news was going out on the telegraph, the missionaries appeared safe and unharmed, led by their guide and defender, John Otherday. Estimates of deaths and destruction varied widely, and there seemed to be no credible source to sort it all out. Compounding the information gap was the fact that so many of the refugees were German immigrants with limited English skills and no relatives or friends in the city to support their credibility. Six months after the outbreak the pioneer newspaper editor and lecturer Jane Grey Swisshelm, lecturing in the East, complained that people still didn't believe it. "People cannot and will not believe it possible that any set of savages committed the outrages that we say they did on the people of a civilized state," she announced.

No one was more at sea about the events in Minnesota than the president. Just before noon the day after he created the Department of the Northwest and put Pope in charge of it, he received another panicky message from Minnesota Governor Ramsey: "Those Indian outrages continue. I ask Secy Stanton to authorize the U.S. Quartermaster to purchase say 500 horses—he refuses. The state cannot purchase on as good terms, if at all, as the General Government. This is not our war, this is a national war. I hope you will direct the purchase or send us 500 horses or order the Minnesota Companies of horse in Kentucky and Tennessee home. Answer me at once. More than 500 whites have been murdered by the Indians." Ramsey added that he had called upon Minnesota Senator Morton Wilkinson to go to the White House and seek aid for Minnesota—arms, supplies, and food for refugees. Episcopal Bishop Henry Benjamin Whipple also was on his way to Washington where, at Ramsey's urging, he was to ask his cousin, General in Chief Henry W. Halleck, to send a regiment of cavalry to Minnesota.

Ramsey's was not the only panicky voice. "A general alarm pervades all of our settlements," said Dakota Territory Governor William Jayne, describing "a few thousand people at the mercy of 50,000 Indians should they . . . fall on us." Iowa Governor Samuel Kirkwood added, "I have reliable information that Yankton Indians on our western border, north of the Missouri River, have joined with the hostile Indians in Minnesota, and threaten our whole northwestern border." Kirkwood foresaw a "terrible massacre" if the president did not intervene immediately.

Indeed, the flood of hysterical reports coming into Washington must have persuaded the president that the situation was even worse than it really was. "Nebraska settlers by the hundreds fleeing," reported officials from that state, who then explained, "A combined effort on the part of the unfriendly Indians is meditated against the entire region." Interior Secretary Caleb Smith endorsed this report, telling War Secretary Stanton, "The statements of the agent are corroborated by other information which has been communicated to this Department."

Lincoln received another report from personal secretary John Nicolay, still in Minnesota, who said negotiations with the Chippewas had broken down and might soon lead to open hostility. All of this did indeed seem to confirm Lincoln's worst fears of a general Indian uprising encouraged by the Confederacy as part of its war effort. True to his nature, John Pope did everything in his power to exacerbate the already volatile situation. He arrived in Minnesota on September 16 and on that same day wired Halleck, predicting "a general Indian war all along the frontier, unless immediate steps are taken to put a stop to it." He said there was panic "everywhere in Wisconsin and Minnesota."

Over the ensuing days Pope's reports to Washington grew increasingly frantic. "I am doing all I can," he said, "but have little to do it with." The Sioux uprising was, he said, a war of "formidable proportions" that demanded priority attention. Stanton was put off by Pope's demand for twenty-five thousand troops, which he considered excessive in light of the war needs against the South. Halleck also tried to calm Pope, telling him, "Your requisitions are beyond all expectations."

Pope responded by becoming even more overwrought. "You do not seem to be aware of the extent of the Indian outbreaks," he said to Halleck, claiming that fifty thousand white settlers were fleeing the country and that "the whole of Minnesota west of the Mississippi and the Territories of Dakota and Nebraska will be entirely depopulated." In fairness to Pope, much of what he reported to Washington was true enough. "You have no idea of the wide, universal and uncontrollable panic everywhere in this country," he reported to Halleck. "Over 500 people have been murdered in Minnesota alone and 300 women and children now in captivity. The most horrible massacres have been committed; children nailed alive to trees and houses, women violated and then disemboweled—everything that horrible ingenuity could devise. It will require a large force and much time to prevent everybody leaving the country, such is the condition of things."

But Lincoln had no extra armies to send to Minnesota. What he had was a large Rebel force roaming the Maryland countryside, dancing circles around McClellan's army, holding fancy balls in Frederick, surrounding the Harpers Ferry arsenal, and posing a very real threat to Washington itself. Not surprisingly, Lincoln eagerly responded to a suggestion by Governor David Tod of Ohio on September 9 to employ Union soldiers paroled by the Confederates against the Sioux.

In the early years of the Civil War it was customary for both sides to parole prisoners of war on the condition that they promise not to fight again until they were officially exchanged. This was deemed preferable to having to feed and care for huge populations of idle men who might otherwise return to their homes and provide for their families. This sensible system began to disintegrate not long after the Union began sending black soldiers into battle, for the South refused to treat blacks with the same respect extended to whites, and the North refused to tolerate discrimination against blacks. But in 1861 and 1862 the functioning parole system seemed an obvious solution to the dilemma presented by the Sioux uprising. At the time there were twenty thousand such Union parolees near Annapolis, Maryland. Lincoln ordered Stanton to send them to Minnesota "with all possible dispatch."

Stanton promised Pope that ten thousand paroled soldiers would soon be on the way to fight the Sioux. But neither Lincoln, Stanton, nor Pope anticipated resistance from the soldiers in question: most of the parolees simply refused to go. Some seized the opportunity to abandon military service altogether and return to their homes. Others insisted military action against the Sioux would violate their terms of parole.

After a few days Pope began to get restive, demanding to know when the soldiers would be on arriving. He complained that he had no cavalry and that "it is impossible to follow mounted Indians on foot." True to form, he ratcheted up his predictions of calamity. "Do not misunderstand the facts," he warned Halleck. "It is not only the Sioux with whom we have to deal. All the Indians—Sioux, Chippewas, and Winnebagos are on the verge of outbreak along the whole frontier."

But still the soldiers in Annapolis refused to move. Union Gen. Lew Wallace (who would later write *Ben Hur)* reported that when he tried to organize the parolees to fight the Sioux, "nearly the whole body protested." The same was true in other parolee camps. There was simply none among them willing to fight Indians in Minnesota. They had done their part, seen action against the Confederates, been captured and paroled. They wanted to go home—at least for a while.

Lincoln grew increasingly annoyed at this intransigence, and Pope grew increasingly distraught about his missing legions, but there wasn't much either could do about it. The following month, in response to a request from the president, Attorney General Edward Bates sent to Lincoln an opinion that the agreement or "cartel" between North and

South regarding paroled prisoners expressly forbade using them for other purposes, such as fighting Indians. In the meantime, Lincoln had other, more pressing issues nearer at hand to deal with—namely Lee and the Army of Northern Virginia.

GEORGE B. McCLELLAN, despite his shortcomings, fully realized the implications of his extraordinary possession of Special Orders 191. It was perfectly clear to him what Lee was doing and that the Confederate army was widely dispersed, leaving each part susceptible to annihilation. In fact, his advantage was even greater than he imagined because the Confederate timetable was behind schedule. The two major segments of the Southern army, Jackson's three divisions and Longstreet's two, were separated by a river and twenty-five miles. D. H. Hill's division, which included the Rebel supply train and one division near Boonsboro, Maryland, was a sitting duck. Other Southern units were scattered about the countryside. McClellan had at his disposal eighty-seven thousand troops, almost exactly twice as many as Lee. Yet McClellan was convinced that Lee outnumbered him. Still, the dispersal of Lee's armies left them vulnerable.

McClellan also knew he needed to move quickly to take advantage of the opportunity. "No time shall be lost," he promised Lincoln via telegraph. But McClellan was simply incapable of fast movement, and perhaps the Union soldiers, who had become accustomed to his style, were likewise averse to alacrity. Still laboring under the assumption that Lee had 120,000 men, it was imperative to make certain the Union supply wagons were full and his flanks adequately covered. A full eighteen hours passed before the first Federal troops began to move.

Lee was awaiting word of the anticipated surrender of the Union garrison at Harpers Ferry when he received the first intimations that something unusual was afoot with McClellan. There is a story that a Southern sympathizer had been on hand when McClellan received Lee's orders, and he relayed the news to Lee through Jeb Stuart. But the name of the sympathizer has been lost, and it seems unlikely that McClellan would have shared the contents of Special Orders 191 with a civilian. At most, a civilian could have reported that something was happening. At about the time Lee might have received this news, he also had intelligence from his cavalry that Union troops were moving toward him. Lee appreciated full well how vulnerable his dispersed forces were at that moment, and he reacted with his customary swiftness.

He raced to catch up with a situation that threatened to get away from him. Union troops got the better of a fight with D. H. Hill's people at South Mountain, threatening to interject themselves between Confederate units and setting them up to be picked off one at a time. Lee sent couriers to gather his forces near Sharpsburg and looked longingly toward Harpers Ferry for a quick resolution of that fight and an early return of his forces from there.

The Union commander at Harpers Ferry, Col. Dixon Miles, was an old army regular who had been disciplined for drunkenness at First Bull Run but allowed to retain his rank. He lacked sufficient wit to see that his position was indefensible and shrugged off suggestions from junior officers that he move his forces into the surrounding mountains, where they might make a stand against the enemy. Once Jackson's artillery was in place, the troops in Harpers Ferry had no chance. Miles was killed during an exchange of artillery, saving him the embarrassment of having to answer for his incompetence. A group of thirteen hundred Federal cavalry did manage to escape the night before the collapse, to the great annoyance of the Rebels who were looking for fresh mounts. About 200 men were killed on each side, a relatively minor count compared to what was coming. As was customary, some 11,500 Union prisoners were paroled on condition that they not take up arms against the South until they were officially exchanged.

As soon as Harpers Ferry was secure, Jackson's men moved to rendezvous with Lee at Sharpsburg. Around the region, other Confederates were moving in the same direction. To the Federals, watching the Rebels march away from them, it seemed as if they were on the run. McClellan thought so too and sent optimistic reports to Washington, where they were received with caution. The euphoria quickly dissipated as reports filtered back to McClellan's headquarters that Lee's army was forming a battle line near Sharpsburg and Antietam Creek. "They are in full view," Capt. George A. Custer reported. "Their line is a perfect one about a mile and a half long. We can have equally good position as they now occupy. We can employ all the troops you send to us."

In reality, Lee had mustered only a portion of his army and was by no means ready for a full onslaught by the Federals. He had with him, including artillery, perhaps fifteen thousand men to face McClellan's host. Of his army's forty brigades, twenty-six were still at Harpers Ferry, and many of his men were barefoot, tired, and hungry. Lee had been surprised by McClellan's uncharacteristic aggressiveness, but he was counting on the Union commander's innate timidity to buy time for the Southerners. Had McClellan hurled his forces on the Rebels at that point, there is little doubt Lee's soldiers would have been routed and a decisive Northern victory would have been achieved.

But that was not McClellan's style. The morning of September 16 dawned damp and foggy, obscuring movements of both armies. Sporadic cannon fire disturbed the peace, but as the hours passed it became clear to both armies that a fight would not come that day. McClellan's hesitancy was no surprise to Lee, who had told his subordinates there would be no fighting that day and probably not the next. McClellan outnumbered Lee four to one—at least two to one in his own imagination. But he dawdled the day away while Lee's lean dispersed units hurried toward him from many different points of the compass.

While McClellan wasted time, word came of the Union surrender at Harpers Ferry. News also reached Washington and caused a predictable round of disgust and finger-pointing. McClellan's critics assumed he was once again busily failing his mission. Around noon the hesitant general finally reached a decision, though his battle plan was vague. He would "make the main attack upon the enemy's left—at least to create a diversion in favor of the main attack, with the hope of something more, by assailing the enemy's right—and, as soon as one or both of the flank movements were fully successful, to attack their center with any reserve I might then have in hand." Orders were sent down the line that the fight would commence the next morning. Joseph "Fighting Joe" Hooker was to lead the initial advance, taking the Union right against the Confederate left. Hooker's preparatory disposition of his troops on the Rebel side of Antietam Creek made McClellan's intentions clear to Lee, who then aligned his defenses accordingly.

The battleground was filled with dips and deceptive ravines that seemed fairly level from a distance, but an up-close look at the field provided a variety of opportunities for clever defenders to thwart their attackers. On the Union left the two armies faced each other across Antietam Creek, a country tributary that was at once too wide and deep to be called a stream but still not a full-fledged river. Most men could wade it easily enough, but in doing so they became sitting ducks for sharpshooters on the opposite bank. And Union troops, not Confederates, would be the ones who had to ford the creek under heavy enemy fire. It rained during the night, and both armies, forbidden to start fires for fear of drawing enemy fire, endured a cold, wet, uneasy evening.

At daybreak both sides opened with artillery, and soon Hooker's troops went forward against Jackson's men and were immediately engulfed by Southern artillery and rifle fire. Much of the fighting was done in a thirty-acre cornfield where the action raged back and forth throughout the morning. At the beginning the corn was taller than a man's head; by the end there was little left but stubble and corpses—hundreds of them. Hooker's advance bogged down by midmorning. The Rebels took the worst of the fighting in terms of casualties, but Hooker himself was wounded and had to be evacuated from the field.

In the center of the Union line, the Second Corps, commanded by Edwin V. Sumner, moved ahead too quickly and without reconnaissance. As Sumner rode out in front with John Sedgwick's leading division, Sedgwick's division was caught by Confederate troops advancing from three directions and was badly mauled, losing more than two thousand men. The second division of Sumner's corps somehow missed the road taken by Sedgwick and came into line far to the left. Sumner's last division finally came into line to the left of the second after being delayed by McClellan. Together these two divisions forced the Confederates back into a sunken road, a heavily rutted roadway that formed a natural trench, later known as "Bloody Lane." There the battle reached a brutal intensity. After savage fighting, the Rebels abandoned Bloody Lane, but the attacking Federals stalled in the face of artillery fire.

At this point McClellan had victory in his grasp. The Rebels had been badly used. All of their forces had been committed. The streets of Sharpsburg were filled with beaten and demoralized Confederates who had, temporarily at least, lost their fight. Most of the left and center of Lee's line was held by a handful of diehards, but not enough to resist a determined attack.

All eyes were on the Union left commanded by Ambrose E. Burnside, a jovial fellow who enjoyed a remarkable degree of public respect based mainly on a couple of minor victories the year before. Burnside was a West Point graduate who sported a unique style of facial hair that has given his name, in a slightly inverted fashion, a certain immortality.

Lincoln had, in fact, offered Burnside the top command before he re-called McClellan after Second Bull Run. But Burnside declined the offer because, he said, he did not consider himself qualified for so high a command. Events at Antietam were to confirm that judgment.

The task given to Burnside's Ninth Corps was to storm Antietam Creek and smash the Confederate right. He had begun his deployment about 7:00 a.m., and about midmorning he received orders to attack. By that time the fighting on the left and the center was abating. Lee had denuded his right to provide desperately needed support to his center, leaving about four hundred Georgians to contest Burnside's creek cross-ing. The Southerners were dug in on a high bank and had a good field of fire.

Burnside had not bothered to scout the creek earlier for possible crossings, so he made his main effort at a stone bridge that today bears his name. The bridge is one of three that span the creek, and at the time was known as the middle bridge. Once the attack was ordered, Burnside sent a unit south to search for other crossings below the mid-dle bridge; then he made two attempts to cross the bridge, being thrown back both times with severe losses. A third attempt about 1:00 p.m. carried the bridge, but by then his troops discovered they could wade across the creek at just about any point. By midafternoon the Ninth Corps had gained the high ground to the east and south of Sharpsburg, though Lee was by then sending reinforcements to contest the Union advance on the town. The fighting became hot, and it was in this exchange that Pvt. David Thompson of New York, as recorded by historian Stephen Sears, was reminded of a quote from Johann Wolf-gang von Goethe regarding the Napoleonic wars, saying it seemed to him that "the whole landscape for an instant turned slightly red."

As Union troops placed renewed pressure on the Confederate cen-ter, Burnside's men drove to the edge of Sharpsburg. There they were suddenly hit on the flank by A. P. Hill's Light Division, which had ar-rived late on the battlefield after a seventeen-mile trot from Harpers Ferry. The Union troops had no warning, because McClellan was hold-ing his cavalry in reserve, not using it for scouting—a bizarre breach of military protocol that was never explained. Adding to the confusion, many of Hill's ragged Rebels were wearing blue uniforms confiscated from the Federal arsenal they had recently seized. Burnside's troops withdrew to the ridges along the creek.

On September 18 the two armies accepted the standoff, much as they had two days before. Early that day McClellan received reinforcements to supplement the two corps and cavalry he had not used the day before. Once again fortune wagged opportunity in his face. Lee's army was spent; one major assault by McClellan's overwhelming force would have caught the Rebels with their backs to the Potomac. They would have had little chance of survival, much less victory.

McClellan, however, did nothing. During that night Lee's troops executed a masterful evacuation across the Potomac and began trekking back toward Richmond. Total Confederate casualties were about 13,700, while Union losses were put at 12,350. It was the single bloodiest day in American military history.

There ensued a war of words North and South about who won the battle of Antietam. Lee at first did not consider it a defeat but rather a setback. Counting the Union prisoners taken at Harpers Ferry, the contest had exacted a much larger toll on the enemy. His plan was to regroup and move immediately back into Maryland to challenge McClellan again. But he soon realized that a substantial part of his army was straggling over a distance of several miles. His men were worn out and beaten, at least for the time being.

McClellan had no doubt he had won a great victory. "Maryland is entirely freed from the presence of the enemy who has been driven across the Potomac," he wired Washington. "No fears need now be entertained for the safety of Pennsylvania." In letters to his wife he exuded confidence in a job well done. "Those in whose judgment I rely tell me that I fought the battle splendidly & that it was a masterpiece of art. I feel that I have done all that can be asked in twice saving the country. I feel some little pride in having, with a beaten & demoralized army, defeated Lee so utterly. Well, one of these days, history will do me justice." He did not identify the people on whose judgment he relied.

Others were less charitable toward the Union commander. Lincoln was exceedingly frustrated by McClellan's failure to pursue Lee's retreating army, as were many of McClellan's subordinates. "I think myself he errs on the side of prudence and caution," said George Gordon Meade in a letter to his wife, "and that a little more rashness on his part would improve his generalship." Others employed more strident criticism.

But Lincoln, as disappointed as he was, was savvy enough to know when a battle could be called a victory. It was he, after all, who had returned McClellan to command over the objections of his cabinet and congressional leaders. He proclaimed Antietam a victory and seized it as the pretext he needed to announce, on September 22, the preliminary Emancipation Proclamation to take effect the following January 1.

AT THE time of the battle of Antietam, Bishop Henry Benjamin Whipple was in Washington at the behest of Minnesota Governor Alexander Ramsey to seek more military aid to suppress the Sioux uprising. While there he heard of the battle of Antietam. He hurried to the battlefield where the First Minnesota Infantry, the only Minnesota unit in McClellan's command, had been caught in the maelstrom and taken heavy casualties. "They had been placed at a point where the battle raged fiercest," Whipple recorded. "The field was covered with the dead. The stone house and barn hard by were filled with the wounded and dying."

The bishop rolled up his sleeves and worked among the wounded men, offering them what comfort he could. He brought them water, words of comfort, and, for many, last prayers. He wrote down messages of hope and farewell to families. While he was going about this work, McClellan heard he was on the scene. The two men had met years before, when McClellan was chief engineer for the Illinois Central Railroad (the same railroad that had employed attorney Abraham Lincoln and awarded him the highest fee he ever earned). McClellan sent a note: "My dear bishop, will you do me the favor to perform divine service in my camp this evening? After the great success that God has vouchsafed us, I feel that we cannot do less than avail ourselves of the first opportunity to render to Him the thanks that are due Him alone. I, for one, feel that the victory is the result of His mercy, and should be glad if you would be the medium to offer the thanks I feel due from this army and from the country."

Whipple went to the camp as requested and held the service. McClellan attended with many of his senior officers. Afterward Whipple and McClellan went to the general's tent and discussed the day's events until long after midnight. McClellan complained that he was being criticized for not bringing the war to a close fast enough. It is not known whether they discussed the Sioux uprising in Minnesota. As Whipple left, McClellan asked him to stop at the hospitals on the way to Washington and see how his men were doing.

Whipple gladly agreed to this request, and on September 23 he wrote to McClellan:

> My dear General, I have spent the day in visiting your brave boys in the hospital. I am sure it will gladden your heart as it did my own, to know the great love they bear you. When I told them how tenderly you had spoken of them and how you knelt with me in prayer for God's blessing upon them, many a brave fellow wept for joy. On every side, I heard, "God bless him! God bless him!" Occasionally, some veteran exclaimed, "God bless little Mac."
>
> I had the opportunity to commend some dying men to God and to whisper to them the Savior's name for the last journey.
>
> If I were not wearying you, I could fill an hour telling you of words of loving confidence spoken by these brave sufferers who had been in good and evil report. But I cannot close without telling you how sweet the remembrance is of the service held in your camp and to assure you it is a pleasure every day to ask God's blessing upon you. Your way is rough. Many do not know you. Let no cloud or thorn trouble you. Above you is God our Father. He will hear our prayers. God bless you.

General Meade shared McClellan's religious conviction and also his admiration for Bishop Whipple. On another occasion, hearing the bishop was in Washington, Meade invited him to army headquarters in Virginia for Easter Communion. William T. Sherman likewise knew Bishop Whipple, though Sherman challenged many of Whipple's doctrines in what may have been a way of venting his own religious disputes with his rigidly Catholic wife. Years later, when Sherman published the history of his campaigns, he sent a copy to Whipple's son, Charles, then a major in the army: "To the son of my great and good friend, Bishop Whipple of Minnesota, with love and veneration for the father and earnest wishes for the honor and happiness of the son."

Following his meeting with McClellan and his visits with the soldiers, Whipple returned to Minnesota to do what he could to mitigate the horrors that attended the Sioux uprising.

9

THE WAR OF
THE RACES

FTER THE FAILURE TO capture either Fort Ridgely or New Ulm, the Sioux leaders realized they would soon be facing a serious military challenge. Scouts reported a column of soldiers nearing St. Peter, and Little Crow knew they would soon be at Fort Ridgely. Someone would have to answer for the killing and looting, and the interrogation did not promise to be pleasant. He and the other chiefs convened a council and decided they had to uproot their families and move away from the Lower Agency before the soldiers arrived in force.

Up to that point, the fighting had generally gone pretty well by the lights of the Sioux, notwithstanding the setbacks at Fort Ridgely and New Ulm. Hundreds of settlers had been killed, perhaps three hundred taken prisoner to be used as hostages later, and tens of thousands more were fleeing the valley. Tons of plunder had been taken—food, wagons, livestock, clothing, and a variety of pioneer implements. The young warriors thought they had done quite well and expressed glowing satisfaction with themselves.

Little Crow agreed the villages of the Lower Agency had to be abandoned to avoid being surrounded and captured, but he was not certain the whites had enough soldiers to extend their control above the Upper Agency. He deemed it possible the Sioux could move to the northwest, above the Upper Agency, retain their plunder, and negotiate a deal with the whites, trading the captives for an agreement that would enable them either to keep their land or what was left of it. He also saw a military advantage to moving to the northwest, for the only trails the soldiers could use to follow them led along the river, where they would be vulnerable to ambush.

It took the Sioux a day to pack their belongings, including the stolen booty, on their wagons and carts, many of which were stolen. The following morning a stream of wagons, carts, and buggies emerged from the villages in one continuous stream. Most of the people walked, including the captives. One captive later described the procession as five miles long and one mile wide and consisting of "every kind of vehicle that was ever manufactured. Nice coaches, ox carts, chaises, bakers' carts, peddlers' wagons, sometimes a cow with poles tied to her back Indian style."

The Sioux warriors adorned themselves with stolen items that caught their fancy, apparently unaware they were women's items. For men who customarily adorned themselves with feather bonnets and smeared their faces with brightly colored pigment it only seemed natural to wrap crepe shawls around their heads and tie gold watches to their ankles. The Indian squaws wore dresses stolen from the white women, along with earrings and brooches. "It was hard to keep from smiling to see how they were used by these poor savage creatures," recalled Sarah Wakefield, one of the captives. "They looked more like a troop of monkeys than anything human."

The procession was a noisy parade of bawling cattle, barking dogs, and screaming children. The warriors rode along each side of the line of refugees to prevent the captives from escaping. They paused for the night at Rice Creek, about halfway between the Lower and Upper Agencies, and proceeded on the next day. When they arrived at the Upper Agency they met a determined band led by Chief Red Iron, who made it clear they were not welcome. He told Little Crow where to camp, between the villages of two Christian chiefs, and that he and his people could camp nowhere else. Red Iron also said that when the whites came for them, if they tried to escape across the lands of the Upper Agency, the northern Sioux would kill them. Little Crow was not a prisoner; he was free to go west or south. But it was abundantly clear he would receive little support from the northern chiefs.

Little Crow's people set up their tepees where they were told, after which Little Crow rallied about 150 of his warriors for a mission into the Big Woods. His plan was to intercept the reinforcements headed for Fort Ridgely from the northeast. He also envisioned raids on the towns of Forest City and Hutchinson. Some of his warriors were on horse-back and some on foot. Little Crow himself rode in a wagon with Joe Campbell, a half-breed who drove the team. Campbell also served as scribe because Little Crow could not write.

While they rode, Little Crow dictated a letter to Governor Ramsey, requesting an end to hostilities and a settlement. When the letter was done, Little Crow asked Campbell to read it to the warriors. It elicited a virulent reaction of jeers and derision and had to be destroyed—and along with it went much of what little was left of Little Crow's prestige. The following morning when he attempted to resume the trek to the Big Woods, only thirty-seven warriors would accompany him. The others thought it would be easier to raid and plunder Forest City and Hutchinson. More than two-thirds of Little Crow's band elected Walker Among Sacred Stones to lead them. That night the two groups camped several miles apart. The mutinous faction settled down for the night about two miles northeast of the Robinson Jones farm, where the uprising had begun three weeks before. Having lost face, Little Crow turned over the leadership of his small band to his half brother, White Spider.

Also camping in the area were fifty-five newly recruited soldiers under the command of Maj. Richard Strout of Minneapolis, comprising Company B of the Tenth Minnesota, along with about twenty other citizens. This group had been sent to protect the settlers in Meeker County and was on its way to Forest City from Glencoe.

Meanwhile, at Forest City, Capt. George C. Whitcomb commanded a volunteer company that had skirmished the previous day with some Sioux near Acton. Informed of Strout's position, Whitcomb sent three messengers to warn him that hostiles were in the area. These riders reached Strout's camp about 3:00 a.m., found it completely unguarded, and raised an alarm. The soldiers spent the rest of the night cutting down minié balls into bullets for their Belgian muskets.

At daylight the soldiers, most of whom were on foot, marched a few miles to the west shore of Hope Lake, where they encountered Little Crow's band, now led by White Spider, and were quickly surrounded. Strout's men fought their way out and back to Hutchinson. Six were killed or mortally wounded and about twenty others were injured. On the Sioux side, one was killed and three wounded. The Sioux counted this a victory, but none of the credit went to Little Crow, who had fought as a warrior, not as a leader.

Flush with victory, the Sioux, reinforced by the arrival of twenty more warriors, reunited to plot attacks on Forest City and Hutchinson. Little Crow went along to Hutchinson, but not as leader. Both towns had erected stockades only a few hours before the Sioux arrived. These were simple structures, ten to twelve feet high and about a hundred feet square with firing ports. They afforded some protection to the people, but houses and livestock were at risk.

People in little towns all around the region built defensive structures, some of which were more ambitious than others. At Maine Prairie the settlers erected a two-story timber fort. The townspeople of St. Joseph built three pentagon-shaped blockhouses with foot-thick green timber. St. Cloud boasted "Fort Holes," a circular construction forty-five feet in diameter with gunports for sharpshooters. It was never tested. Settlers at Sauk Centre built a stockade of tamarack logs that was later converted into a substantial fort by soldiers. At Little Falls the people fortified the Morrison County courthouse where women and children slept at night while the men guarded their fields and animals.

For settlers who had not taken refuge within stockades, the consequences were the same as for the isolated white families around the Lower Agency. A Sioux warrior named Sacred Rattle led an attack on the homestead of Jack Adams near Forest City. Adams was killed and his wife and baby boy were taken hostage. When the baby cried, Sacred Rattle snatched the child from his mother and, swinging the child by its feet, dashed its head against a rock.

In the early morning hours the combined band of Sioux, screaming war whoops and firing their weapons, rode into Forest City. As the residents cringed behind their stockade, the Sioux looted their shops and set fire to five houses.

Hutchinson, which had a timber stockade eight feet high and sheltered four hundred people during an attack, fared worse, with more houses looted and burned. The Hutchinson Academy, a source of great pride to local residents, was burned to the ground. Hundreds of horses and oxen were stolen, along with wagons, to transport the booty back to the temporary Lower Sioux encampment near the Upper Agency. Little Crow rode atop one of the wagons. When he arrived, there was a letter for him from Henry Hastings Sibley offering a peace parley. Little Crow studied the paper for a moment, as if he could read it, and then passed it to Campbell. "If Little Crow has any proposition to make,"

Sibley wrote, "let him send a half-breed to me and he shall be protected in and out of camp."

HENRY HASTINGS SIBLEY had been appointed a colonel in the Minnesota militia by Governor Ramsey and charged to take care of the Sioux uprising as best he could. Sibley and Ramsey were quintessential examples of how the Indian system enriched certain men and paved their way to political power. Fifty-one years old, Sibley was from a middle-class family in Detroit, Michigan. At the age of eighteen he had taken a job as a clerk with the American Fur Company in the Minnesota region. By age twenty-four he was a partner in the firm and based in Mendota, where he built an elaborate mansion of stone. He employed a variety of servants, including a French chef, and lived a luxurious life, at least by frontier standards. He married and within eight years had nine children. Though he had retired from the fur trade, he still managed to successfully file a claim for $145,000 under the Sioux treaties on his own behalf and that of the American Fur Company for alleged overpayments for furs. The Sioux protested this obvious fraud to no avail. Sibley's claim was approved by the Indian agent, who at the time happened to be Alexander Ramsey.

Gen. Zachary Taylor had described the American Fur Company as "the greatest set of scoundrels the world ever knew." Clearly Sibley was one of the primary scoundrels, but somehow he was esteemed as an honest, public-spirited citizen. This was no doubt in part because his reputation was measured among whites who cared nothing about Indian exploitation and because Sibley had a knack for public relations.

Sibley had served as a territorial delegate to Congress from Minnesota and was elected its first governor in 1858, beating Republican candidate Alexander Ramsey by about 240 votes. The margin of victory came from a district where all the voters were Sioux customers of Sibley's business, but a protest of this suspicious arrangement came to nothing. When his term of office was up, Sibley retired from public life, preferring "the peace and quiet of private life to the thorny path of public office." His successor was Ramsey, who quite naturally turned to Sibley to lead an expedition to subdue the unruly Indians.

"There was no one who was as eminently qualified for the position as he was incapable of seeking it, Ramsey's old political foe and personal friend, Henry H. Sibley, and it was to him that Governor Ramsey instantly turned," historian William F. Folwell noted. "Sibley, still in middle life, was robust and athletic and accustomed to outdoor life; he was widely experienced in great affairs and greatly trusted and respected; he spoke the French and understood the Dakota language; he was familiar with Sioux country and acquainted with many of the leading men of the four tribes; and above all he possessed profound knowledge of the Indian character and habits. Ramsey at once drove over to Mendota, where Sibley was still living in his stone house, and laid the duty upon him."

On the minus side of Sibley's qualifications for this duty was a total absence of any military training or experience as well as a penchant for dawdling and dithering that offered a distant echo of the beleaguered George B. McClellan. It took Sibley a full day to get out of Fort Snelling because he felt obliged to write a letter to Ramsey about the shortage of ammunition, tents, and camping gear supplied to him. He also didn't care for the Austrian-made muskets he was given, saying he would much prefer Springfield rifles. But the first-rate equipment had gone to the soldiers fighting the Confederacy, and he had to make do with what was available.

It had taken Pvt. William Sturgis all night and part of a day to ride from Fort Ridgely to Fort Snelling. The missionaries escaping from the Upper Agency, led by John Otherday over winding backwoods trails, had gone even farther than Sturgis to reach Fort Snelling in seven days. It was to take Sibley eight days to make the journey—eight days that left the soldiers at Fort Ridgely and the citizens of New Ulm fighting desperately to survive. Sibley's sluggishness evoked critical comment from many quarters, the most plaintive from the beleaguered defenders of Ridgely and New Ulm. But to Sibley his deliberation was simply prudent. McClellan himself would have understood the need for a wise commander to make sure his men were well supplied and rested before they sallied forth to confront their wily and deadly enemies.

At the outset Sibley had in his command about 225 men, a force that would be augmented by a company commanded by Capt. Hiram Grant that had taken a different route before they met at Fort Ridgely. Their first action was to exacerbate the misery of the throngs of refugees who were fleeing the Sioux. Some were in small family groups and others in larger assemblies, representing entire towns and villages that had packed up and fled the terror. Most of the families were riding or walking beside wagons laden with their possessions—beds, furniture, clothing, farm implements, and poultry. They were all clearly glad to see the soldiers. Many of them told stories of terrible outrages, and more than a few of them bore wounds as evidence of what they had been through. Sibley's troops listened sympathetically and then commandeered the wagons from the refugees. They gave the settlers receipts, unloaded them, and headed toward Indian territory. Long after the militiamen had gone, the bewildered settlers sat forlornly amid their possessions by the road and wondered what they should do.

As Sibley proceeded with all deliberate speed, he received word that Fort Ridgely was under attack and had been partly burned. This news did not prompt him to increase his speed or to send word to Captain Grant to move more quickly toward the fort. The first leg of Sibley's trip took him and his command to St. Peter, through the eastern edge of the Big Woods. It was considered a good road by frontier standards, and most people were able to traverse it in a long day. It took Sibley and his troops two and a half days. When he got to St. Peter, he complained the trip had worn out his people because the road was "execrable."

Sibley did not deem it necessary to send scouting parties to reconnoiter the Sioux, because at St. Peter he encountered an old friend, Jack Frazer, a half-breed who had escaped the Lower Agency and claimed to have a full grasp of what was going on. Frazer told Sibley the Sioux were seven thousand strong and could field fifteen hundred mounted and well-armed warriors. This news daunted Sibley, who did not believe his small force stood much chance against such a large, well-equipped host of savages. He sent word to Ramsey calling for "five hundred additional troops officered by the best men and armed with Springfield rifles, and a goodly supply of fixed ammunition." His reluctance to send mounted cavalry to scout the enemy and his willingness to embrace wildly exaggerated estimates of enemy strength, like his propensity to hesitate, was positively McClellanesque.

While pausing at St. Peter, Sibley received word that New Ulm was under attack. He had no way of knowing the status of things at Fort Ridgely. Rather than move precipitously toward either objective, he elected to await the arrival of more troops and the Springfield rifles he had requested. He got what he wanted—six companies of infantry armed with Springfields—plus three hundred mounted troops and a train of wagons loaded with food and ammunition. With a force of fifteen hundred well-armed men, plus a significant contingent of cavalry, Sibley at last felt able to move toward Fort Ridgely. But before going, ever mindful of his public image, he sent a note to Ramsey requesting copies of recent Minnesota newspapers.

Two days later his force at last arrived at Fort Ridgely, eight days after they started out. "The war of races," he proclaimed, "has begun, renewed in its old and simplest form."

After he arrived at Fort Ridgely, Sibley received the newspapers requested from Ramsey, and he could not have liked what he read. The *St. Cloud Democrat* called him "the state undertaker with his company of grave diggers." The *Hastings Independent* labeled him "a snail who falls back on his authority and assumed dignity and refuses to march." He would have been even more dismayed to read some of the scorching comments about him sent to Governor Ramsey by private citizens, few of whom believed Sibley was up to the task. "That a man who defrauded you out of the executive chair on the strength of Indian votes is continued in power while murder, rapine, and plunder surround his imbecility staggers us all," wrote St. Peter attorney Horace Austin.

AT FORT RIDGELY, Sibley's first priority was to drill his soldiers into some sort of battle order, though he himself was conspicuously ill-trained for the undertaking. While he did this, several people persuaded him to send troops into the devastated Lower Agency area to bury the bodies of the dead settlers still lying where they had been slain. After scouts assured him there were no Sioux nearby, he sent a burial party composed of Company A of the Sixth Minnesota under Hiram Grant, about 50 mounted men led by Capt. Joseph Anderson, 17 teamsters and wagons, and a fatigue detail of other soldiers and volunteers—about 170 men in all. Also present was Joseph Brown, a former Indian agent and now a major in the volunteer army. Sibley charged Brown, who knew the country well, to find the Sioux and learn what their plans were, a task Brown took to heart because his wife and family were being held hostage by Little Crow. Brown's actual status among the military expedition's leadership later provided a source of some controversy.

Meanwhile, the Lower Agency Sioux left behind at the Upper Agency by Little Crow received word that New Ulm had been evacuated and its property left unguarded. Gray Bird, whom Little Crow had left in charge, met with Big Eagle, Mankato, and others to determine what to do. They decided to lead 350 warriors to New Ulm, take whatever they could, and cross the river below Fort Ridgely to head off any reinforcements that might be coming from the southeast.

Not long after Grant's burial detail had begun its grim work, it was divided into two groups. Brown crossed the river with Anderson's cavalry, leaving Grant's infantry on the north side. At the Lower Agency, Brown's team buried several victims, including Andrew Myrick. Grant's party buried Marsh's soldiers who had been ambushed at Redwood Ferry. Then they moved upstream, burying bodies as they went, and stumbled upon twenty-eight-year-old Justina Krieger, wandering in a daze. Krieger's first husband had died five years before, leaving her with two sons and a daughter. She then married Frederick Krieger, who had three children from a previous marriage. He and Justina had three daughters, and in the spring of 1862 the family had moved to Sacred Heart in the Lower Agency vicinity. The family was one of thirteen fleeing the massacres when they were assailed by the Sioux. The encounter began in the usual way, with the Indians feigning friendship then suddenly attacking. Frederick was killed and Justina hit with buckshot, but not before she managed to get eight of her brood safely into the woods. She passed out and lay on the ground for hours. Indians later returned to look for valuables. One felt Justina's pulse, concluded she was dead, and cut off her dress, leaving a four-inch gash in her abdomen.

"I saw one of these inhuman savages seize Wilhelmina Kitzman, my niece, hold her up by her foot, her head downward, her clothes falling over her head," Justina recalled. "While holding her with one hand, in the other he grasped a knife, with which he cut the flesh around one of her legs, close to the body. Then, by twisting and wrenching, he broke the ligaments and bone, until the limb was entirely severed from the body. The child screamed frantically, 'Oh God! Oh God!' When the limb was off the child was thrown on the ground, stripped of her clothing, and left to die."

Of the eight Krieger children who made it to the woods, one died of starvation and the others reached sanctuary at Fort Ridgely and were among the refugees there when Sibley arrived. The soldiers tended Justina's wounds and put her in one of the wagons. About sunset, Grant's troops turned back and pitched camp near a depression where Birch Coulee Creek met the Minnesota River. There they were joined a bit later by Brown's group. Together the two groups had buried fifty-four victims of the uprising, and neither had seen any Indians. They assumed the Sioux had gone north to the Upper Agency.

Brown was uncomfortable with the site on which Grant chose to camp; it was near woods on one side and a hill on the other that could provide cover for an attack. He expressed his concern then dropped the matter because he accepted the argument that the Sioux were far away. Wagons were arranged in a horseshoe shape, with ropes connecting each vehicle and securing the horses. Anderson's cavalry arrived while Grant's and Brown's men secured the area. He accepted an invitation to share the camp. A few men, including Nathan Myrick, who had found and buried his brother, returned to Fort Ridgely.

The men were weary after a day of riding and burying the dead. Grant set up ten picket posts at equal intervals, each manned by three soldiers. They ate an evening meal, and soon all were asleep except for the pickets. They were inside what amounted to a corral about a hundred yards in diameter with the tents in the middle.

While the soldiers were making camp, Sioux scouts reported to Big Eagle, Gray Bird, and Mankato that 75 soldiers were camped nearby. During the night 200 warriors quietly surrounded the camp; 150 additional Sioux were kept in reserve. Just before dawn a sentry saw movement in the grass and fired. Suddenly Sioux popped up all over. The camp came alive with gunfire as the warriors shouted war whoops and charged from all sides. Groggy soldiers reached for their rifles and tried to figure out what was happening. One officer cried out, "Fall down," so his men would avoid the converging fire, but many believed he said "Fall out," a familiar command. Several stood at attention and were quickly shot down. On orders from Grant, troops overturned the wagons—except for the one sheltering Justina Krieger—to create breastworks. Within moments 22 men lay dead or mortally wounded; another 60 were wounded less seriously. Of 87 horses, only two remained alive.

The Sioux quickly realized they were up against more than 75 soldiers and sent for the other 150 warriors waiting a short distance away. Only two of the Sioux had been killed during the attack, leaving them with a five-to-one advantage over the soldiers who were still capable of fighting. The soldiers were totally cut off on all sides, and they had only one bucket of water in the compound and almost no food. They suffered through the day from thirst and hunger as well as sporadic attacks from the Sioux. The guns of the dead and wounded were distributed to those who could still fight, equipping each soldier with two weapons, but they were low on ammunition. Only those guarding direct approaches into the camp were permitted to fire.

The Sioux continued fitfully firing all night while the soldiers languished from lack of water, food, and sleep. At daybreak a warrior approached under a white flag. He said the Indians had been reinforced during the night and would soon attack and kill all the whites, but the half-breeds were free to leave unharmed. Among the company were nine men with some Indian blood, including a few with relatives among the attackers. They responded to the emissary that they would stay with the soldiers. It was an encouraging moment for the besieged detachment, but they all knew they could not hold out much longer. All eyes turned toward Fort Ridgely, only sixteen miles away. The sound of the shooting had to carry that far, and relief was surely on the way.

Back at the fort, Sibley continued to receive reinforcements, boosting his command to at least 1,500 men, even after the departure of the 270 of the burial detail. Sentries reported gunfire from the direction of Birch Coulee. Sibley rode out with two officers to listen more closely. Convinced something was going on, he sent 50 mounted rangers, three companies of infantry, and a few artillery pieces to see what was happening. When the relief party got to within about three miles of Birch Coulee, they came under fire and hunkered down. The detachment commander, Col. Samuel McPhail, reported that the Sioux had his group completely surrounded and requested reinforcements from Sibley. Later, Big Eagle claimed that only a handful of warriors attacked McPhail's party, making a lot of noise to trick the soldiers into a defensive position. The Birch Coulee detachment heard the firing at McPhail's party but did not know what it was. Meanwhile, Sibley reacted with unusual speed, sending a second relief party of more than 1,000 men with artillery to McPhail's group. The two groups linked up about midnight. By that time the survivors at Birch Coulee had been under attack for almost a full day, two more of the wounded had died, and the remainder were running low on powder, water, and stamina.

At daybreak Sioux scouts reported a three-mile-long relief party was headed toward Birch Coulee. McPhail was only three miles from Birch Coulee, but it took his men eight hours to get there. By the time they arrived, it had been thirty-one hours since the party had come under attack and twenty-eight hours since the firing was first heard at Fort Ridgely. When they saw they were greatly outnumbered, the Sioux fired parting shots and rode away. No one pursued them.

When Sibley arrived at the camp, he reported a "sickening sight" of death and destruction. All of the horses and thirteen men were dead. Another forty-seven soldiers were severely wounded, four of whom later died. And everyone was in bad shape. Most were streaked with blood and panting for water. Many were unable to stand without support.

As the relief party investigated the devastated camp, they found the one wagon upright in the middle, its sides slashed and pitted with hundreds of bullet holes. Looking inside, they were amazed to discover Justina Krieger. "They seemed perfectly astonished on finding me alive," she recalled. "The blanket on which I lay in the wagon was found to have received over 200 bullet holes during the fight." She was taken later to St. Paul. There she met John Jacob Meyer, a settler whose wife and children had been killed in the massacres. They later married.

In the battle of Birch Coulee, white soldiers suffered their worst losses of the war. Big Eagle later reported that the Sioux lost only two men. It was a desperate business and did not augur well for Sibley's "war of the races." During the prolonged Sioux war that followed, "Remember Birch Coulee" was to become a watchword for anyone who pitched camp without anticipating attack or looking for a good defensive position.

Ever anxious about his public image, Sibley tried to distance himself from the disaster by reporting that Brown had been in command at Birch Coulee. When Grant made his report, as military officers are required to do, Sibley gave it back to him. "I was coolly informed that I should make my report to Maj. Joseph R. Brown, who was in command of the expedition," Grant said. "This was the first I had heard of it. We had been gone four days, two of which we had been engaged in deadly fight; no order had been given to me by Major Brown, not an intimation that he considered himself in command. To say that I was angry, when told to make my report to him, would only express half what I felt. I then and there destroyed my report."

Joseph Brown at the time was not formally a militia officer and did not use the rank of major until two months later. "If any blame rests on anyone for selection of camps, or in carrying out any of the details of the expedition, it rests upon me," Grant claimed. "I had the full charge."

10

ENVIRONED WITH DIFFICULTIES

L INCOLN DECIDED TO ANNOUNCE the Emancipation Proclamation after long and laborious reflection influenced by intense lobbying by abolitionists, religious leaders, and congressmen. At the same time he was under intense pressure from others who believed such a move would disrupt the war effort and create problems in the slave states still in the Union—Delaware, Kentucky, Maryland, and Missouri. To further compound his dilemma, there were serious questions whether the Union army would rally to a crusade against slavery. There was no question that many senior officers were resistant to such a move.

In the western theater, Ulysses S. Grant was liberating slaves and putting them to work for his army, but not out of any commitment to emancipation. In a letter to his wife, Julia, Grant affirmed that his sole objective was to put down the rebellion. "I have no hobby of my own with regard to the Negro, either to effect his freedom or to continue his bondage," he wrote. "I am using them as teamsters, hospital attendants, company cooks and so forth, thus saving soldiers to carry the musket." Like most thoughtful leaders of his time, including Lincoln, Grant could not conceive of a world in which black and white lived side by side as equals. "I don't know what is to come of these poor people in the end," he said, "but it weakens the enemy to take them from them."

If Grant was ambivalent about slavery, McClellan was adamant that the war should not evolve into a crusade for emancipation. Three months before, in an act of typical McClellan chutzpah, he asserted his views in a memorandum to Lincoln. Neither "confiscation of property" nor "forcible abolition of slavery" should be considered viable policy, he said. That was not what the war was about. "Military power," he said, "should not be allowed to interfere with the relations of servitude." And then, menacingly, he added, "A declaration of radical views, especially upon slavery, will rapidly disintegrate our present armies."

It seems clear that the majority of Union soldiers, like their counterparts in gray, had no compelling opinion of slavery one way or the other. Most of them had answered the call to arms for other reasons, usually defense of the Union in the North or defense of home in the South. Many recruits North and South no doubt answered the call to war as an invitation to glory and adventure and an escape from the dawn-to-dusk drudgery of farm life. There were outspoken people in the North who felt strongly that slavery should be destroyed, but they were a distinct minority in the overall population, usually associated with radical abolitionist societies. It is fair to say that the great majority of whites considered blacks, like Indians, to be inferior to themselves in most respects.

Thus what seems in retrospect an inevitable focus of the Civil War did by no means seem inevitable at the time—either to its advocates or its opponents. It is fair to say Lincoln struggled with this decision like he did with no other.

Lincoln had always been opposed to slavery, but he clearly understood, unlike most emancipation advocates, that the first step toward the abolition of slavery was to win the power necessary to make it happen. He recognized that, though some strident abolitionists could win congressional seats and even governorships, a presidential candidate had to cast a wider net. Just as he had muted his opposition to slavery in his debates with Stephen A. Douglas in 1858, he took a more moderate stand on slavery than his main competitor for the 1860 Republican presidential nomination, William H. Seward. He made his case in a well-reported speech at the Cooper Union in New York City in 1860, a closely articulated position that he reprised later in other speeches in New England.

There is no question that Lincoln's most compelling wartime passion was the preservation of the Union. In his famous response to Greeley, he made clear that this was his paramount concern. "The Union with him," said Lincoln's longtime friend Alexander H. Stephens, who served ironically as vice president of the Confederacy, "in sentiment, rose to the sublimity of a religious mysticism."

But Lincoln had passion enough for more than one cause, and his opposition to slavery was abundantly clear to the public, at least in the run up to the 1860 election. That is why Northern abolitionists worked to secure his election and why Southern states resorted to secession once the outcome of that election became apparent. In the months prior to his inauguration, Lincoln said and did all he could, short of endorsing slavery, to mollify the Southern bloc and prevent the rupture of the Union. His efforts were in vain, however, because Secessionists entertained no doubts whatever regarding Lincoln's core opposition to their cherished "peculiar institution" and his determination to get rid of it.

Lincoln also understood the delicate limits of democratic government, which were probably never more delicate than at that moment. He instinctively knew the peril of a politician who gets too far ahead of his constituents, and he saw no compelling evidence of a consensus for abolition. To the contrary, the absence of such a consensus was glaring.

In his struggle to decide, Lincoln resorted increasingly to the realm of faith, where he had been at best a sometime visitor, at least before he became president. Two years of office wore him down. The deaths in his family and on the battlefield weighed heavily on him, and he sought support wherever he could find it. To the Chicago Christians who petitioned him on September 13 to take a clear stand against slavery, he conveyed his most sincere desire to know the will of God in the matter. "And if I can learn what it is, I will do it!" he said. Since midsummer he had been anxious for a military success that would strengthen his hand politically so he could justify such a public pronouncement. While Lee and McClellan played cat and mouse in Maryland, the president listened intently to news reports and hoped for a victory on which he could set the stage for emancipation. Later he said to his cabinet he had made a personal "vow, a covenant, that if God gave us the victory in the approaching battle, he would consider it an indication of Divine will, and that it was his duty to move forward in the cause of emancipation."

By this time Lincoln had adopted an eccentric daily regimen that impressed his aides with its abnegation. In his biographical novel of Lincoln, Gore Vidal suggested the president suffered severe digestive problems, and the memoirs of personal secretary John Hay hint at something of the sort. "Lincoln used to go to bed ordinarily from ten to eleven o'clock unless he happened to be kept up by important news, in which case he would frequently remain at the War Department till one or two," Hay recorded. "He rose early. When he lived in the country at the Soldiers' Home, he would be up and dressed, eat his breakfast (which was extremely frugal, an egg, a piece of toast, coffee, etc.) and ride into Washington all before eight o'clock. In the winter at the White House, he was not quite up so early. He did not sleep well, but spent a good while in bed. Tad [his son] usually slept with him. He would lie around the office until he fell asleep and Lincoln would shoulder him and take him off to bed. He pretended to begin business at ten o'clock in the morning, but in reality the ante-rooms and halls were full before that hour—people anxious to get the first ax ground." Hay added:

> He was extremely unmethodical. It was a four years' struggle on Nicolay's part and mine to get him to adopt some systematic rules. He would break through every regulation as fast as it was made. Anything that kept the people themselves away from him he disapproved, although they nearly annoyed the life out of him by unreasonable complaints and requests.
>
> The House remained full of people nearly all day. At noon, the president took a little lunch—a biscuit, a glass of milk in winter, some fruit or grapes in summer. He dined between five and six, and we went off to our dinner also. Before dinner was over, members and Senators would come back and take up the whole evening. Sometimes, though rarely, he would shut himself up and would see no one. Sometimes he would run away to a lecture or concert or theater for the sake of a little rest. He was very abstemious—ate less than anyone I know. He drank nothing but water, not from principle, but because he did not like wine or spirits.

Lincoln spent many late nights at the War Department before and after the showdown at Antietam, and though the result was less than the overwhelming rout he had sought, it was sufficient to finally steel his will to make the war a crusade against slavery. He took a weekend to tweak the final language, then he summoned his cabinet to meet on September 22. He began with a humorous reading and quickly turned to business, reminding them they had discussed an emancipation proclamation the previous July. He said the time had come to redeem the promise he had made to himself and his maker. He did not invite comment on this issue but invited them to address "any other minor matter."

The document itself was remarkably dry and free of the soaring rhetoric usually associated with Lincoln. Whatever tweaking he did during the previous forty-eight hours did not include adding lofty phrases. The Emancipation Proclamation begins with a bit of bureaucratic double-talk about compensating slave owners in loyal states for lost property and repeats an earlier promise to repatriate blacks to Africa. Even at this late date, Lincoln had no idea that blacks could live among whites as equals, nor did anyone else in his cabinet espouse such a radical notion. To do so would put them beyond the pale of public discourse. The issue before them was not racial equality but slavery, and on that pivotal matter they stood together. The heart of Lincoln's Emancipation Proclamation was that "all persons held as slaves within any state or designated part of a state, the people whereof shall then be in rebellion against the United States, shall be then, thenceforward, and forever free."

Lincoln made it clear to his cabinet that he was taking the action with more than a little trepidation, and he expressed a plaintive wish to pass the responsibility to someone more qualified but recognized that such was not possible. "I must do the best I can and bear the responsibility for taking the course which I feel I ought to take," he said. As happened when he broached the matter in July, the only dissenter was Postmaster General Montgomery Blair of Maryland, who expressed concern about the decree's impact on the Border States and also that the pronouncement would provide fodder to the Democrats in the midterm elections. Lincoln said he had considered both possibilities—no doubt through many sleepless nights—and gave the order to Secretary of State Seward to be officially published. The proclamation was released to the newspapers the next day, and fifteen thousand copies were printed and distributed among the Union armies.

It is a measure of Lincoln's depth and resilience that he had a private meeting with Allan Pinkerton, the detective who provided McClellan's faulty intelligence on Confederate military strengths, on the same day that the preliminary emancipation proclamation was published. At the time Pinkerton was assuring McClellan—and Lincoln—that the Confederates had 140,000 men arrayed against the Army of the Potomac. The actual number was closer to 52,000. It was not clear why Pinkerton kept feeding McClellan these inflated statistics unless he, like any savvy consultant, was telling his client what he believed his client wanted to hear. The ostensible purpose of Pinkerton's visit to the White House was to brief the president on national security concerns, though historian David Herbert Donald attributes it to mutual intelligence gathering: McClellan sent Pinkerton to sound out his standing with the president while the president wanted to plumb McClellan's loyalty.

Both parties received what they wanted. Lincoln effusively praised McClellan, citing the nation's "great debt of gratitude" to the general for his "great and decisive victories." Pinkerton dutifully reported to McClellan that Lincoln was solidly in the general's corner. For his part, Lincoln was reassured that McClellan was not plotting an insurrection against the civilian government. But he also deduced from Pinkerton's report that Antietam was less a victory than had been reported initially and that a great opportunity to crush the South had been lost.

Two days later Lincoln suspended habeas corpus in its application to persons accused of "discouraging volunteer enlistments, refusing militia drafts, or guilty of any disloyal practice, affording aid and comfort to the rebels." Donald believes this was done almost as an afterthought, but it seems unlikely a cunning lawyer like Lincoln did not appreciate the significance of the move. Few legal principles are more fundamental to English common law than habeas corpus, which essentially restrains the government from incarcerating people indefinitely without demonstrating sufficient legal cause. In the autumn of 1862, amid civil conflict and Indian uprising, there were many people in the North openly agitating against the government, urging soldiers to desert and citizens to withdraw their support. It was Lincoln's purpose to suppress such activities aggressively, even if it meant imprisoning people without formal charges.

But Donald is surely right that most of Lincoln's attention in late September was on emancipation. That night, when a group came to the White House to serenade the first family and celebrate the proclamation, Lincoln was still ambivalent about the wisdom of the move. "I can only trust in God I have made no mistake," he told the singers. "It is now for the country and the world to pass judgment on it." Almost as an afterthought, he added, "In my position, I am environed with difficulties."

AMONG HIS difficulties was the distant thunder of the Sioux uprising in Minnesota that was still being reported as a massive outbreak of several tribes along the frontier at the instigation of the Confederacy, an assessment that John Pope did nothing to allay while demanding permission to exterminate the Sioux. With all he had on his plate, Lincoln had to keep in mind the Indian menace and be ready to do whatever was necessary to alleviate the situation, though he scarcely had enough men and material to satisfy the incessant demands of McClellan and the other armies in the eastern and western theaters, never mind the Indian war.

His understanding of the Minnesota situation was undoubtedly clarified by a letter from George A. S. Crooker, an articulate and knowledgeable Minnesotan. Crooker was acquainted with Seward and through him submitted his October 7 missive to the president.

"From all proofs yet offered," Crooker wrote, "there is no evidence whatever to induce the belief that the Secessionists of the South had anything to do with it. The possession of a few Sharps Rifles by the Indians has been referred to as evidence of it. But the Sioux Indians engaged in the murder and pillage never had more than ten such rifles and these it can be proved were bought in St. Paul."

The outbreak of the Sioux, Crooker explained, "was caused by the wretched condition of the tribes, some of them were almost to the point of starvation, the neglect of Government agents to make the annuity payments at the proper time and the insulting taunts of the Agents to their cries for bread" and also to "the rapacious robberies of the Agents Traders and Government officials who always connive together to steal every dollar of their money that can be stolen."

Crooker asserted that the military dimension of the Sioux threat had been greatly exaggerated. "There has never been at any time 500 Indians in this war in arms against the whites and there is not a shadow of probability that Little Crow can muster over 250 warriors today. They are great cowards and 450 well equipped soldiers with one six pounder would drive them out of the state if the upper chiefs of the same tribe would let them pass through their lands. But these upper chiefs not only refuse to join him but refuse to let him cross their territory to run away. 2000 infantry and 500 Cavalry rightly officered equipped and directed would exterminate the whole nest of these outlaws in thirty days."

Ridiculing Pope's demand for twenty-five thousand men "and all the necessary munitions and paraphernalia and pomp of Eastern warfare" to crush the rebellion, Crooker claimed that Henry Sibley could, with the addition of some cavalry, accomplish the task by himself in ten days. But Crooker hastened to add that Sibley would be reluctant to visit violence upon the Sioux because "he does not wish to shed the blood of his brethren." Like most of the white men who had made fortunes in the Indian trade, Crooker noted, Sibley had children by Indian women and depended upon the government largess to Indians for his own ample income.

Crooker warned Lincoln that the citizens of Minnesota were enraged, demanding the extermination or banishment of all Sioux well beyond the Missouri River. "The first would be a harsh judgment to pronounce against those who faithfully withstood all the appeals of Little Crow when he came to them fresh from the slaughter of those whom they may well believe to be their common enemies. A more Christian and a wiser policy would counsel a judgment better 'tempered with mercy.' I should visit Little Crow, and the leaders of his band, with the most severe penalties of the law. They should hang, the only death that the Indian dreads. To the residue I should be more lenient.

"The people of Minnesota will never consent that the war (if indeed it is entitled to that name) shall be settled without the removal of all Sioux tribes far from the confines of the state," Crooker added. "We all know that of all the Indian Tribes living upon the borders of civilization, the Sioux are the most utterly faithless and barbarian. The people of Minnesota will not therefore bear a longer residence of this tribe among them. If the Government does not remove them, her people will avenge themselves by cutting them off in detail."

Crooker continued in this vein for several pages, offering a detailed description of the corruption of the Indian system that Lincoln had read before in letters from Bishop Henry Whipple and others. But the essence of Crooker's message, that the scale of the uprising had been exaggerated, must have come as a relief to the president if he took it at face value. (Crooker underestimated the number of Sioux on the warpath, but most of his assessment was accurate.) His most cynical observation was that Pope's call to exterminate the Sioux would be resisted, not by the enraged citizens of Minnesota who were wholeheartedly behind it, but by the vast conspiracy of Indian agents, traders, and politicians who were feeding off the annuity system. They know all too well "that the dead Indian draws no money from the government" and that their chance for plunder "would be proportionately lessened and destroyed."

BUT AN even more vexing difficulty facing the president was the war that continued despite the Union's momentary advantage after Antietam. McClellan strutted like a peacock on the strength of his tenuous "victory" over Lee. He seized every opportunity to bask in the triumph but made no effort to pursue the Rebels into Virginia. More than a week after the guns had been silenced, McClellan was still in Maryland.

Lincoln was concerned that McClellan's "case of the slows" might reflect more than mere lethargy, very possibly a lack of commitment among the highest echelons of the army to conquer the Rebels and restore the Union. He heard some scuttlebutt attributed to Maj. John J. Key that the army had not "bagged" Lee's force after Antietam because "that is not the game." The idea, the officer supposedly explained, was that both armies would remain in the field until everyone was exhausted, after which "we will make a compromise and save slavery."

On September 27 Lincoln convened a summary court-martial in the White House and declared that public expressions of such sentiments by any Union officer were unforgivable. He forthwith ordered Key to be expelled from the army. The president ominously vowed that if there were any such game in play to accommodate the Confederacy, "It was his objective to break up that game." In choosing Key as a scapegoat to make his point, it is unlikely Lincoln was unaware that Key's brother, Thomas M. Key, currently served as acting judge advocate on McClellan's staff and was a trusted adviser to the general.

John J. Key, an earnest and promising young officer, appealed for clemency, which Lincoln denied, responding that he "had been brought to fear that there was a class of officers in the army, not very inconsiderable in numbers, who were playing a game to not beat the enemy when they could, on some peculiar notion as to the proper way of saving the Union. I dismissed you as an example and a warning."

In the company of an old friend from Springfield, Ozias M. Hatch, Lincoln slipped out of Washington on October 1 to visit the battlefield and talk to his top general. It was a surprise visit that unnerved McClellan. Lincoln stayed in camp for four days, visiting the wounded in hospitals and reviewing troops. His gawky appearance did not inspire many who saw him. Some thought him a humorous character and others were less charitable. "He looks the same as his pictures," a young private wrote to his parents, "though much more careworn; one of his feet is in the grave." Said another, "Not only is he the ugliest man I ever saw, but the most uncouth and gawky in his manners and appearance."

McClellan guided Lincoln around the battlefield and attempted to explain how the fighting had transpired, but Lincoln quickly took his leave and returned to a tent adjacent to McClellan's. Early next morning Lincoln awoke Hatch and took him on a walk to the crest of a nearby hill from which much of the army encampment could be seen.

"Hatch, Hatch, what is all this?" Lincoln whispered.

"Why Mr. Lincoln, this is the Army of the Potomac," Hatch replied.

"No, Hatch, no," Lincoln said. "This is General McClellan's bodyguard."

During their unrecorded meetings, Lincoln and McClellan were apparently deferential to each other. That day the general wrote to his wife, "I incline to think his real purpose of his visit is to push me into a premature advance into Virginia." Explaining that the army wasn't ready for such a move, he nonetheless reported that the president treated him with great kindness and consideration. "He was very affable, and I really think he does feel very kindly towards me personally."

Lincoln tried by every means he knew to prod McClellan to action. He told a friend later that he hoped to make McClellan understand he would be a ruined man if he did not move forward, "rapidly and effectively." To his secretary John Hay he said he went to Sharpsburg to urge McClellan to move "and came back thinking he would move at once. But when I got home, he began to argue why he ought not to move."

A couple of days later Lincoln sent to McClellan—via Henry W. Halleck—an order to "cross the Potomac and give battle to the enemy. Your army must move now while the roads are good."

But McClellan would not move and seemed to possess no end of explanations and rationales why action against the Rebels would be imprudent. Lee's army was "undoubtedly greatly superior" to his own, he said, and without reinforcements, "I may have too much on my hands in the next battle." He raised the specter of another Rebel invasion of the North and complained about a lack of supplies—shoes, clothing, blankets, tents, horses—all the things an army needed to stay in the field. In fact, there were supply mix-ups that led to shortages of key equipment here and there among the Union troops, but none of these compared to the scarcity afflicting Lee's barefoot troops. Halleck grew dismayed with McClellan. "There is an immobility here that exceeds all that any man can conceive of," he reported. "It requires the lever of Archimedes to move this inert mass. I have tried my best, but without success."

While McClellan remained camped safely in Maryland, Lee's army also rested and replenished its ranks. For once they had enough to eat.

As if to underscore a growing confidence among the Army of Northern Virginia, Jeb Stuart led a peripatetic band of about eighteen hundred horsemen on a huge swing around McClellan's army and through Pennsylvania, where they liberated hundreds of Yankee horses and caused another general alarm throughout the North.

Meanwhile, Lincoln continued his frantic efforts to cultivate a military education. This is reflected in a letter he wrote to his reluctant general on October 13: "You remember my speaking to you of what I called your over-cautiousness. Are you not over-cautious when you assume that you can not do what the enemy is constantly doing? Should you not claim to be at least his equal in prowess, and act upon the claim?"

One of McClellan's chief complaints was that he could not possibly supply a part of his army at a base in Winchester, nearer Richmond, unless the railroad from Harpers Ferry was in working order. Lincoln was unimpressed. "But the enemy does now subsist his army at Winchester at a distance of nearly twice as great from railroad transportation as you would have to do without the railroad last named," he countered. "He now wagons from Culpepper Court House which is just about twice as far as you would have to do from Harpers Ferry. He is certainly not more than half as well provided with wagons as you are. I certainly should be pleased for you to have the advantage of the railroad from Harpers Ferry to Winchester, but it wastes all the remainder of autumn to give it to you; and, in fact, ignores the question of time, which can not, and must not be ignored." The president went on to discuss a variety of strategic options as if lecturing a student. Though he closed with an assurance that his missive was not an order, the tone was not lost on the general.

Lincoln continued to send McClellan pointed notes that, according to Nicolay, "amounted to poking sharp sticks under Little Mac's ribs." Predictably, McClellan resented these "mean and dirty dispatches," writing to his wife that he was being bombarded with insults, innuendos, and accusations "from men whom I know to be greatly my inferior socially, intellectually and morally! There never was a truer epithet applied to a certain individual than that of the 'Gorilla.'"

To a friend, McClellan said, "Lincoln is down on me," and later intimated that he expected to be relieved of command and transferred to the western theater of operations. On October 17 he replied to Lincoln's letter, promising to give it his "full and respectful consideration

. . . the moment my men are shod and my cavalry are sufficiently renovated." Five days later he again promised to heed the president's instructions, but he needed more infantry and cavalry.

A week after that, McClellan seemed to experience some sort of catharsis of spirit even worse than normal. He raised the specter of Rebel forces under Gen. Braxton Bragg, then four hundred miles away in Tennessee, linking his army with Lee's. That same day McClellan forwarded to Washington a report that his cavalry horses were "absolutely broken down from fatigue and want of flesh."

That message ignited Lincoln. "Will you pardon me for asking what the horses of your army have done since the battle of Antietam that fatigues anything?" he barked at McClellan.

McClellan protested this message, and predictably, Lincoln followed up on October 27 with a conciliatory note, or at least one he clearly intended to be conciliatory. "Yours of yesterday received. Most certainly I intend no injustice to any; and if I have done any, I deeply regret it. To be told after more than five weeks of total inaction of the Army, and during which period we have sent to that Army every fresh horse we possibly could, amounting in the whole to Seven thousand nine hundred and eighteen, that the cavalry were too much fatigued to move, presented a very cheerless, almost hopeless prospect for the future; and it may have forced something of impatience into my dispatch. If not recruited and rested then, when could they ever be? I suppose the river is rising and I am glad to believe you are crossing."

The powers in Washington had already judged McClellan and found him wanting, and now condemnation began to spread. Northern newspapers stepped up their calls for more aggressive leadership, and reporters chronicled growing dissatisfaction about the inaction among officers and infantry. Everyone, including McClellan himself, seemed to know his star was falling. Lincoln bided his time because the off-year election was just days away, and he feared yet another shift in senior leadership might undermine his credibility at a delicate time.

11

WE HAVE GOT TO DIE

OL. HENRY HASTINGS SIBLEY lingered a long time at Fort Ridgely purportedly out of concern that his force was inadequate to the task of pursuing the Indians and assuring the safe release of the hostages. By this time 91 whites and about 150 half-breeds were being held by the Sioux, most of them at Little Crow's camp. Among the whites was George Spencer (sources disagree whether Spencer was the only white man in captivity; some say as many as three of the captives were men); all the others were women and children. They were hungry and frightened, but the fate of the women was particularly cruel. "The female captives," reported Spencer, "were, with few exceptions, subjected to the most horrible treatment. In some cases, a woman would be taken out into the woods, and her person violated by six, seven, and as many as ten or twelve of these fiends."

Others reported that the younger, more attractive women were routinely taken to special tepees set aside for purposes of sexual abuse. After several weeks of regularly having their clothes ripped off, many of the women were barely clad in rags, haggard from want of food and rest, and quite understandably traumatized. But they struggled to survive in defense of their lives and children, and they bore the scars of their treatment for the rest of their lives. Reports of this situation reached the whites at Fort Ridgely, and there was no reason to question their credibility, but still Sibley dawdled. He was distressed by the loss of ninety horses at Birch Coulee and the departure of virtually all his volunteer cavalry, called away to other service in the Civil War, leaving him with only twenty-five mounted men. He also had few experienced officers to rely upon, which in his case was a major problem because Sibley was the most inexperienced of the lot.

But whatever Sibley lacked in military acumen, he was a master of public relations and knew he had a problem other than the Sioux. Already under fire from the newspapers in St. Paul and other leading citizens for his slow journey to relieve Fort Ridgely, Sibley was now being labeled a "snail," a coward, and the "state undertaker" for his even slower pursuit of the Indians. He expressed concern that his troops were inadequately prepared to march on the Sioux and also concerned that the hostages might be killed if he attacked prematurely. Finally recognizing he was out of his depth, he tendered his resignation on September 4, whether to Governor Ramsey or General Pope isn't clear. For a man of his standing, it was an extraordinary admission of inadequacy. That same day he lamented his quandary in a letter to his wife. "Well, let them come and fight these Indians themselves, and they will have something to do besides grumbling." His resignation, however, was rejected.

During this time Sibley sent the message to Little Crow to negotiate the release of the captives. He had no way of knowing that Little Crow was losing control of the situation and lacked any authority to dictate terms to his warriors. Working with his captive scribe, Little Crow replied to Sibley's entreaty with a rambling justification for the uprising, reciting many of the by-now-familiar grievances against the Indian agents. Sibley responded: "You have murdered many of our people without sufficient cause. Return [to] me the prisoners, under a flag of truce, and I will talk with you then like a man."

Once again the Sioux were at odds about what to do. Two Sioux chiefs, Wabasha and Taopi, wrote to Sibley without Little Crow's knowledge and asked to be taken under his protection. Sibley replied that he would soon be on the march and the Indians should gather with the captives "in full sight of my troops" under a white flag. Some of the Sioux chiefs were eager to make a deal, but others disagreed. Among these was Rdainyanka ("Rattling Runner"), Wabasha's son-in-law, whose chilling arguments were later recorded by Isaac V. D. Heard, an attorney from St. Paul who had signed on in Sibley's service:

I am for continuing the war, and am opposed to the delivery of the prisoners. I have no confidence that the whites will stand by any agree-

ment they made if we give them up. Ever since we treated with them
their agents and traders have robbed and cheated us. Some of our people have been shot, some hung; others placed upon floating ice and
drowned; and many have been starved in their prisons. It was not the
intention of the nation to kill any of the whites until the four men returned from Acton and told what they had done. When they did this,
all the young men became excited and commenced the massacre. The
older ones would have prevented it if they could, but since the treaties
they have lost their influence. We may regret what has happened, but
the matter has gone too far to be remedied. We have got to die. Let
us, then, kill as many of the whites as possible, and let the prisoners die
with us.

Meanwhile, Sibley reported he was drilling his raw soldiers into a
force he hoped could be relied upon to fight effectively. Presumably
some of the noncommissioned officers among his troops were attending to this drilling. And after a while the fellows seemed to acquire a
certain military bearing. Also, by the second week of September, Sibley
received substantial quantities of ammunition, clothing, and provisions.
With them came something even better—270 men from the Third
Minnesota Infantry who had seen action at the battle of Murfreesboro
in Tennessee and been captured and paroled. Unlike the parolees near
Annapolis, they were not averse to fighting Sioux, especially in their
home state. As for the legal opinion by Attorney General Edward Bates
that parolees could not be used against Indians, he had not yet written
it. The officers of the Third Minnesota remained in Confederate prisons, but the enlisted men offered Sibley what he most needed—well-
trained infantry. Sibley took heart and made plans to march against the
Sioux, but then it rained, causing a two-day delay.

On September 17, the day Federals and Confederates clashed near
Antietam Creek, John Pope urged Sibley to push on and "exterminate"
the Indians. On September 19 Sibley marched out of Fort Ridgely and
up the Minnesota River Valley toward the Upper Agency, where he was
told the Sioux from the Lower Agency were camped. In addition to the
Third Minnesota, his command included fifteen companies of infantry,
thirty-eight Renville Rangers, twenty-eight mounted citizen guards,
and sixteen citizen artillerists—a total of more than sixteen hundred
men. The Reverend Stephen Riggs, one of the missionaries who had

worked with the Sioux for years and knew their language, was with this group to act as interpreter.

To no one's surprise, Sibley's column moved at a leisurely pace. The Upper Agency was about forty miles from the fort, and wagons usually made the trip in a day, but some of the refugees fleeing the massacres had made it in half a day. Sibley's group took four days—during which the hostages continued to fear for their lives and the women were repeatedly raped. In the colonel's defense, he had few horses and little cavalry to scout the Sioux, so he felt obliged to proceed carefully. On the night of September 22, the same day on which Lincoln issued the Emancipation Proclamation, Sibley's force camped on the east shore of Lone Tree or Battle Lake (which no longer exists), about five miles north of present-day Echo. Sibley's guide mistakenly told him it was Wood Lake, which was more than three miles to the west. (Thus, like the battle of Bunker Hill that was not fought on Bunker Hill, the ensuing battle of Wood Lake was not fought at Wood Lake.)

Lone Tree Lake drains through a small, meandering stream that curves northeast through a deep ravine and eventually turns east. One group of soldiers camped to the left, facing the lake, another group dug in on the right and held the crest of the southern slope to the ravine, and another group took the far right, behind the ravine. The camps were aligned in a triangular pattern. Despite his lack of cavalry and the rough experience at Birch Coulee, Sibley assumed the Sioux were farther up the valley, and thus he carelessly posted his pickets too close to the camp to provide much warning of an attack.

Unlike Sibley, the Sioux did have scouts in the countryside and soon knew the whereabouts of his camp. As was their custom, they convened a powwow to determine a course of action. Little Crow, Shakopee, Rdainyanka, Mankato, and other chiefs from the Lower Agency proposed a night attack to maximize the element of surprise. But before launching the attack, they sent an invitation to the chiefs of the Upper Agency to join in the attack and then waited for the invitees to appear. The chiefs from the Upper Agency, however, were put off by the idea of a night attack, which they considered unworthy of warriors. After extended discussion, they all agreed on a morning attack as the soldiers broke camp and moved north toward the Upper Agency camps. It isn't clear how many braves were involved, but the best estimates put their total number between seven hundred and twelve hundred, a large group, but smaller than Sibley's. The Sioux hid in the deep grass along the river road and waited for dawn.

Fortunately for Sibley, the rigorous training he had attempted to impose on his men had limited impact. A group of about a dozen men, which included Pvt. Grove Kimball from the Third Minnesota, decided to search for fresh food. They had heard there were ample potatoes, melons, sweet corn, and other foods at the Upper Agency. So they took four wagons in which to haul back whatever they found. Some of the men said later they assumed they would have received permission for this adventure but thought it more prudent not to ask. They left camp around 7:00 a.m. while the other solders were preparing breakfast.

"They came over the prairie," said Big Eagle, "right where our line was. Some of the wagons were not in the road, and if they had kept straight on would have driven right over our men as they lay in the grass. At last they came so close that our men had to rise up and fire." Kimball was shot through the thigh and later died of his wound. Back in camp, the other soldiers heard the shooting and grabbed their weapons. The battle was on.

The fighting was premature and upset all of Little Crow's carefully laid plans. "Little Crow felt very badly," said Big Eagle. "Hundreds of our men did not get into the battle and did not fire a shot. They were too far out." Probably no more than three hundred Sioux were actively engaged.

But a lot of them did get into it. As soon as the foragers realized they were under attack, they took refuge behind their wagons and returned fire. Realizing they were greatly outnumbered, the twelve men fell back toward camp. The rest of the Third Minnesota moved toward the shooting under the command of Maj. Abraham Welch. As they formed a line and began pushing the Indians toward the river, another group of Sioux emerged from the tall grass and attempted to take the soldiers from the rear. The Renville Rangers moved into the fray to counter that threat, and other Indians appeared on all sides.

Sibley rose to the occasion by sending several units into action plus a howitzer and a 6-pounder. As was the situation with the Sioux, a relatively small portion of Sibley's soldiers were actively engaged, probably no more than a third. The cannon quickly took a heavy toll on the Indians and, as happened at Fort Ridgely, seemed to break their spirit.

Mankato was killed by a cannonball, which witnesses say he refused to dodge. His body was taken from the field, but another fourteen or fifteen dead warriors lay scattered on the ground, and most of them were scalped by the soldiers. Sibley was offended by this and threatened dire repercussions if any more scalpings occurred. "The bodies of the dead," he said, "even of a savage enemy shall not be subjected to indignities by civilized and Christian men." Supposedly this work was done by the Renville Rangers, who were half-breeds and thus at least partly heir to Indian battle traditions. About fifty Sioux were wounded, and one was taken prisoner.

Seven soldiers, including Private Kimball, were killed. Major Welch was wounded in the leg, and another thirty-three or thirty-four soldiers were wounded, mostly among the Third Minnesota and the Renville Rangers. With Indian casualties outnumbering white by two to one, the battle of Wood Lake was claimed as a victory. Sibley said in a letter to his wife that the Indians had received "a severe blow" and "will not dare to make another stand."

IT SHOULD come as no surprise that Sibley, savoring his victory, decided to remain at the Lone Tree camp for two days to attend his wounded and take stock of the situation. Again he lamented the shortage of cavalry needed for swift pursuit of the Sioux and also his concern for the safety of the hostages. He was optimistic that the defeat at Wood Lake would create a rift among the Sioux that could lead to a settlement. He knew that several Christian chiefs from the Upper Agency had wanted no part of the insurrection and had spoken against it.

As the failures of the insurrection multiplied, the Christian chiefs did become more outspoken and more bold in their resistance. While Little Crow and the others were fighting at Lone Tree, some of the Christian chiefs seized the opportunity to take control of the hostages and took them to their own camp at the Upper Agency, near the deserted mission. They dug fortifications for defense in case Little Crow and the others were successful and came searching for the captives.

But the warriors returned defeated and, perhaps more important, realized that the insurrection was all but over. Little Crow announced his intent to flee with his people. Wabasha said he would stay, hoping to trade the hostages still alive for leniency. When the Sioux warriors ar-

rived at the Upper Agency and learned the captives had been moved,
they made no effort to retrieve them. Little Crow went to his camp to
spend his last night in the Minnesota River Valley. The next morning he
ordered his wagons loaded with his possessions for a long trek to the
west and summoned his people for a final statement.

"I am ashamed to call myself a Dakota [Sioux]," he said. "Seven
hundred of our best warriors were whipped yesterday by the whites.
Now we had all better run away and scatter out over the plains like buffalo and wolves. To be sure, the whites had wagon-guns and better
arms than we, and there were many more of them. But that is no reason why we should not have whipped them, for we are brave Dakotas
and the whites are cowardly women. I cannot account for the disgraceful defeat. It must be the work of traitors in our midst."

Then Little Crow, along with about one hundred of his people, set
out for the west along with other groups led by Shakopee, Red Middle
Voice, and the four young warriors who had initiated the uprising with
the killings at Acton. Not all of the Sioux who were most active in the
killings fled, but most of them did.

Sibley, of course, dithered and dawdled for two more days and finally moved out on the third day, September 25, advancing at a
leisurely pace toward the camp where the hostages were being held—a
distance of about ten miles that most travelers of the time could handle
in half a day. By way of explanation of his tardiness, before setting out,
he wrote to Wabasha, in response to the message brought by Joseph
Campbell, "If I advanced my troops before you could make your
arrangements the war party would murder the prisoners. Now that I
learn from Joe Campbell that most of the captives are in safety in your
camp, I shall move tomorrow."

Some of the active leaders of the uprising stayed in their camps to
accept whatever retribution was coming. Among these was Big Eagle,
Traveling Hail, Wabasha, Wacouta, and the Christian chiefs—Little
Paul, Simon, Akipa, and Cloudman. As soon as Little Crow, Red Middle Voice, Shakopee, and their followers were gone, the Christian chiefs
who had taken charge of the hostages sent Campbell, Little Crow's
onetime scribe, to inform Sibley that the captives were safe and waiting
for his arrival.

The hostages grew increasingly anxious about Sibley's casual advance, and many of them were highly critical of him afterward. "We at

last concluded he was afraid," reported Sarah Wakefield. "The Indians began to get uneasy for fear Little Crow would return and kill us if Sibley did not come soon."

On the first day Sibley's soldiers traveled only eight miles, whereupon they stopped in the afternoon to conduct a "dress parade," after which they spent hours digging defensive trenches in case they were attacked again. Sarah Wakefield later found this action infuriating. "God watched over us and kept those savages back," she said. "To him, I give all the honor and glory; Sibley I do not even thank, for he deserved it not."

About noon on September 26 Sibley's troops finally reached their goal, setting up camp a short distance above the tents where the captives were being held. During all the time it took for Sibley's column to reach the hostages, the rapes continued. "The night before the troops came," reported Nancy Faribault, "twenty or thirty Indians came in with a young white girl of sixteen or seventeen. She was nearly heartbroken and quite in despair."

Sibley's troops' first act was to name the site Camp Release. On foot but with a troop escort, Sibley entered the Sioux camp at about two o'clock in the afternoon "with drums beating and colors flying" and requested a council. Much of the afternoon was whiled away in speechmaking as various chiefs took turns protesting their innocence. In a report to General Pope, Sibley said the Indians and half-breeds were assembled "in considerable numbers, and I proceeded to give them very briefly my views of the late proceedings; my determination that the guilty parties should be pursued and overtaken, if possible, and I made a demand that all the captives should be delivered to me instantly, that I might take them to my camp." The Christian chiefs and other "friendlies" instantly complied and brought out 91whites, almost all women and children, and about 150 half-breeds. Subsequently, other captives were brought from other nearby camps, bringing the total to 107 whites and 162 half-breeds.

Isaac V. D. Heard was on hand to record the scene. "The poor creatures wept for joy at their escape," he said. "They had watched our coming for many a weary day, with constant apprehension of death at the hands of their savage captors, and had almost despaired of seeing us. The woe written on the faces of the half starved and nearly naked women and children would have melted the hardest heart."

Though most of the hostages had been starved and abused in a variety of ways, there were a few conspicuous exceptions. In a letter to his wife, Sibley recorded that Harriet Adams "whose six months old child was killed when she was captured" and "who is exceedingly pretty" told him she had not been molested but rather protected by a friendly Indian who treated her like a sister.

Sibley reported also that a second "rather handsome captive" had "become so infatuated with the redskin who had taken her for a wife that, although her white husband was still living . . . and had been in search of her, she declared that were it not for her children, she would not leave her dusky paramour." Readers of a later century will have more knowledge of the behavior of people who are held hostage and who, after a while, tend to identify with their captors.

In succeeding weeks others straggled in from diverse points of the compass in various states of distress. In late October a foraging party of soldiers under Sibley's command found Justina Boelter, with her three-year-old daughter Ottilie, wandering around the Upper Agency near the Minnesota River. Her husband, John, had been killed with his parents and other family members in August. In the nine weeks since, she and her daughter had lived in the woods without fire or shelter, eating whatever plants they could find to survive. A second daughter, five-year-old Amelia, had died of starvation near the end of September. Reportedly, Justina and Ottilie were so pathetic looking that the soldiers wept to see them. They both recovered, and the woman later married her brother-in-law, Michael Boelter, whose wife and three daughters had been killed during the massacres.

Sibley sent some of the freed captives back to Fort Ridgely and the orphans to other settlements where they could be cared for. He kept several of the women at the camp to testify against the Indians who had assaulted them so he could take them into custody. Many of the Sioux were eager to surrender in exchange for the prospect of being fed. The uprising had disrupted their meager economic prospects, not the least of which was the loss of the annuity payments. They were all looking at a long, cold winter.

From Camp Release, Sibley wrote again to Pope and asked to be relieved of duty. He said he had achieved his two primary missions—defeating the Indians and liberating the captives—and that a "strictly military commander" would be better suited to the task of hunting down the Sioux who remained at large. Once again his request was not granted. Instead, upon recommendation of General Pope and Governor Ramsey, President Lincoln recommended Sibley for promotion to brigadier general of the Minnesota volunteers. Congress eventually ratified his promotion—after a long delay.

Predictably, most of the ringleaders of the uprising had taken Little Crow's advice and headed west, but a few set up camp across the river to see what would happen. Over a period of weeks Sibley employed various promises and inducements to get more of them to surrender. He sent out half-breed messengers to promise the fugitives they would be treated honorably, as prisoners of war, and he argued that their "only hope of mercy, even to the women and children, will be immediate return and surrender." By October Sibley had two thousand Sioux in his immediate vicinity, though many of them were armed and living in their own tepees. Feeding them in addition to his sixteen hundred soldiers became a problem. On October 4 he dispatched more than one thousand Sioux under guard to harvest corn and potatoes from the fields and to look for other provisions. Meanwhile, other soldiers scoured the countryside for more refugees.

When Sibley was satisfied that most of the Sioux were under his control, he pounced—sending his soldiers to round up the chief suspects near his camp, disarm them, and hold them in a hastily erected log enclosure. The Sioux camped farther away were invited to a council then surrounded and arrested. Most of the captives were manacled together in pairs. Almost immediately Sibley had about two hundred men under guard, and within a couple of weeks that number expanded to more than four hundred.

On October 9 General Pope wired Washington, "The Sioux War may be considered at an end." But within a day he was reporting a new set of problems. "We have about 1,500 prisoners—men, women and children—and many are coming every day to deliver themselves up."

Sibley had made his intention clear to his superiors two days after his arrival at Camp Release to create some sort of tribunal "to try summarily the mixed bloods and Indians engaged in the raids and massacres." He called it a "military commission," which was good enough for General Pope, but Governor Ramsey, in a letter to President Lincoln, called it a "military court." Not to be outdone, Charles E. Flandrau, who had led the defense of New Ulm, referred to it as a "court martial" and a "military tribunal." There was in fact no clear legal precedent for the undertaking, and given the temper of the time and place, it could have easily degenerated into a lynch mob. To Sibley's credit this did not happen, though many people—including General Pope—were eager to dispense with the formalities and get on with the hangings. A week before the end of the fighting, Pope had written to Sibley: "I altogether approve of executing the Indians who have been concerned in these outrages."

Pope also made it clear that he was not overly concerned about the legal refinements of the proceedings. "I don't know how you can discriminate now between Indians who say they are and have been friendly, and those who have not." He advised Sibley to hold on to all the prisoners, and "all who are guilty whatever the number should in my judgement be hung." Pope made it abundantly clear to Sibley that his task was to achieve "a final settlement with all these Indians," and step one was to hang them. "Do not allow any false sympathy for the Indians to prevent you from acting with the utmost rigor," he instructed Sibley. "Be assured I will sustain you in whatever measures you adopt to effect this object."

Sibley knew he had grim work on his hands, and he was not thrilled at the prospect. "This power of life, and death, is an awful thing to exercise," he wrote to his wife. "And when I think of more than three hundred human beings are subject to that power lodged in my hand, it makes me shudder."

Whatever the court was called, it was comprised of five of Sibley's officers: Col. William Marshall, who commanded five companies in the battle of Wood Lake; Col. William Brooks, who commanded the Sixth Minnesota Infantry at the battles of Birch Coulee and Wood Lake; Capt. Hiram Grant, who commanded a company at the battle of Birch Coulee, taking full command when his superiors were wounded in the fighting; First Lt. Rollin C. Olin, who was second in command at the battle of Wood Lake; and Capt. Hiram Bailey of the Sixth Minnesota. Major George Bradley of the Seventh Minnesota later replaced Marshall, who was called away to other service after the first twenty-nine trials. No defense counsel was provided. Sibley directed St. Paul attorney Isaac V. D. Heard to serve as court recorder, and most of the record of the proceedings stems from his pen. (Heard later wrote a history of the Sioux uprising that remains a primary source on the matter.)

At the beginning of the trials, Sibley announced his intention to hang everyone found guilty. "They will be forthwith executed," he wrote to Pope. "Perhaps it will be a stretch of my authority. If so, necessity must be my justification."

Pope was on the same page, as Sibley well knew by this time. "It is my purpose to utterly exterminate the Sioux," Pope replied to Sibley. "They are to be treated as maniacs or wild beasts."

The Reverend Stephen Riggs, who had accompanied Sibley as chaplain and interpreter, was asked to interview the women captives and record their testimony about the abuses they had suffered and to witness against their abductors. Perhaps unwittingly, Riggs went on to play a key role in what followed. "The prisoners were arraigned upon written charges specifying the criminating acts," Heard wrote.

> These charges were signed by Colonel Sibley or his adjutant general, and were, with but few deceptions, based upon information furnished by the Rev. S.R. Riggs. He obtained it by assembling the half breeds; and others possessed of knowledge, in a tent, and interrogating them concerning suspected parties. The names of the witnesses were appended to the charge. He was, in effect, the grand jury of the court. His long residence in the country, and extensive acquaintance with the Indians, his knowledge of the character and habits of most of them, enabling him to tell almost with certainty what Indians would be implicated and what ones not, either from their disposition or their relatives being engaged, and his familiarity with their language, eminently qualified him for the position.

Riggs was clearly uncomfortable in this role and fretted even more about it later. He said at the time that the conduct of the trials was too hasty to permit proper elucidation of the evidence, and he anticipated that the meagerness of the record would lead to new trials. Some who knew Riggs had spent the better part of his life among the Sioux as a missionary accused him of a bias for them. But he admitted that "a terrible necessity—the demand of public justice—requires that the great majority of those who are condemned should be executed."

12

BENT BY
HIS BURDENS

LINCOLN WOULD IN TIME come to regard the Emancipation Proclamation as the crowning achievement of his career, but for the first few weeks he fretted greatly that it could prove to be a catastrophic miscalculation. There was an election only a few weeks away that would afford the voters ample opportunity to register their approval or disapproval.

There was no way to predict what impact the proclamation would have. Postmaster General Montgomery Blair warned the president that the Emancipation Proclamation would not go down well in his home state of Maryland. Though the proclamation specifically exempted slave states still loyal to the Union, such as Maryland, it clearly did not bode well for the slaveholding class. In the months leading up to the announcement, Lincoln engaged in a dialogue with Border State politicians and sought some amicable way to free their slaves, possibly by providing financial compensation. The talks went nowhere because the loyal slaveholders could not conceive of giving up their slaves or imagine what was to be done with millions of freed slaves.

Perhaps even more troubling was the very real prospect that the Emancipation Proclamation would transform the Democrats into an antiwar party. The Republicans were still a fledgling party in 1862, and their ability to sustain a political movement through several election cycles was unknown. In the election of 1860 the Democrats had accounted for 44 percent of the vote in the free states and a majority in the Border States that remained loyal to the Union. The Thirty-seventh

Congress that convened on July 4, 1861, included 102 Republicans, 44 Democrats, 21 Unionists, and three others.

By the fall of 1862, as casualty lists carried heartbreak into every city and village, there was a small but growing opposition in the North to a war that seemed to be going nowhere. And virtually all of the opposition was expressed through the Democratic Party. While many, if not most, Democrats supported the war, the Peace Democrats, derided as Copperheads, openly called for reunion of North and South through negotiation, not subjugation.

But while there was division among the Democrats about the war, there was little disagreement about emancipation—they were virtually unanimous in opposition to such an extreme measure. During 1862 there were four votes in Congress directly related to the slavery question: a prohibition on the return of fugitive slaves to their masters, the emancipation of slaves in the District of Columbia, a ban on slavery in the territories, and a confiscation act empowering the army to commandeer slaves from their masters in states that had rebelled against the Union. On all of those questions the Democrats were almost unanimously opposed and the Republicans almost unanimously in favor. The party-line split could not have been more starkly drawn. Lincoln was fully aware of this Democratic commitment to the continuation of slavery, and it troubled him deeply.

Still, Republican legislators had the majority and were clearly antislavery, but racist attitudes remained prevalent even among their ranks. One gets a general sense in reading the personal correspondence of the period, including letters home from Union soldiers, that the white majority conceded humanity to blacks—but just barely. There were anti-black riots in Cincinnati and New York in the summer of 1862, and as if to highlight the point, the voters of Lincoln's home state of Illinois once again voted—with two-fifths of Republicans joining Democrats—for exclusion of freed blacks from their states. "Our people want nothing to do with the Negro," said Illinois Senator Lyman Trumbull.

New York City was a hotbed of racism and antiwar sentiment. A former mayor denounced Lincoln's administration and called for active resistance to emancipation. Peace Democrat Horatio Seymour, who was running for governor, favored restoring the Union as quickly as possible, even if it meant granting concessions to the South. He said emancipation meant "niggerism for nationality."

"The Irishman sees the Negro as a dangerous competitor," wrote Karl Marx in an analysis of the 1862 election for Vienna's *Die Presse*. "The efficient farmers in Indiana and Ohio hate the Negro almost as much as the slaveholder. He is a symbol, for them, of slavery and the humiliation of the working class, and the Democratic press threatens them daily with a flooding of their territories by 'niggers.'"

The political realities of such sentiments explain why, as late as August 1862, Lincoln was still floating his notion of colonizing freed blacks in Central America or "returning" them to Africa—though few American blacks thought of anywhere other than America as home.

Lincoln struggled to navigate the turbulent political waters to reach the higher ground of emancipation, but his erstwhile allies either could not or would not recognize his dilemma. The black abolitionist leader Frederick Douglass decried that Lincoln was becoming "a miserable tool of traitors and rebels" and that he had "contempt for Negroes." He noted that Lincoln's flirtation with colonization would incite "ignorant and base" white men to "commit all kinds of violence and outrage upon the colored people."

But Douglass and the other fiery abolitionist leaders were free to indulge their abstract ideals in part because they did not have to win elections to assert their views. Lincoln understood that only people who won elections could do anything about slavery. There was an uneasy sense among the Republicans, including the man in the White House, that they had to offer a plausible scenario for dealing with freed blacks once emancipation became reality. In fact, partially in response to the president's urging, Congress appropriated six hundred thousand dollars for an experiment in colonizing blacks on an island near Haiti. A few hundred were induced to participate in this experiment, but their ranks were devastated by disease and hunger. By 1864 the survivors were on their way back to the States.

The early reactions to the Emancipation Proclamation were predictable. Confederate President Jefferson Davis denounced it as an obvious attempt to provoke insurrection. Though a slaveholder, Davis was a curiously passive one who owned no whips and generally treated his servants well, at least comparatively speaking, to the point that they often declined to work and got away with it. His great failing was an inexplicable inability to see that the great majority of slaveholders around him were not so benign.

Elsewhere in the South the politicians and newspapers were virtually unanimous in their excoriation of the proclamation. If anyone in Dixie thought it to be a good idea, he prudently kept his thoughts to himself. There is little question the proclamation undermined the position of Southerners who opposed secession. One pro-Union Southerner in Eastern Tennessee, where Republicans enjoyed significant support, was appalled by the "atrocity and barbarism" of Lincoln's announcement. The slaves, of course, had no voice.

The more radical elements in the Republican Party, who had been highly critical of Lincoln's failure to transform the war into an anti-slavery movement, were at least for the time being silent or positive. Abolitionist Senator Charles Sumner of Massachusetts, who had been severely beaten on the Senate floor by South Carolina Representative Preston Brooks, said he stood "with the loyal multitudes of the North, firmly and sincerely by the side of the President." The Republican governors who had convened in Altoona, Pennsylvania, to critique Lincoln's war leadership found he had beaten them to the punch and took a train to Washington to congratulate him. Even Douglass was temporarily silenced.

Horace Greeley, editor of the *New York Tribune,* who had been vicious in his attacks on Lincoln's slowness to embrace emancipation, now sang a different tune. "God bless Abraham Lincoln," he wrote. The *Chicago Tribune* called it "the grandest proclamation ever issued by man." All across the North, and especially in New England, there were cheerful rallies and upbeat speeches praising the president's action. Abolitionists sent letters of fawning praise to the White House. Predictably, prominent academics lined up in Lincoln's corner—the poets John Greenleaf Whittier and William Cullen Bryant wrote to him in support—and even Ralph Waldo Emerson, who had been among those most critical of Lincoln's alleged timidity about slavery, now said the president "had been permitted to do more for America than any other American man."

On September 25 in Bangor, Maine, Vice President Hannibal Hamlin put pen to paper to write the president a note remarkable in its humility: "I do not know, as, in the multiplicity of the correspondence with which you are burthened, this note will ever meet your eye—But I desire to express my undissembled and sincere thanks for your Emancipation Proclamation. It will stand as the great act of the age. It will

prove to be wise in Statesmanship, as it is Patriotic—It will be enthusiastically approved and sustained and future generations will, as I do, say
God bless you for the great and noble act."

Lincoln responded kindly to his vice president but was sharp to note
that the initial reaction of flowery words was not the final word. "Com-
mendation in newspapers and by distinguished individuals is all that a
vain man could wish," he responded. "The North responds to the
proclamation sufficiently in breath, but breath alone kills no rebels."

Others in the North were lukewarm to hostile about the proclamation, including some close to the president. Secretary of State Seward
officially supported the action and had not opposed it when Lincoln
presented it to the cabinet, but privately he derided it as pointless and
unnecessarily provocative. Montgomery Blair held his tongue, but others in the influential Blair family labeled the proclamation a mistake.
And the proclamation was probably the last straw for Interior Secretary
Caleb Smith, already caught up in the scandals that provoked the Sioux
uprising, and he soon resigned from office.

Not surprisingly, the most heated criticism in the North came from
Democrats, and it was expressed vehemently in the Democratic newspapers. The *New York World* said Lincoln was "adrift on a current of
radical fanaticism." The *New York Evening Express* said it would make
impossible "the restoration of the old Constitution and Union." The
New York Journal of Commerce predicted it would lead to a "continuation of the war, in a dark future, in which the end is beyond our vision."

"The effect produced by the appearance of the proclamation did
much to justify the previous hesitation of the President," recorded
Union Gen. Carl Schurz, who engaged in some heated exchanges with
Lincoln on the subject. Schurz had been active in Lincoln's presidential
campaign, serving as his main liaison with German American immigrants, for which he was rewarded with a generalship:

> In the first place, it did not bring about the confusion in the internal
> conditions of the Southern states that had been expected by the anti-
> slavery men who advised the measure. They had, indeed, not looked for
> nor desired a servile insurrection. But they had expected the ruling class,
> and with it the Confederate government, to fear the possibility of such a
> calamity, and for that reason to withdraw a part of their forces from the
> fighting line to watch the Negroes. They had also expected that the

number of Negro fugitives from the Southern country would become much larger, and that thereby the laboring force of the South necessary for the sustenance of the army would be greatly reduced.

One of the most remarkable features of the history of those times is the fact that most of the slaves stayed on the plantations or farms, and did the accustomed work with quiet, and in the case of house servants, not seldom even with affectionate fidelity, while in their heart, they yearned for freedom, and prayed for its speedy coming. Only as our armies penetrated the South, and especially when Negroes were enlisted as soldiers, did they leave their former masters in large numbers and even then there was scarcely any instance of violent revenge on their part for any wrong or cruelty any of them may have suffered in slavery.

Naturally, the Emancipation Proclamation became a major bone of contention in the November elections—there was never a chance it would not—strengthening the president's standing among abolitionists and weakening his appeal to moderates and conservatives. As the election approached, the political heat on Lincoln intensified. "In the autumn of 1862, Mr. Lincoln was exposed to the bitterest assaults and criticisms from every faction in the country," recorded Nicolay and Hay in their biography of the president. "His conservative supporters reproached him with having yielded to the wishes of the radicals; the radicals denounced him for being hampered, if not corrupted, by the influence of the conservatives. On one side, he was assailed by a clamor for peace, on the other by vehement and injurious demands for a more vigorous prosecution of the war."

Schurz added, "Much seditious clamor was heard about the blood of white fellow citizens being treacherously spilled for the sole purpose of robbing our Southern countrymen of their Negro property, and all this in direct violation of the Federal Constitution and its Laws." Though this activity seemed to affect mainly Democratic partisans, Schurz noted, "it served to consolidate their organization, to turn mere opposition to the Republican administration into opposition to the prosecution of the war. On the other hand, it greatly inspired the enthusiasm of the antislavery people, and gave a new impetus to their activity."

Lincoln had expected to lose support because of the Emancipation Proclamation and was somewhat taken aback when he came under fire also for the suspension of habeas corpus. Democrats accused him of assuming dictatorial powers. The *Illinois State Register,* a Democratic paper, foresaw a "reign of terror in the loyal states" with mass arrests and convictions without trials to stifle dissent. In New York, Seymour thundered he would resist "even if the streets be made to run with blood" if arbitrary arrests continued after his election. An Ohio editor wrote, "A large majority can see no reason why they should be shot for the benefit of niggers and Abolitionists."

To Schurz it seemed "the political situation in the North assumed a threatening aspect. Hundreds of thousands of Republican voters were in the army, away from home. Arbitrary arrests, the suspension of the writ of habeas corpus, and similar stretches of power had disquieted and even irritated many good men. "But more than this," he continued, "our frequent defeats in the field and the apparent fruitlessness of some of our victories, like that of Antietam, had a disheartening effect upon the people. Our many failures were largely ascribed to a lack of energy in the administration."

By late October, beset by frustrations about lack of military action against the Rebels and the prospects of a massive setback in the campaign, Lincoln impressed one visitor as haggard, worn out, and "literally bending under the weight of his burdens."

BUT THERE was at least a little good news coming Lincoln's way. By mid-October he knew the Sioux uprising in Minnesota had been effectively suppressed and that the outbreak was not as widespread as he had feared. Further, there was no evidence that the Confederacy was involved, at least not in stirring up the Sioux. John Pope was making characteristically harsh noises about retributions due the Indians, openly advocating their extermination, but Lincoln sent clear word to him to stage no executions without sanction from Washington.

Lincoln offered no explanation for his decision to intervene in the Minnesota affair when virtually everyone there was crying out for Indian blood, but it may have had something to do with a visit from one of the few white champions of the Sioux in that state, or anywhere west of the Alleghenies—Bishop Henry Benjamin Whipple.

Few in Minnesota at the time or since would question Bishop Whipple's commitment to the Sioux, but in his own way he had helped foster the environment that fed the Indian's resentments and led to the

uprising. His clearly stated goal and that of the other Christian missionaries was not only to convert the Sioux to the Christian faith but to
wean them from their traditional customs and beliefs in favor of the
white man's lifestyle. "In Whipple's mission churches, the first significa-
tion of an Indian man's conversion to Christ was to give up braids for a
short Euroamerican-style haircut and the sporting of Euroamerican
clothing in lieu of breech cloth and buckskins," wrote social commentator and historian George E. Tinker. "Throughout Whipple's episco-
pacy, the Indian missions in Minnesota among the Ojibway were
engaged in an ongoing struggle against the influence of all forms of Indian spirituality, from daily face painting to the power ceremonies of
the Grand Medicine Lodge and the Medewin."

Whipple clearly regarded the Sioux culture as savage and was committed to bringing them to terms with modern civilization. "Eventually,
it becomes clear that civilizing—that is, Europeanizing—Indian people
evidently took precedence over conversion," Tinker observed. "Indeed,
the two discrete acts seem to have been thoroughly intermingled in the
minds of the missionaries, evidenced by Whipple's repeated invocation
of 'Christian civilization.'" In his letters to authorities—first President
Buchanan and later Lincoln—Whipple criticized "the glaring defects in
our Indian system" because in part it "placed no seal of condemnation
on savage life."

Whipple made no bones about his desire to convert the Indians to
the white man's values, and a key part of that was instructing them to
become farmers in the manner of whites. This was at sharp odds with
the traditional nomadic lifestyle of the Indians, who roamed the prairies
and plains in search of game and rarely put down roots in any one spot
for long. Over the course of the three-and-a-half-century struggle between red and white men, the Indians time and again were persuaded
to deed their land to the whites in part because the Indians had no con-
cept of land ownership and no desire to learn farming. Whipple wanted
them to abandon their ancient ways in favor of white ways.

"Here again the solution backfired in ways that exacerbated the
problem," Tinker commented. "In attempting to teach—that is,
impose—their own model of civilization on Indian people, the missionaries generated a disintegration of the societal structures of Indian civilization. European-style agriculture with its farms spaced at a distance
from each other contributed to the breakdown of Indian communities

just as readily as did the removal of children from the community. The attempt highlights Whipple's goal of detribalization and assimilation, but it just as readily highlights the devastation he brought to Indian people, which resulted in such cultural dislocation and disintegration."

It is not likely that Whipple would accept that interpretation of his life's work anymore than Lincoln would accept a condemnation of his racist presumption that blacks were inferior to whites. Whipple and Lincoln dealt with the harsh realities of the nineteenth century, not the political correctness of the twenty-first, and did their best to lift two despised peoples above their mean condition over the vociferous, often violent, objections of white Americans.

Since 1859, when Whipple had been inaugurated as bishop, he had tried to rally Minnesota's settlers to the plight of the Sioux, but he had had little success. The settlers simply had no respect or concern for the tribes and generally regarded them as nuisances or threats, incapable of civilized values. The bishop had communicated to Presidents Buchanan and Lincoln the corruption in the Indian system, and he had warned Lincoln that an uprising was inevitable. Whipple never wavered in his commitment to the Sioux, even in the wake of the massacres when his white constituents vilified him for his trouble. He was in St. Paul when news of the outbreak came and was immediately put to work by Sibley in recruiting volunteers to suppress the outbreak. Soon after, the governor sent the bishop to Washington to seek military aid through his cousin, Henry W. Halleck. Thereafter he was active in organizing relief for the victims and arguing against excessive reaction to the Sioux, a position that most whites found incomprehensible. But no one reading his words 150 years later can doubt his sincerity or conviction.

"I should have preferred that other and abler hands plead for the poor race," he wrote later. "To me, it is grievous to be placed in antagonism to others. I love peace, not strife. But God led me to those poor wretched souls. I heard their cries for help. I saw the dark record of crime heaped upon them. I dare not be silent. Some day people will tell in hushed whispers our shame. They will marvel that their fathers dared to trifle with truth and righteousness and, with such foolhardiness, trifle with God."

In October 1862, Whipple went to New York for the General Convention of the Episcopal Church. He took with him a paper he proposed to submit to Lincoln with the idea that other bishops should sign it:

We respectfully call your attention to the recent Indian outbreak, which has devastated one of the fairest portions of our country as demanding the careful investigation of the government. The history of our relations with the Indian tribes of North America shows that after they enter into treaty stipulations with the United States, a rapid deterioration always takes place. They become degraded, are liable to savage out breaks and are often incited to war.

The paper presented specific proposals for reorganizing the Indian Department and improving relations between Indians and whites:

We feel that these results cannot be obtained without careful thought, and we therefore request you to take such steps as may be necessary to appoint a commission of men of high character, who have no political ends to serve, to whom may be referred this whole question, in order that they may devise a more perfect system for the administration of Indian affairs, which will repair these wrongs, preserve the honor of the Government, and call upon us the blessings of God.

Several of the bishops balked at this draft, saying they preferred to avoid political issues. Whipple reacted vigorously, jumping to his feet. "My diocese is desolated by an Indian war," he protested. "Eight hundred of our own people are dead. I have just come from a hospital where more are dying. I have drawn up a paper to present to President Lincoln and all I want is your signatures, yet many of you dare to call this politics." Bishop Alonzo Potter of New York stood in support of the fiery young evangelist from the frontier. He took the paper and had it signed by nineteen bishops and twenty deputies.

Whipple went to Washington, and Halleck took him to call on Lincoln. There is no transcript of the discussion, but Whipple recorded years later that he described to Lincoln the abuses that had fostered the uprising. It is not known if Lincoln read the letter Whipple sent to him the previous March, but he probably did, because Whipple was a prominent man in Minnesota, and Lincoln was nothing if not alert to the concerns of prominent citizens. If he had not read the letter, he received a vivid verbal summary this time. Whipple reported that, as he related the events leading up to and during the massacres, tears came to Lincoln's eyes. "I gave an account of the outbreak, its causes and the suffering and evil which had followed in its wake," the bishop recalled. "Mr. Lincoln had known something of Indian warfare in the Black Hawk War. He was deeply moved. He was a man of profound sympathy, but he usually relieved the strain upon his feelings by telling a story."

"Bishop, a man once thought that monkeys could pick cotton better than Negroes because their fingers were smaller," Lincoln replied. "He turned a lot of them into his cotton field. Then he found it took two overseers to watch one monkey. I guess we have the same problem. We need two honest men to watch each Indian agent. This Indian service must be reformed. If I get through this war, I am going to see that it is done."

Lincoln read the paper brought by Whipple and signed by the other bishops. He gave Whipple a card of introduction to the secretary of the interior, Caleb Smith. "Give Bishop Whipple any information he wants about Indian affairs," it said. He gave the paper back to Whipple and instructed him to share it with Smith.

A bit later Lincoln met a friend from Illinois and inquired whether their mutual friend, Luther Dearborn, had moved to Minnesota. Told that he had, Lincoln said, "When you see Lute, ask him if he knows Bishop Whipple. He came here the other day and talked with me about the rascality of this Indian business until I felt it down to my boots."

ON OCTOBER 29 McClellan proudly wired Lincoln, "We occupy Leesburg." Then and now, Leesburg is a small Virginia town about five miles south of the Potomac River, about twenty-five miles from Washington. "I am much pleased with the movement of the army," Lincoln replied, in what was probably one of Honest Abe's few blatant lies. "When you get entirely across the river, let me know." This dry exchange suggests that Lincoln had finally given up on McClellan and decided to waste no more time exhorting him to fight.

The president had been anticipating a reverse at the polls. In September he had warned his cabinet, "I believe that I have not so much confidence of the people as I had some time before." He was right. On November 4 the Democrats scored major gains in several states that had voted heavily Republican two years before—New York, Pennsylvania, Ohio, Indiana, and even the president's home state of Illinois, including his home district that he had once served in Congress. Wisconsin split, and New Jersey went Democratic. The Republicans would still be a majority in the Thirty-eighth Congress, which was not to convene until December 1863, but by only a twenty-five-seat margin. Democrats won the governorships of New York and New Jersey and would have likely picked up more if there had been more in play. It was a big night for the Democrats, and they weren't slow to crow about it, asserting an end to abolition and boasting they would win an outright majority next time around.

But in truth the rout was not as bad as it seemed at first blush. Republicans held seventeen of nineteen free state governorships, elected several Republican representatives in Missouri for the first time, and actually gained five seats in the Senate. Even where the Democrats won, their margins of victory were slim and probably due in large measure to the absence of so many soldiers away to the war. Lincoln's Republicans would not allow that to happen again in 1864.

Karl Marx reported to his readers in Europe that the election results obscured a real shift in the American political landscape. If Lincoln had made emancipation a cause in 1860, he said, there is no doubt he would have been defeated. But "matters were quite different in the latest election. The Republicans made common cause with the Abolitionists. They came out emphatically for immediate emancipation, whether for its own sake or as a means of ending rebellion. If this circumstance is taken into account, the majority in favor of the government in Michigan, Illinois, Massachusetts, Iowa and Delaware, and the very significant majority vote it obtained in the states of New York, Ohio, and Pennsylvania, are equally surprising. Before the war, such a result would have been impossible."

Minnesota returned its two Republican congressmen to Washington. The *St. Paul Pioneer* reported that twelve counties in the southwest quadrant of the state that had reported votes in the 1860 election, five in the first district and seven in the second, did not report votes. The great majority of their citizens were either dead or had fled. There were not enough left to conduct an election.

13

A SOFT VOICE

THE FIVE-MAN COMMISSION appointed to try the Sioux accused of crimes in the uprising convened first at Camp Release on September 28, but they were ill-prepared to sort out the confused situation. They did not speak the Sioux language. They had more than two thousand prisoners to sort through, though many of the worst offenders, including Little Crow and Red Middle Voice, were long since fled to more hospitable climes. It quickly became clear that missionary Stephen Riggs—who did speak Sioux fluently, knew the customs and habits of the Sioux well, and was intimately acquainted with many of the prisoners—was the key to the operation. Prior to the trials he had interviewed hundreds of the captives privately, as well as many of the former hostages, to determine which of the prisoners were most culpable. And it was the ones singled out by Riggs who were put on trial.

Without a doubt, Riggs was uniquely qualified for the task. Court recorder Isaac V. D. Heard noted that Riggs served as "the Grand Jury of the court" and could tell "almost with certainty" who had been implicated. Riggs rejected Heard's analysis and wrote a lengthy letter to Lincoln, urging clemency for several prisoners. But there is no question he was the dominant force in the proceedings and stood by the results.

It is perhaps not surprising that the first trial was of a Negro or mulatto named Godfrey, or Otakle, the son of a Canadian Frenchman and a Negro woman, who was married to a Sioux woman, lived with the Sioux at the Lower Agency, and had been caught up in the violence. There were witnesses who offered damning testimony against him. To have been both black and Sioux in that place and time, accused of atrocities against helpless whites, would appear to have exhausted the possibilities of human misfortune. It does not seem by accident that Godfrey was singled out as the first of the accused to be put on trial.

He was charged with murder. Subsequent trials reflected some confusion about which Sioux did what to whom, but none of the witnesses confused Godfrey with anyone else. One of the hostages, Mary Woodbury, said she had seen Godfrey two or three days after the outbreak at Little Crow's village all decked out in war paint, well armed with gun and tomahawk, whooping it up with the other warriors, and apparently eager to fight the whites. He went off with the warriors to attack New Ulm, and when he returned, other Indians said he was the bravest of all. She said also she heard him brag of killing seven whites. Other hostages testified that Godfrey was with the Sioux who took them captive and, though unarmed, he seemed in favor of the outrages taking place around him. Still others testified they saw him fighting enthusiastically with the Sioux at both New Ulm and Fort Ridgely.

By all odds, Godfrey had no chance for acquittal, but subsequent events suggest that the challenges of living as a mixed-blood black man of uncertain status among red and white people, with a certain French element mixed in, imbued Godfrey with a wily intelligence that served him well in his predicament. Before the first witnesses were called, he readily admitted his presence at the battles at New Ulm and Fort Ridgely and that he had struck a man with a tomahawk in a house in which several were killed. However, he insisted he had been threatened with death if he did not participate and that he had bragged of his exploits "to keep the good will of the Indians."

"He had such an honest look, and spoke with such a truthful tone, that the court, though prejudiced against him in the beginning, were now unanimously inclined to believe there were possibilities as to his sincerity," recorded Heard. "His language was broken, and he communicated his ideas with some little difficulty. This was an advantage in his favor, for it interested the sympathetic attention of the listener, and it was a pleasure to listen to his hesitating speech. His voice was one of the softest I ever listened to."

No one charged Godfrey with rape or claimed to have seen him commit murder. Nevertheless the commissioners convicted him to "be hung by the neck until he is dead," as they were to do with most of the accused, but since the evidence was ambiguous and because they came to trust him, they commuted his sentence to ten years. As if to convey his gratitude, Godfrey turned state's evidence against the other accused and provided testimony that convicted more than a few of them. "He was the means of bringing justice to a large number of the savages," Heard recalled. "Not the least thing had escaped his eye or ear. Such an Indian had a double barreled gun, another a single barreled, another a long one, another a short one, another a lance, and another one nothing at all. One denied that he was at the fort. Godfrey saw him there preparing his sons for battle, and recollected that he painted the face of one red, and drew a streak of green over his eyes."

Heard noted that Godfrey recalled in detail conversations in which the Sioux allegedly boasted of their violent acts against the whites. In several instances Godfrey's testimony was substantiated by other evidence that after a while began to persuade the commissioners of Godfrey's veracity. "It was a study to watch him, as he sat in court, scanning the face of every culprit who came in with the eye of a cat about to spring," Heard observed. "His sense of the ridiculous, and evident appreciation of the gravity which should accompany the statement of an important truth, was strongly demonstrated."

When a prisoner declared his innocence and Godfrey knew otherwise, Godfrey would "drop his head upon his breast and convulse, with a fit of musical laughter." From time to time the commissioners called upon Godfrey to interrogate the accused, which he did to great effect, though it was, to say the least, a highly unusual legal procedure. On several occasions he led the accused into confessions of guilt.

When the trials began on September 28 only sixteen prisoners were on the docket, and the commissioners were working deliberately to assure justice was done. But Riggs was busily debriefing many others and producing more candidates for judgment. By October 4 only twenty-nine cases had been disposed of while the backlog was growing rapidly. By October 21 more than a hundred had been sentenced to death while several hundred more cases remained to be heard. And Pope was leaning on Sibley to resolve the cases faster.

"The trials were elaborately conducted until the commission became acquainted with the details of the different outrages and battles and then, the only point being the connection of the prisoner with them, five minutes would dispose of a case," Heard reported. "As many as 40 were sometimes tried in a day."

Riggs noted: "In a few weeks, instead of taking individuals for trial, the plan was adopted to subject all the grown men, with a few exceptions, to an investigation, trusting the innocent could make their innocency appear. This was not possible in the case of the majority, as conviction was based upon admission of being present at the battles."

A few of the accused, such as Cut-Nose, were clearly guilty of heinous crimes, and their verdicts were never in doubt. But for most the charges were of a general nature—that they had been present at the battles of Fort Ridgely, New Ulm, Birch Coulee, or Wood Lake. To the Indians, admitting they were present at a battle was not the equivalent of admitting to a crime. They had surrendered with an expectation of being treated as prisoners of war. They did not understand the proceedings they were caught up in and did not have legal counsel. Most of those sentenced to die, said Riggs, "were condemned on general principles, without any specific charges proved."

Heard recorded that some of the defenses offered by the accused seemed ludicrous to the commissioners. "In at least two thirds of the cases, the prisoners admitted that they fired, but in most instances insisted that it was only two or three shots, and that no one was killed," he said. "A fiery-looking warrior wished the commission to believe that he felt so bad at the fort to see the Indians fire on the whites that he immediately laid down there and went to sleep, and did not awaken until the battle was over! Several of the worst characters, who had been in all the battles, after they had confessed the whole thing, wound up by saying that they were members of the Church!"

The court reporter added: "One young chap, aged about 19, said that he used always to attend divine worship at Little Crow's village below St. Paul, and that he never did a bad thing in his life except to run after a chicken at Mendota a long time ago, and that he didn't catch it. The evidence disclosed the fact that this pious youth had been an active participant in some of the worst massacres on Beaver Creek."

On October 14 Lincoln's cabinet, meeting in the White House, listened to a report on the Sioux uprising sent by General Pope, read aloud by Secretary of War Stanton. Pope made clear his intent to hang a large number of Indians. "I was disgusted with the whole thing," said Secretary of the Navy Gideon Welles. "The tone and opinions of the dispatch are discreditable." In his diary Welles wrote that he had no doubt that the outrages committed by the Sioux were horrible, "but what may have been the provocation we are not told."

Lincoln also was upset by the report that once again underscored Pope's eagerness to start hanging people despite the president's instruction to stand by. He immediately instructed Assistant Secretary of the Interior John Usher to go to Minnesota to make certain Pope did not start the hangings without permission from the White House. Lincoln wrote to Minnesota Senator Henry Rice (another close friend of Bishop Whipple's) asking him to work with Usher to keep things under control. Usher met with Pope and conveyed to him Lincoln's stern reminder of his earlier admonition. On October 17 Pope informed Sibley, "The President directs that no executions be made without his sanction."

It seems likely that without Lincoln's active intervention at this point, the executions would have commenced quickly if only in response to public demand. The newspapers in St. Paul were rabidly anti-Sioux. "I see the press is very much concerned, lest I should prove too tender hearted," Sibley wrote, promising that the number of executions "will be sufficiently great to satisfy the longings of the most blood-thirsty."

With winter coming on, Sibley became concerned that the area would not provide sufficient food for his prisoners or forage for the animals. Altogether, he had thirty-six hundred people—prisoners, Sioux, freed hostages, soldiers, and others in his encampment. Early snows could make the roads impassable and prevent supplies from getting in—creating a potential for serious health problems. He suspended the trials for a few days, and on October 23 he moved almost the entire group to the Lower Agency. This time his movement was not so dilatory, and two days later the trials resumed. "The avenging nemesis had brought the guilty to an appropriate spot," Heard commented, "for it was here the mad saturnalia began."

The pace quickened as the commissioners warmed to their task and responded to urgings from Pope and Sibley to move more quickly. Two hundred seventy-two more cases were tried between October 25 and November 5. In a space of little more than one month, the military tribunal had tried 392 accused prisoners and sentenced 303 of them to hang. Sibley forwarded the names of the accused to Pope in St. Paul, who telegraphed them to President Lincoln and requested instructions

to proceed. Pope sent the names also to Governor Ramsey, with the ad-
dendum, "The Sioux prisoners will be executed unless the President
forbids it, which I am sure he will not do."

Pope's telegram to Washington cost more than four hundred dollars, a substantial sum in those days, probably because the complex Indian names baffled the telegraph operators. For some reason this sum
riled the editors of the New York Times, who suggested it be deducted
from Pope's salary.

"Military justice," said Groucho Marx, "is to justice as military
music is to music." It was abundantly evident to most observers at the
time and since that the perfunctory legal proceedings involved in these
cases did not meet even the most rudimentary standards for capital
crimes. In many instances the convictions were based upon the testimony of a single eyewitness who, given the nature of the fast-moving
traumatic episodes involved and the unfamiliar garb of brightly painted
Sioux warriors, was highly suspect. Much of that testimony was from
other defendants presumably trying to save their own skins. Godfrey
provided testimony against fifty-five of those convicted. Another defendant, Thomas Robertson, acquitted in his own trial, testified against
fifty-five defendants. At least eight other defendants testified as witnesses for the prosecution.

And as noted earlier, the defendants had no defense counsel. (Only
one request for counsel was made, and it was denied.) In the absence of
legal advice, it seems clear few of the defendants had any idea what they
were up against. One half-breed defendant, David Faribault, wrote later
that he did not realize he was on trial for his life but rather involved in a
proceeding to determine if he should be brought to trial. With counsel
it is probable many of the accused would not have readily admitted to
firing shots or presented preposterous excuses.

Case number 388 was typical of the proceedings. One witness said
he saw the prisoner "and he stated to me that he was wounded at the
Fort, and that he there fired one shot." The prisoner was not allowed
to speak in his own defense. He was immediately condemned to death.
The accused in case 389 said he saw nothing "but fired. I fired twice."
That was the sum of the proceeding. "And thereupon the case being
closed, the commission was cleared and proceeded with their finding
and sentence," recorded Heard. The accused was found guilty and sentenced to hang.

It is also reasonable to presume that at least some of the commissioners were prejudiced against the accused, for many of them had fought in the battles against the Sioux. Court member William Marshall, before he was called away to military duty after hearing the first twenty-nine cases, had fought the Sioux at Birch Coulee and later admitted, "My mind was not in a condition to give the men a fair trial." Even Stephen Riggs had doubts about the process. "I have a very high regard for all the gentlemen who composed the military commission," he said in a letter published in a St. Paul newspaper. "I count them among my personal friends. But they were trying Indians; and my sense of right would lead me to give Indians as fair and full a trial as white men. This was the difference between us."

The crucial question was the true status of the accused—whether that of common criminals or belligerents. The Sioux considered themselves warriors engaged in battle, but their opinions did not count. Though there were a few pitched battles between soldiers and warriors, the great majority of the victims were noncombatants—women, children, and unarmed farmers. Minnesota Senator Morton S. Wilkinson likely spoke for most of his constituents in a letter to Lincoln: "These Indians are called by some prisoners of war. There was no war about it. It was wholesale robbery, rape, murder. These Indians were not at war with the murdered victims."

Heard commented: "No one was sentenced to death for the mere robbery of goods, and not to exceed a dozen for mere presence in battle, although the prisoner had gone many miles to it, or on a general raid against the settlements. It was required that it should be proven by the testimony of witnesses, unless the prisoner admitted the fact, that he had fired in the battles, or brought ammunition, or acted as commissary in supplying provisions to the combatants, or committed some separate murder."

NO ONE at the time had much of a fix on where Abraham Lincoln stood with regard to Indian relations in general and the Sioux in particular. It was generally assumed that he, like most frontiersmen of his age, had an abiding disdain for the red man as part of a heritage of three centuries of unremitting warfare punctuated with periods of uneasy coexistence. There were hardly any white families in the western

states who had not lost relatives and friends to the endless Indian con-
flicts, and if one went back two or three generations—probably few in
the entire country. Lincoln's grandfather had been killed by Indians in
1784, making Lincoln's father an orphan at age six, which presumably
was a factor in the family's modest economic circumstances.

Animosity toward the Indians was enshrined in the Declaration of
Independence signed fourscore and six years before. Among the charges
against George III were his alleged efforts "to bring on the inhabitants
of our frontiers, the merciless Indian Savages, whose known rule of warfare, is an undistinguished destruction of all ages, sexes and conditions."

Yet Lincoln seemed to carry no animosity toward Native Americans
beyond a casual assumption, based upon observation, that they were a
Stone-Age people struggling to cope with a more advanced culture that
was sweeping away their world. Lincoln volunteered to serve in the
Black Hawk War but did not see any fighting. He later joked about a
mishap in which he damaged a musket left in his care and some
"bloody struggles" with mosquitoes. There is a story related by Carl
Sandburg of an incident during that time when an elderly Indian wandered in among the soldiers with whom Lincoln was serving. Reportedly some of the rough frontier boys were preparing to make short
work of the old man when Lincoln intervened to stop them. When one
of them accused Lincoln of cowardice, Lincoln invited him to test his
theory. This story has a taste of Parson Weems to it, but Lincoln was a
rough-and-tumble frontier boy who often engaged in pranks and
roughhousing among other young men. And he earned the respect of
the toughest of them, many of whom told admiring stories about him
years later. From what we know of his character, it seems plausible that
something like this actually happened.

As president, Lincoln welcomed the occasional visits from Indian
chiefs in their ceremonial regalia if only for the comic relief from his
burdens of office. It was his custom to assume the role of Great White
Father and offer them advice that Bishop Whipple would have appreciated, that they should learn "the arts of civilization." He instructed one
group of Native American visitors that "the world is a great round
ball," a phrase that strikes contemporary historians as condescending
but probably came as a revelation to the Indians.

In a different visit he attributed the "great difference between this
pale-faced people and their red brethren" to the fact that the white men

were farmers instead of hunters. Here, too, Bishop Whipple and many other missionaries to the Indians would have taken confirmation of their own life's work. On at least one occasion, the president wandered into quicksand when he told some visiting Indians that even though the white people were engaged in a great war with each other, "We are not, as a race, so much disposed to fight and kill one another as our red brethren." It is unlikely the most gullible Indian would have accepted that line at face value and hard to believe Lincoln had invested much thought in it.

It is to Lincoln's credit that he did not feign any specific knowledge of Indian matters. In September, while the Sioux uprising was very much on Lincoln's mind, he was visited by Cherokee Chief John Ross, who was seeking Union aid for his tribe that had fallen under Confederate control. "In the multitude of cares claiming my constant attention," Lincoln said to him candidly, "I have been unable to examine and determine the exact treaty relations between the United States and the Cherokee nation."

As president, Lincoln knew his government had some serious issues related to the Indians beyond using the system to reward political supporters. Whipple had written to him about the rampant corruption in the system and later conveyed the same information to him in person. But Lincoln was preoccupied with the war and had little time to invest in Indian affairs.

REGARDLESS OF how busy he was, the report from John Pope that he intended to hang more than three hundred people grabbed Lincoln's attention away from other matters. On November 10 he sent a telegram to Pope. "Please forward, as soon as possible, the full and complete record of these convictions," ordering the general to include information that might help him determine the most guilty parties. He demanded "a careful statement" from Pope about the results of the trials.

"The only distinction between the culprits is as to which of them murdered most people or violated most young girls," Pope replied testily, warning that the people of Minnesota "are exasperated to the last degree, and if the guilty are not all executed I think it nearly impossible to prevent the indiscriminate massacre of all the Indians—old men, women and children." As if to underscore the threat, Pope intimated that his own soldiers shared the sentiments of the citizens toward the prisoners.

Governor Ramsey chimed in with the same message, possibly after consultation with Pope. "I hope the execution of every Sioux Indian condemned by the military court will be at once ordered," he wrote to Lincoln. "It would be wrong upon principle and policy to refuse this" lest "private revenge would on all this border take the place of official judgement on these Indians."

But Lincoln refused to be stampeded. He summoned George Whiting and Francis Ruggles from the attorney general's office to review the convictions. It became readily apparent to them that the court records were sketchy at best and that few of the convictions could pass muster.

WHILE WHITING and Ruggles reviewed the convictions, Sibley decided to transfer the seventeen hundred remaining Sioux who had not been convicted to Fort Snelling, where it would be simpler for the government to feed them. As the four-mile-long procession passed through the town of Henderson, as if to confirm Pope's dire warning about citizen reprisals, the locals set upon the Sioux with clubs, knives, and stones. One Indian child died of his wounds before the guards could restore order. The others eventually reached Fort Snelling. There they were assembled in a fenced area on the north bank of the Minnesota River and allowed to live in 250 tepees on army rations.

Two days later the 303 condemned Sioux were taken from the Lower Agency toward a stockade named Camp Lincoln on the Minnesota River southwest of Mankato, near a settlement called South Bend that is no longer there. This procession passed through New Ulm and, not surprisingly, received an even rougher reception than the earlier group. Hooting women lined the streets with rocks, pitchforks, bricks, and tubs of scalding water. "The Dutch she-devils were as fierce as tigresses," Sibley wrote to his wife. At least 15 prisoners and some of the guards were injured.

SOON EVERYONE knew the president was holding up the executions, and there followed a spate of aggressive lobbying from interested parties seeking to influence his decision. Sensing his indecision, Pope and Ramsey offered the president a way to duck the issue. "I would suggest that if the govt be unwilling at so great a distance to order the execution of the condemned Indians the criminals be turned to the State Govt to deal with," Pope suggested on November 12.

The newspapers in St. Paul were calling for quick executions of all the convicted Sioux. Dr. Thaddeus Williams wrote Lincoln an impassioned letter, depicting many gruesome scenes of murder, rape, and dismemberment perpetrated by the Sioux during the uprising, speaking of "400 human beings butchered, their entrails torn out & their heads cut off & put between their lifeless thighs, or hoisted on a pole; their bodies gashed & cut to strips, & nailed or hung to trees; mothers with sharp fence rails passed through them & their unborn babes; children with hooks struck through their backs & hung to limbs of trees—these are the shadows which flit in the backgrounds of the picture, and cry, not only for justice, but for vengeance."

The newspaper in Stillwater, Minnesota, as if trying to outdo the St. Paul papers, demanded that the president deal harshly with the Sioux. "We tell you, Abraham Lincoln, that the remaining twenty thousand men of Minnesota will never submit to such ingratitude and wrong. We tell you plainly and soberly, if these convicted murderers are dealt with more leniently than other murderers, the people of the State will take law and vengeance in their own hands, and woe to any member of the hated race that shall be found within our borders."

Even Stephen Riggs, erstwhile friend of the Sioux, weighed in on Lincoln in a November 17 letter. "My long connection with these Indians and personal acquaintance with many of those who are condemned, would naturally lead me to desire that no greater punishment should be inflicted upon them than is required by justice," he wrote. "But knowing the excited state of this part of the country, the indignation which is felt against the whole Indian people in consequence of these murders and outrages, the indignation being often unreasonable and wicked, venting itself upon the innocent as well as the guilty, knowing this I feel that a great necessity is upon us to execute the great majority of those who have been condemned by the Military Commission."

Riggs used his letter to make a special appeal for one of the condemned, Robert Hopkins or Chaskaydon, who "saved Dr. Williamson's family and others. In the testimony of this case a witness states that he heard Robert Hopkins say he had killed one—witness understanding that it was a person while it was only a cow. This testimony was taken and recorded when the prisoner was not before the commission. I hope you will reprieve this man." Lincoln issued the reprieve, but it was to prove ineffective.

Against this drumbeat Lincoln heard a few contrary voices, the most notable being that of Bishop Whipple, who never gave up. He sent a letter to the president via Minnesota Senator Henry M. Rice on November 12: "We cannot hang men by the hundreds. Upon our own premises we have no right to do so. We claim that they are an independent nation & as such they are prisoners of war. The leaders must be punished but we cannot afford by an wanton cruelty to purchase a long Indian war—nor by injustice in other matters purchase the anger of God."

Rice enjoyed a "long interview" with Lincoln in which the Whipple letter was read aloud and led to a discussion of the proposed executions, reform of the Indian system, and—not surprisingly—intrigues among the Minnesota politicians. Rice sent an encouraging report to Whipple, including an assurance that Lincoln was committed to reforms of the Indian system.

Two days later Ramsey sent another telegraph to Lincoln: "Nothing but the speedy execution of the tried and convicted Sioux Indians will save us from scenes of outrage. If you prefer to turn them over to me & I will order their execution." That same day Senator Wilkinson came to the White House with Minnesota Congressman Cyrus Aldrich to seek speedy executions. Lincoln promised to address the subject in his annual report to Congress due December 1. (In those days, the president's annual report to Congress was sent in writing and not delivered as a speech.)

As promised, Lincoln addressed the issue in his report. "The State of Minnesota has suffered great injury from this Indian war," he said, calling upon Congress to consider reforms of the Indian system. But he did not say what he was going to do with the condemned Sioux.

It was a busy week in the Sioux story. The other Minnesota congressman, William Windom, introduced a bill, quickly approved by the Committee on Indian Affairs, to consider ways of removing all Indians from the state. And President Lincoln requested advice from Judge Advocate General Joseph Holt. "I wish your legal opinion," he said, "whether if I should conclude to execute only a part of them, I must myself designate which, or could I leave the designation to some other officer on the ground." Holt replied he had to do it personally.

On December 5 Senator Wilkinson introduced a resolution, subsequently passed, demanding that Lincoln give an accounting of his handling of the Sioux prisoners. He and other Minnesotans kept up the drumbeat for mass executions. Citizens of St. Paul petitioned Lincoln saying they had heard "with fear and alarm reports of an intention on the part of the United States government to dismiss without punishment the Sioux warriors captured by our soldiers. Against any such policy we respectfully but firmly protest."

Governor Ramsey weighed in again with Lincoln. "Our people have had just reason to complain of the tardiness of executive action," he said. Ramsey went further, claiming that an agent from Lincoln, a reference to John Usher, had assured him all the convicted prisoners would be hanged, or words to that effect. "No official intimation has been received that the president contemplates any other course," the governor noted. No doubt Usher made some promises, but there is no evidence to suggest he sought to supplant the president's will with his own.

On December 6 Lincoln began drafting a message to General Pope. It listed 39 Sioux from the total of 303 who were to be hanged.

14

I COULD NOT HANG MEN FOR VOTES

INCOLN PAINSTAKINGLY WROTE OUT on White House stationery the names of the thirty-nine Sioux to be hanged. It was no simple task for many of the convicted Indians shared the same name or similar names. For example, the man Lincoln reprieved at the request of Riggs, Chaskaydon, was confused with Chaska, Chaskay, and Chaskastay. Lincoln deliberately spelled out the consonants by their sound, using dashes to convey pronunciation as best he could, and alongside each name he added the number of the case attached to that particular Indian. He did everything possible to make certain the reprieved were not confused with the guilty. Even so, the officers on the scene had a difficult time sorting out the condemned from the reprieved, and the case numbers did not help much, because after several weeks no one could remember which Indian had which number.

Without question many of those condemned to die were guilty of murder and/or rape. Cut-Nose may not have killed twenty-seven people, as he claimed, but he killed several. Napashue may not have killed the nineteen he claimed, but he had killed enough to hang. Two of his comrades who had accompanied him on his forays, Tehehdonecha and Dowanea, were seen to commit murder and rape. Tazoo was convicted of rape on the testimony of a victim. Hapan confessed to being with the group that killed Francis Patoile and took his family hostage. Mazabomdoo killed an elderly woman and two children. Others were clearly guilty of heinous crimes in various degrees.

It is equally certain that the worst offenders were not among the convicted awaiting execution: Little Crow, Red Middle Voice, Sacred Rattle, Hapan, Walker Among Sacred Stones, Plenty of Hail, White Lodge, Medicine Bottle, White Spider, Shakopee, and the four hunters who started it all—Brown Wing, Killing Ghost, Runs Against Something When Crawling, and Breaking Up. Historian C. M. Oehler estimates that probably one out of twenty, and certainly no more than one in ten, of the murderers and rapists Sibley set out to apprehend were in the snare. The others had fled west, where they would continue their depredations for years to come.

Not everyone involved in the leadership of the uprising was sentenced to die. Big Eagle had led warriors at most of the key battles, but he had not participated in massacres or rapes. He was sent to prison.

While the names of the condemned were on their way to Minnesota, Lincoln was writing an explanation of his action in response to the senate resolution introduced by Senator Wilkinson. In it he recounted the events leading up to the trials, his request for the transcripts, and the many appeals he had received—a few for clemency for the Indians, the vast majority for their speedy execution. "Anxious to not act with so much clemency as to encourage another outbreak, on the one hand, nor with so much severity to be real cruelty, on the other, I caused a careful examination of the records of trials to be made, in view of first ordering the execution of such as had been proved guilty of violating females," he said. "Contrary to my expectations, only two of this class were found. I then directed a further examination, and a classification of all who were proven to have participated in massacres, as distinguished from participation in battles. This class numbered forty, and included the two convicted of female violation. One of the number is strongly recommended, by the commission which tried them, for commutation to ten years' imprisonment. I have ordered the other 39 to be executed on Friday, the 19th instant."

What Lincoln did not explain to the senators was why he chose to intervene in the Sioux proceeding in the first place when he could have easily ignored it or passed responsibility along to state or army officials. It was a risky move politically at a time when Lincoln's political career seemed to be hanging by a thread. He and his party had lost ground in the off-year elections only a few weeks before, and the war was going badly. The overwhelming majority of voters in Minnesota were crying for Indian blood and opposed clemency for any convicted Sioux. Bishop Whipple advocated mercy and reform of the Indian system, but Lincoln was politically astute enough to know that Whipple's position was unpopular in Minnesota (and even Whipple and Riggs conceded that many, if not most, of the convicted Indians should be hanged). Assuming a tight contest when Lincoln sought reelection two years hence—and everyone assumed a tight contest inevitable—the loss of Minnesota could have ended his political career and even been the decisive factor in the irreparable breakup of the Union. His action in the Sioux matter was politically reckless.

Lincoln offered no explanation for his intervention, perhaps because he thought none was necessary. A grave injustice was about to be done against a despised people who had no friends in power to help them. It was clear from the admittedly sparse records of the trials that most of the convicted were marginal players in the drama and that the worst culprits had escaped. Lincoln had the power to extend mercy where mercy was appropriate, and he did.

Some historians have suggested this singular deed was motivated by concern about foreign opinion, but it seems unlikely that thought even crossed Lincoln's mind. He had been concerned that the British might recognize the Confederacy as a belligerent power, but the Emancipation Proclamation blunted that possibility. In any event, it was unlikely the countrymen of Rudyard Kipling would become exercised about aggressive suppression of rambunctious natives.

Lincoln's intervention was not the result of a complex political calculation but rather a simple expression of his character. Though he was, without question, a wily and calculating politician, his defining characteristic was a passionate nature. He might take a roundabout path to reach his goals, but he never wavered from them. Alexander H. Stephens observed that Lincoln's passion for the Union amounted to a "religious mysticism," and Walt Whitman noted, "The only thing like passion or infatuation in the man was the passion for the Union of these states." But even Lincoln's passion for the Union was a human one. It was born of his conviction that the Union was a compact among people, not states, and that only a unified people could together redress the most shameful stain on the nation's soul—slavery.

Lincoln was first and foremost a man of passion: passion for a wife who was more burden than helpmeet; passion for sons dead, dumb, and distant; passion for fellow humans held in bondage; passion to reach out to those most in need of succor. Secretary John Hay noted in his diary: "Today we spent 6 hours deciding on Court Martials, the President, Judge Holt, & I. I was amused at the eagerness with which the President caught at any fact which would justify him in saving the life of a condemned soldier. He was only merciless in cases where meanness or cruelty were shown. Cases of cowardice he was especially averse to punishing with death. He said it would frighten the poor devils too terribly, to shoot them. On the case of a soldier who had once deserted & reenlisted he indorsed, 'Let him fight instead of shooting him.'"

Lincoln's solicitude for society's despised held firm despite a daily regimen that required him to send tends of thousands of men to death—and to issue calls for more volunteers to take their places in the line of fire. Amid the clamor of war he was surely tempted to distance himself from the papers on his desk that represented lives in the balance, taking refuge in the lofty rhetoric of principle and noble purpose. But he never failed to see the people in the papers—whether casualty lists from the battlefield, farm boys condemned for cowardice, or Indians in the shadow of the gallows—and to extend compassion wherever he could find a pretext for its purchase.

Lincoln did not devote much of his oratory or personal communication to exhortations about justice, perhaps recognizing that term's vulnerability to various interpretation. The Minnesotans clamoring for mass executions of Indians were demanding justice. Lincoln's motivation for intervening on behalf of the convicted Sioux was the same that underlay most of the crucial decisions in his extraordinary life—an abiding passion for mercy.

In the election of 1864 Lincoln won reelection and carried Minnesota, albeit by a slim margin. Alexander Ramsey, who by then was in the U.S. Senate, told Lincoln he would have taken more votes if he had hanged more Indians. "I could not hang men for votes," the president replied.

WHILE LINCOLN was going to such great pains for the distant Sioux, he had one ear to the telegraph monitoring events closer to home. The Union army, now under new leadership, was once again squaring off against Lee's legions.

Three days before he wired Pope to hold off on the executions on November 10, Lincoln had fired McClellan for the second and final time, replacing him with Ambrose E. Burnside. Officially, McClellan was told to go home and await orders that never came. To Nicolay, Lincoln explained that as McClellan was "delaying on little pretexts of wanting this and that I began to fear that he was playing false—that he did not want to hurt the enemy." Lincoln said further that if McClellan were to permit Lee to block his advance toward Richmond, he would be removed. "He did so & I removed him."

Predictably, some of McClellan's senior staff muttered dark threats against Lincoln and other senior politicians. To his credit, McClellan passed the baton with dignity. "Stand by General Burnside as you have stood by me, and all will be well," he said amid parting cheers from his loyal troops.

And to his credit, Burnside tried to avoid the assignment. It had been offered to him twice, first after McClellan fell into disfavor after his campaign on the Virginia Peninsula, and again after Second Bull Run, and both times he turned it down. Now he tried to turn it down again, partly out of loyalty to McClellan and partly out of his own well-founded sense that he was not up to the job.

Burnside's undoing was a certain aura of success that he had not quite earned and didn't know how to handle. A West Point graduate, he had served in the Mexican War and been wounded fighting Apaches in 1849 in the New Mexico Territory. Like McClellan, he had won a couple of small engagements early in the war that earned him rave reviews from a public desperate for winners. Like McClellan, he cut an impressive figure. He was handsome and well tailored and noted for a hearty good humor. When he rode before the troops, he wore buckskin gauntlets and a loose pistol holster. He looked like a confident general, and his troops responded to him.

Burnside reluctantly took the job supposedly because it would go to his hated rival Joseph Hooker if he did not. He immediately plunged into his new assignment, investing long hours to the point of exhaustion. He came up with a plan to besiege Fredericksburg, about fifty miles north of Richmond and halfway between Richmond and Washington. The main problem was that, to get to Fredericksburg, Burnside had to get his army across the Rappahannock River, and for that he needed pontoon bridges. He ordered them through Halleck and, because of

Burnside's characteristically confused communications, delivery was eight days late. By the time the boats arrived it was the first week of December. By the time the Army of the Potomac began to move, Lee's Confederates were dug in on the heights overlooking the city and their artillery commanded virtually every conceivable approach.

Burnside had an awesome force of 110,000 men opposed to Lee's 75,000. He also had excellent artillery, well directed and superior to that of the Rebels, on Stafford Heights, which overlooked the scene. And he had a hidden advantage—a gap in the Confederate defensive line of some five hundred to six hundred yards, an area of swampy undergrowth manned by Stonewall Jackson's corps. Jackson apparently did not know about this gap. The local Rebel commanders saw it and had troops positioned around it, but it remained empty, an inviting opportunity for the Federals to crash through the Southern lines and rout their defenses.

Winter came early, and the ground was cold. Lee was willing to spend the winter in hibernation, but Burnside was under pressure from Washington to make things happen. The Federal commander decided a frontal assault would take Lee by surprise. If Lee was surprised, it was only by the rank stupidity of the move. He had Longstreet's corps arrayed along four miles of front on high ground overlooking the town with an excellent vantage point over the open ground the Union troops would have to cross. As one of Longstreet's artillery officers said, "A chicken could not live on that field when we open up on it."

The Union troops began laying their pontoon bridges in the predawn hours of December 11, three in Fredericksburg and three more a few miles downstream. A group of Mississippi sharpshooters contested the work opposite the town but apparently only as a delaying action while Longstreet and Jackson linked up to form a continuous line. After some sharp fighting, Federals routed the sharpshooters and crossed the river. They spent the next day trashing Fredericksburg. Historian Douglas Southall Freeman recorded the scene: "Splendid alabaster vases and pieces of statuary were thrown at 6 and 700 dollar mirrors. Closets of the finest china were broken into and their contents smashed onto the floor and stamped into pieces . . . rosewood pianos piled in the street and burned, or soldiers would get on top of them and kick the keyboard and internal machinery all to pieces . . . wine cellars broken into and the soldiers drinking all they could and then opening the faucets and let the rest run out. . . . Libraries worth thousands of dollars . . . thrown on the floor and in the streets." If Burnside knew about this, he did nothing to deter it.

For many of the Federals it was their last hoorah. That night Union troops surveyed the scene before them, the open ground leading up to the entrenched Rebels on the high ground, and had an idea of what was to come. Hundreds of them wrote their names on pieces of paper and pinned them to the back of their uniforms so their bodies could be identified later. The next morning the Federal artillery opened up on the section where the gap remained, whether by chance or discovery is not known. The Southern artillery did not answer because it could not match the range of the Union guns. Just after lunch the Federal columns began to move, a vast phalanx of disciplined men moving like a giant beast to grapple with its foe. When the first ranks came within about eight hundred yards of the Rebel lines, the Southern artillery opened up, cutting huge swaths in their lines. Other Federals filled the gaps and kept on coming. When they were within rifle range, the battle began in earnest.

The Union troops forced their way through the southern gap in the Confederate line and for a brief moment stared at an opportunity such as they rarely encountered. "Through the gap," records Freeman, "the enemy could now pour thousands of men." Of course, nothing of the sort happened. Confederate officers in the area rallied their men to meet the threat. The Union command did nothing to exploit the opportunity. The Rebels counterattacked, and the Yankees withdrew.

Just before noon, while the action on the gap was beginning to sputter out, Burnside launched his main attack on the center of Lee's line. In response to the attack order, Union troops ran through the cluttered streets of Fredericksburg and into the open ground below the Rebel positions. Federal artillery provided support as the advance picked up momentum. A line of Federal soldiers kicked down a board fence "as if it were paper" and double-timed toward the enemy who lay waiting, rifles loaded and ready. When the Union troops came into range, the Southerners opened up with canister fire—hundreds of small lead shot fired from cannons—that cut huge swaths through the Federal lines. The first charge broke, but soon another took its place with the same results. Soon the entire plain was covered with the dead and dying, freezing in the winter cold while their comrades charged forward to take their turn in the dance of death. The carnage was shocking even to men who had become accustomed to it. "Oh great God," cried Union Gen. Darius Couch, "see how our men, our poor fellows, are falling."

And still they came. It was by all accounts one of the bravest and most heartbreaking efforts ever rendered by a U.S. military force. At one point, despite his advantage, Lee thought his lines might be over-run by the sheer doggedness of the attacking troops. He called up rein-forcements, giving him a solid phalanx of infantry standing four deep and pouring fire into the advancing Federals. "Never," said Douglas Freeman, "had Lee presented so many muskets on so narrow a front."

Lee himself perhaps offered the most memorable if enigmatic com-ment about the spectacle taking place before his eyes. "It is well that war is so terrible," he said, "else we should become too fond of it."

The Federals never had a chance, but they kept coming, as if every-one in command were dumbfounded and unable to halt it. When they finally withdrew, they left thousands of dead and wounded men on the sloping ground. Through it all, Burnside watched helplessly as if he, the commander, were an innocent bystander unable to influence events. He was clearly moved by the bloodletting. "Oh those men, those men over there," he said. "I cannot get them out of my mind."

The Union army officially recorded 12,653 casualties at Freder-icksburg, including 9,600 wounded, many of whom died later. The Confederates recorded 595 killed, 4,061 wounded and another 653 missing. Few battles in the Civil War, or any war, have been so one-sided. "It was the worst defeat in the history of the American army," commented historian David Herbert Donald.

Lincoln had fretted throughout the day of December 13 for news of the battle, and when it was brought to him by a journalist who came directly from the scene, he said, "I hope it is not as bad as all that."

But it *was* as bad as all that. And public reaction was severe. The *Chicago Tribune*, citing the failures of the army, weight of taxes, closure of the Mississippi River, lack of cotton, and mounting national debt, lamented, "The war is drawing toward a disastrous and disgraceful ter-mination." Senator Wilkinson, smarting over Lincoln's reprieves of the Sioux, saw no hope for the country "except in the death of the Presi-dent and a new administration."

The battle of Fredericksburg precipitated the worst crisis of Lin-coln's presidency. An influential group of senators, secretly encouraged by Treasury Secretary Chase, concluded that Lincoln was getting bad advice from Secretary of State Seward, and this was the cause of so many battlefield reverses. Without question, Lincoln's cabinet was an abrasive lot who got on each other's nerves, but their differences were more personal than political or philosophical. When Seward learned the Senate had voted to censure him, he tendered his resignation to Lincoln. When it became clear that the senators' opposition to Seward stemmed, at least in part, from Chase's influence, the treasury secretary also submitted his resignation. Coming on the heels of the Fredericksburg disaster and amid the clamor of criticism about his reprieves for the Sioux, Lincoln slipped into depression. "We are on the brink of destruction," he said to his friend Illinois senator Orville Browning. "It appears to me the Almighty is against us, and I can hardly see a ray of hope."

But Lincoln was never more resilient than when his back was to the wall. He managed his testy cabinet and rebellious senators like a maestro would conduct an unruly orchestra. He deftly contrived to have the cabinet and senators come together one evening, quite to each other's surprise, for a showdown in the White House. There he invited them to openly express their disregard for each other and their dissatisfaction for his administration. None of the agitators had sufficient heart to continue the squabble in that setting. The senators pulled in their horns and returned to the Hill, no doubt muttering beneath their breath. Lincoln refused to accept the resignations of Seward and Chase. As he said later to Senator Ira Harris of New York, using a country expression to describe his political balancing act, "I can ride now. I've got a pumpkin in each end of my bag."

WHILE LINCOLN was managing his cabinet crisis, he received a message from Pope in Minnesota conveying a request from Sibley for a week's delay in the executions of the Sioux. He needed more time to make preparations, particularly to construct a scaffold large enough to handle thirty-nine men and also to assure security. He was concerned the occasion might evoke public demonstrations by thousands of Minnesotans eager to see the culprits pay for their crimes.

His concern was not baseless. On December 4 a mob of drunks from Mankato had attempted to storm the stockade to kill the prisoners. The guards had managed to dissuade them without anyone being killed, but there was a potential for disorder. Lincoln delayed the executions until December 26.

It fell to Stephen Riggs to inform the prisoners of the president's decision. The missionary entered the enclosure where the convicted men sat or stood leaning against the walls. He was well acquainted with many of them and had provided the intelligence that put many of them there. "I have known you for many years," he intoned. "I have pointed you to the cross and prayerfully endeavored to convince you allegiance to God and the Great Father in Washington was your duty. With a broken heart, I have witnessed your cruelty to inoffensive men, women and children; cruelty to your best friends. You have stained your hands in innocent blood, and now the law holds you to strict accountability. It pains me to inform you that your Great Father in Washington says you must die for your cruelty and murders, and I am directed to inform you that some of you will be hanged by the neck until you are dead."

Riggs read out the names carefully, stressing the key consonants that defined who would live and who would die. There was no reaction from the Sioux, either of anger or relief. Riggs folded the letter and put it back into his pocket, looking around the room. "May God have mercy on your souls," he said.

It fell to Joseph Brown, a guard who knew the Sioux well, to separate the condemned from the spared. It was to prove a daunting challenge, and in the end the job was imperfectly done. Those selected to die were taken from the larger group and housed in a stone building to await their fate. As the impact of the message began to sink in over the following days, some of those condemned to die spoke out. Several insisted they had been convicted unfairly or were prisoners of war. Wahehna said he had not killed anyone and no one had claimed to see him do so. Had he thought he might be sentenced to hang, he said, he would have fled with Little Crow.

White Dog, the handsome Sioux who had called out to Marsh's men at Redwood Ferry, insisted it was all a big mistake, that he was trying to warn the soldiers away, though the survivors of that fight thought differently. No one claimed to have seen White Dog participate in any massacre or rape, but he would hang.

No crimes against settlers or rapes of women were charged against Rdainyanka, the one who had spoken so eloquently that they would all die anyway so they might as well take as many whites with them as they could. Rdainyanka's eloquence did not fail him when he learned of his death sentence. "You have deceived me," he wrote to his father-in-law while awaiting execution. "You told me if we gave ourselves up to the whites, all would be well. I have not killed or injured any white person, and yet today I am set apart for execution and must die in a few days, while men who are guilty will remain in prison. When my children are grown up, let them know their father died without having the blood of a white man to answer for to the Great Spirit. My wife and children are dear to me. Let them not grieve for me. Let them remember the brave should be prepared to meet death. I will do as becomes a Dakota."

As soon as they were housed in the stone building, the condemned began the traditional death chant, an eerie dirge that upset the guards who feared a breakout attempt. They doubled the guard and put the prisoners in chains. On Wednesday night, Christmas Eve, those with family held elsewhere in the stockade were permitted visits. They passed along trinkets or other personal possessions to their relatives. On Christmas Day, Riggs was there to provide comfort, along with a Catholic priest, Father Augustin Ravoux, because at least one of the condemned was Catholic. Word came from Washington that President Lincoln had reprieved one more prisoner, Tatemina, upon appeal of settlers who said he had helped them.

The next morning dawned clear and unseasonably warm. Shortly after nine o'clock, after the captives had eaten their final breakfast, the guards came and put white muslin caps on each one. Each man's hands were tightly bound in front of him, and then his manacles were removed. The provost marshal announced that the time had come, whereupon the muslin caps were pulled down over their faces. Many of them objected to this treatment, but there was nothing they could do about it. They stumbled as they were forced into line and blindly moved toward the huge square scaffold the soldiers had erected beside the river. "The gallows were in a circular shape scaffold," recorded Jacob Nix, the German American who helped organize the defense of New Ulm and who came to see the executions. "The platform, on which the condemned prisoners stood fairly close to each other, was held in place by a long rope."

They marched through the lines of fourteen hundred soldiers who surrounded the scaffold to make certain the proceedings were not disrupted and to bear witness to the retribution. Inside the stockade other prisoners crowded to observe the proceeding. The provost marshal led the prisoners up on the scaffold, where soldiers stood them over the drops and placed nooses around their necks. The condemned men began again their death chant, swaying back and forth and stomping their feet. The scaffold began to shudder from the movement. They called out each other's names and tried to link hands. The soldiers descended from the scaffold as a drum beat slowly. On the third beat, a young man came forward with a knife or hatchet in his hand. He was William J. Duley, the killer of Lean Bear at Slaughter Slough and the father of two victims. At a signal from the provost marshal, he cut the rope that opened all thirty-eight trapdoors simultaneously. The Sioux fell together, their legs kicking wildly.

"As the platform fell, there was one, not loud, but prolonged cheer from the soldiery and citizens," recorded one eyewitness. "And then all were quiet and earnest." Nix, who was unapologetic about his contempt for the Sioux, whom he described as "a predator of the blood-thirstiest and most cruel type," was nonetheless impressed by their composure. "I must admit they faced death courageously," he said.

One of the ropes broke. Rdainyanka fell to the ground motionless, his neck broken. He made no sound or movement when he was carried back up on the scaffold and hanged a second time.

The bodies were cut down, examined to ascertain death, and taken to a mass grave near the river where they were interred. Later that night doctors from local towns disinterred the remains on the pretext that rising river water might flood the common grave. The record is not clear what they did with them. Only the fate of Cut-Nose is known. Dr. William Mayo took his body, cleaned and articulated the skeleton, and used it for teaching. Years later, when his famous sons developed an interest in medicine, they studied the bones of Cut-Nose.

EPILOGUE
APPENDIX
BIBLIOGRAPHICAL NOTE
INDEX

EPILOGUE

THE SIOUX UPRISING OF 1862 was the bloodiest massacre in the three-century-long history of white-Indian conflict in North America.* The actual death toll is unknown. The countryside was populated with immigrants from other states and Europe who had not put down roots and whose names were not yet recorded anywhere. Many of them did not speak or write English. Hastily organized burial details disposed of victims over a period of several weeks, leaving chaotic records of their work or, in some cases, none at all. As thousands of people were fleeing in panic through wilderness areas, under random assault, it is safe to assume many bodies were never found. "It is our impression that nearer two thousand than one thousand have been massacred," said the *St. Peter Tribune* six weeks later. "Doubtless hundreds that have been slain and left upon the surface will never be found, as decomposition is nearly complete, and the prairie fires now ravaging the whole upper country will consume what may yet remain."

Senator Wilkinson informed Lincoln that the death toll was "nearly or quite one thousand." The pioneer editor Jane Grey Swisshelm said later that 1,500 lives were lost. Indian agent Thomas Galbraith attempted a tally and came up with 644 civilians and 93 soldiers, putting the overall total at 737. "More there may be," he said, "and I think they are." Abraham Lincoln put the total at 800, and that is probably a fair estimate.

The hanging of thirty-eight Sioux on December 26, though substantially fewer than was intended, was still the largest public execution in the history of North America. And it seems highly probable, despite a tasteful lack of specific numbers, that this Indian uprising also occasioned the largest and most prolonged gang rape in the country's history. Though contemporary historians displayed a

---

*The destruction of the American army under Gen. Arthur St. Clair in the Ohio Territory in 1791 at the hands of the Miamis and Shawnees, in which perhaps seven hundred people, mostly combatants, were slain, was a battle between warriors and soldiers, not a massacre of defenseless farm families.

conspicuous reticence to examine this topic in detail, the record suggests that several dozen white women were raped repeatedly over a period of more than six weeks.

Perhaps even more significant, the Sioux uprising of 1862 sounded the first shots of a great Sioux war that would continue for twenty-eight years, culminating in the massacre of Indian women and children at Wounded Knee in 1890. The Minnesota Sioux were the easternmost branch of the Sioux nation, which up until then had had minimal exposure to white people. The Sioux warriors who fled west carried with them stories of the white man's perfidy—helping poison relations, sow distrust, and foment more violence. The destruction of George Armstrong Custer and 208 soldiers at Little Big Horn in 1876 was a joint operation of the Sioux and Cheyenne. At least one Sioux veteran of the 1862 uprising participated in that fight, and there were probably others.

Fleeing the scene, Little Crow led his wives and children westward and then north into Canada, trying to rally other Sioux bands as well as other tribes to his war with the settlers. He was heard respectfully in many tribal campfires, but none responded to his call to arms. He appealed to the British in Canada for help without success.

In the weeks after the executions, additional acts of random violence of Indians against white pioneers were reported along the frontier. At least thirty more settlers were butchered in the spring while John Pope was raising an army to pursue the Sioux who had escaped. Little Crow decided he needed horses to take his extended family farther west to escape Pope's army. The following year, he returned with one of his sons to Minnesota, and while there, attempting to steal horses, was killed by a trigger-happy farmer who, like most of the settlers by that time, was paranoid about Indians.

Seeking to avoid Pope's army, Red Middle Voice and his group set out for Canada but encountered a group of their traditional enemies, the Chippewas, along the way. Fighting broke out, and Red Middle Voice was killed.

Several other participants in the Minnesota uprising found sanctuary in western Canada. Plenty of Hail lived into the twentieth century there. Shakopee and Medicine Bottle hid out in Canada for a while but were turned over to Federal authorities in 1864 for a reward offered for their capture. They were returned to Fort Snelling and hanged there in November 1865. Little evidence was introduced against them. "We do not think serious injustice will be done by the execution," said the editors of the *St. Paul Pioneer* the day before the execution, "but it would be more credible if some tangible evidence of guilt had been obtained."

Godfrey (Otakle) was released three years into his ten-year sentence and moved with other Sioux to the Nebraska Territory. There he farmed industriously until his death in 1909.

Most of the Sioux left in prison stayed there for a long time. By April 1864 at least sixty-seven of them had died, more than perished on the gallows. On April 26 Lincoln issued pardons for twenty-five men, and in October ordered the release of Big Eagle. For some reason, his order was not obeyed. Four weeks later he repeated it. "Let the Indian Big Eagle be discharged. I ordered this some time ago." Big Eagle was one of the few Sioux warriors to return to Minnesota. He lived another forty years on a farm near Granite Falls. Most of the Sioux still imprisoned were later pardoned by President Andrew Johnson and transported out of the state to the West.

In February 1863 Congress set up a commission to consider damage claims from Minnesota, and by March the Interior Department reported it had paid out $1,370,374 to claimants. Not surprisingly, traders and merchants received the lion's share.

Lincoln did not live long enough to honor his pledge to reform the Indian system, but President Ulysses S. Grant took up the cause when he became president in 1869, along with a determination to defend the freed slaves from repression. The latter did not endear Grant to a generation of Southern historians who have painted his administration with a dark brush of venality. But Grant did what he could to clean up the Indian system, at one point turning over control of the program to Quakers and professional army soldiers under the pretext that at least they would not steal the Indians' money. Several senior army officers who had fought under Grant's command in the Civil War later displayed a marked consideration of the Indians. For example, Benjamin Grierson, who had led cavalry under Grant during the war, worked closely with Lawrie Tatum, a Quaker agent, to improve the lot of the Kiowas and Comanches and protect them from abuse. Whenever the Indians' food ran out, Grierson ignored regulations and fed them from army rations. Perhaps the most humanitarian of the generals was George Crook, a noted Indian fighter who nonetheless championed the rights of red men. "The American Indian is the intellectual peer of most, if not all, the various nationalities we have assimilated," Crook observed. "He is fully able to protect himself, if the ballot be given and the courts are not closed to him."

Even John Pope, who did a superb job of defending freedmen in the South after the war, earned a reputation for solicitude for the Plains Indians, though he never repented his hard attitude toward the Minnesota Sioux. He commanded the Department of the Missouri from 1870 to 1883, and though he led several campaigns against the Plains Indians, he tried to avoid conflict and zealously suppressed the rapacious whites who sought to defraud them. Pope believed the western Indians were different from the eastern tribes, and contended they had a natural affinity for raising livestock. He spent army funds, probably illegally, to buy cattle for the Indians who proved adept at raising livestock.

George B. McClellan never returned to active duty. He was the Democratic candidate for president in 1864 but was hampered by the party's platform, which called the war a failure and demanded peace, even if it meant the continuation of slavery. He refused to adopt that plank and resolutely called for victory. He carried only three states and resigned from the army on Election Day. He later served as governor of New Jersey in the 1870s and 1880s.

Ambrose E. Burnside was relieved of command of the Army of the Potomac not long after Fredericksburg and placed in command of the Military District of Ohio. There Burnside earned Lincoln more headaches by trying to suppress dissidents in his infamous General Orders Number 38 that essentially banned free speech. He had his agents arrest Clement Vallandigham, a notorious copperhead who openly advocated a peace platform. The event stirred up a ruckus, and Lincoln felt obliged to intervene and commute Vallandigham's sentence to banishment "within the limits of the Confederacy." But Southerners did not want Vallandigham either. Apparently he was something of a dissolute character, and they banished him to Canada. He eventually found his way back to Ohio and dropped out of sight.

By 1864 Burnside was commanding a corps under Grant at the siege of Petersburg. It fell to him to manage a grand plan to tunnel beneath the Rebel positions and blow them up with gunpowder, creating a hole in their lines to enable Union troops to pour through and presumably put Lee's army to rout. The explosion worked as planned, but there had been little thought about informing the troops about how to take advantage of the situation. They poured into rather than around the crater while the Southerners recovered from their shock and mounted a counterattack. From the Union point of view it was a fiasco, as the Federals lost four thousand men to the Rebels' one thousand. "The saddest affair I have witnessed in the war," commented Grant. Lincoln was even more sardonic. "Only Burnside could have managed such a coup," he said, "to wrest one last defeat from the jaws of victory."

None of Burnside's conspicuous failures seemed to diminish his standing with the public. After the war he occupied prominent positions in business and was elected governor of Rhode Island to three two-year terms. In 1874 he was elected senator from that state and held that office until his death in 1881.

On March 23, 1863, Sarah Wakefield wrote a letter to Lincoln lamenting the wrongful execution of Chaskaydon "who saved me and my little family." He was, she said, "executed in place of the guilty man." The intended convict of a similar name had murdered a pregnant woman and cut her baby from her corpse. Despite Lincoln's best efforts, it is clear in this case that the wrong man was executed. Wakefield quoted Stephen Riggs as saying "there was no testimony against the man of any kind" and that Riggs considered it "a horrible affair." She added a P.S.: "It would be gratifying to me to have this guilty man executed although I am in favor of the majority of the poor fellows being pardoned. I can not deem them guilty as many persons, as they were so very kind and honorable to me while I was with them."

In June 1919 Edward Gleek, living near New Ulm, cut down a large white oak tree that broke in two as it fell. Inside he found the mummified corpse of, according to his journal, Jean La Rue. When the first soldiers arrived in New Ulm in 1862, they had fired their rifles in an apparent act of exuberance that terrified many residents who feared it was a Sioux attack. La Rue grabbed his rifle and other belongings and ran to a hollow tree to hide. Apparently he got wedged in, was unable to extricate himself, and his cries for help went unheard. With his body were found his rifle, bullet pouch, powder horn, and $783.50, a not inconsiderable sum in those days. He had written: "Can not get out; surely must die. If ever found, send me and all my money to my mother, Suzanne La Rue, near Tarascon, in the province of Bouches Du Phone, France." Efforts to contact his family were futile.

APPENDIX

In the collection of the Minnesota Historical Society are the papers of Edward D. Neill and his family that document his work as a Presbyterian missionary and minister, state superintendent of education and chancellor of the University of Minnesota (1858–61), wartime chaplain of the First Minnesota Infantry, private secretary to Abraham Lincoln and Andrew Johnson (1864–66), American consul at Dublin, Ireland (1869–71), and president of and professor at Macalester College (1873–93). In this collection are documents from the Lincoln administration relating to the execution of the Indians convicted in the aftermath of the Sioux uprising (the Dakota Conflict) of 1862, including the president's December 6, 1862, letter ordering by name the execution of thirty-nine Indians, thirty-eight of whom were hanged at Mankato on December 26, 1862. The text of which follows.

Executive Mansion

Washington, December 6, 1862

General H. H. Sibley
   St. Paul
      Minnesota

Ordered that of the Indians and Half-breeds sentenced to be hanged by the military commission, composed of Colonel Crooks, Lt. Colonel Marshall, Captain Grant, Captain Bailey, and Lieutenant Olin, and lately sitting in Minnesota, you cause to be executed on Friday the nineteenth day of December, instant, the following names, to wit

"Te-he-hdo-ne-cha"	No. 2 by the record
"Tazon" alias "Plan-doo-ta"	No. 4 by the record
"Wy-a-teh-to-wah"	No. 5 by the record
"Hiw-han-shoow-ko-yaz"	No. 6 by the record
"Mwz-za-bonv-a-dis"	No. 10 by the record
"Wah-pey-du-ta"	No. 11 by the record
"Wa-he-hud"	No. 12 by the record
"Snas-ma-ni"	No. 14 by the record

"Ta-te-mi-na"	No. 15 by the record
"Rda-in-yaw-kna"	No. 19 by the record
"Do-waw-sa"	No. 22 by the record
"Ha-pen"	No. 24 by the record
"Shoos-ka-ska" (White Dog)	No. 35 by the record
"Toow-kew-e-cheh-tey-mano"	No. 67 by the record
"E-tay-hoo-tay"	No. 68 by the record
"Am-da-cha"	No. 69 by the record
"Hay-pee-dow or, Wamme-omau-ha-tas"	
	No. 70 by the record
"Mehpo-o-ko-na-ji"	No. 96 by the record
"Henry Miloroo" a Half-breed	No. 115 by the record
"Cheskay-dow" or "Cheskey-etay	No. 121 by the record
"Baptists Camplotes" a Half-breed	No. 138 by the record
"Tah-ta-kay-gey"	No. 155 by the record
"Ha-pinha-pa"	No. 170 by the record
"Hypolite Ango" a Half-breed	No. 175 by the record
"Na-pay-Shue"	No. 178 by the record
"Wa-kaw-taw-ka"	No. 210 by the record
"Toow-kaw-ka-yag-e-na-jiw"	No. 225 by the record
"Ma-kat-e-na-jiw"	No. 254 by the record
"Pa-zee-koo-tay-ma-na"	No. 264 by the record
"Ta-tey-hdo-dow"	No. 279 by the record
"Wa-She-choow" or "Toow-kaw-shkan-shkan-mano-hay"	
	No. 318 by the record
"A-e-cha-ga"	No. 327 by the record
"Ha-taw-iw-koo"	No. 333 by the record
"Chay-tow-hoow-ka"	No. 342 by the record
"Chew-ka-hda"	No. 359 by the record
"Hda-hiw-hday"	No. 373 by the record
"O-ya-tay-a-koo"	No. 377 by the record
"Maz-hoo-way-wa"	No. 382 by the record
"Wo-kew-yaw-na"	No. 383 by the record

The other condemned prisoners you will hold subject to further orders, taking care that they neither escape, nor are subjected to any unlawful violence.

Abraham Lincoln,
President of the United States

BIBLIOGRAPHICAL NOTE

OST OF THE INFORMATION related herein is derived from existing works about the Civil War, the political career of Abraham Lincoln, and the 1862 Sioux uprising. I have also made ample use of the substantial cache of Lincoln papers in the Library of Congress and a variety of other sources available online, many of them from organizations devoted to Native American history. The purpose of this work is not to break new ground in terms of scholarship—I have unearthed no obscure documents or missing facts—but rather to tell the story of the Sioux uprising not as a discrete event but rather as part of the mosaic of the Civil War. My purpose is to gain insight into the extraordinary pressures visited upon Abraham Lincoln as he attempted to grapple with the events in Minnesota and to put them into perspective. A secondary purpose is to make more readers aware of the Sioux uprising, which was a pivotal event in the history of North America but has been largely overlooked. To the extent that this work challenges existing historical treatment of Lincoln, it is my assertion that the Sioux uprising of 1862 was far from an irrelevant sideshow but rather a major issue for Lincoln and his cabinet during a time when they were wrestling with a series of crises that threatened the survival of the nation. I believe also that it was, as one of my sources contends, the pivotal event that provoked Lincoln to begin drafting black men into military service, a decision that had far-reaching repercussions. To the given facts that it was the bloodiest Indian massacre in our history and led to the largest execution, I add also my conjecture that it was the occasion of the largest and most prolonged gang rape in our history.

As stated earlier, my inspiration for this work was drawn from David Herbert Donald's magnificent *Lincoln*, and I also have drawn liberally on parts of that fine book in pursuit of understanding the events of August–December 1862. For the intricate details of the Sioux uprising I am indebted in equal measure to *The Great Sioux Uprising* by C. M. Oehler and *The Sioux Uprising of 1862* by Kenneth Carley—both of which directed me to a variety of primary sources that I have sought out for further explication of these tumultuous events. I obtained much useful information from Phillips Endecott Osgood's *Straight Tongue: A Story of Henry Benjamin Whipple, First Episcopal Bishop of Minnesota*. Osgood contends that it was Whipple's influence that led Lincoln to intervene in the Sioux matter and reduce the number of men sentenced to death, and I have no doubt, as this book makes clear, that Whipple's counsel weighed heavily in the president's mind.

I must apologize to the reader for one bit of confusion regarding Bishop Whipple's visit with Abraham Lincoln. David Nichols, author of *Lincoln and the Indians,* reports the meeting occurred in September. Osgood says it was in October. An original note in the Library of Congress from Gen. Henry W. Halleck to Lincoln introducing Whipple is unfortunately undated. (A Library of Congress scholar has added a note suggesting it was written in December, but that is almost certainly wrong.) In his memoirs, written many years after the fact, Whipple says only that he met with Lincoln in the autumn. I have weighed the evidence and accepted Osgood's interpretation. I think it would have been premature for Whipple to visit Lincoln in September to urge clemency for the Sioux when the uprising was still under way and no one in Washington yet knew its extent. From other sources I deduce Whipple was in Washington that month at the behest of Governor Alexander Ramsey to seek more military aid to suppress the uprising.

For accounts of the Civil War battles, I have relied primarily upon *The West Point Atlas of American Wars, Volume I, 1869–1900,* edited by Brig. Gen. Vincent J. Esposito. But I have also used information and insights from James McPherson's *Battle Cry of Freedom,* Stephen Sears's *Landscape Turned Red,* and Charles Fair's *From the Jaws of Victory.*

In varying degrees I also have relied upon the following:

Anderson, Gary, and Alan R. Woolworth. *Through Dakota Eyes: Narrative Accounts of the Minnesota Indian War of 1862.* St. Paul: Minnesota Historical Society, 1988.

Berlin, Ira. *Generations of Captivity: A History of African-American Slaves.* Cambridge, MA: Harvard University Press, 2004.

Bishop, Chris, and Ian Drury. *1400 Days: The Civil War Day by Day.* New York: Gallery Books, 1990.

Carley, Kenneth. *The Sioux Uprising of 1862.* St. Paul: Minnesota Historical Society, 1976.

Davis, David Brion. *Challenging the Boundaries of Slavery*. Cambridge, MA: Harvard University Press, 2004.

Donald, David Herbert. *Lincoln*. New York: Simon & Schuster, 1995.

———. *We Are Lincoln Men*. New York: Simon & Schuster, 2003.

Dubin, Michael J. *U.S. Congressional Elections, 1788–1997: The Official Results*. Jefferson, NC: McFarland, 1998.

Fair, Charles. *From the Jaws of Victory*. New York: Simon & Schuster, 1971.

Esposito, Vincent J. *The West Point Atlas of American Wars*. New York: Praeger, 1959.

Heard, Isaac V. D. *History of the Sioux War & Massacres of 1862 and 1863*. New York: Harper & Brothers, 1863.

Jordan, Robert Paul. *The Civil War*. Washington DC: National Geographical Society, 1969.

Keenan, Jerry. *The Great Sioux Uprising: Rebellion on the Plains, August–September 1862*. New York: Da Capo Press, 2003.

McPherson, James M. *Battle Cry of Freedom: The Civil War Era*. New York: Oxford University Press, 1988.

Nichols, David A. *Lincoln & the Indians: Civil War Policy & Politics*. Urbana: University of Illinois Press, 2000.

Nicolay, John G., and John Hay. *Abraham Lincoln: A History*. New York: Century, 1917.

Oehler, Chester M. *The Great Sioux Uprising*. 1959. Reprint, New York: Da Capo Press, 1997.

Osgood, Phillips Endecott. *Straight Tongue: A Story of Henry Benjamin Whipple, First Episcopal Bishop of Minnesota*. Minneapolis: T. S. Denison & Company, 1958.

Nix, Jacob. *The Sioux Uprising in Minnesota, 1862: Jacob Nix's Eyewitness History*. Bloomington: Indiana University Press, 1994.

Schultz, Duane. *Over the Earth I Come: The Great Sioux Uprising of 1862*. New York: St. Martin's Press, 1993.

Schurz, Carl. *Abraham Lincoln: A Biographical Essay*. Boston: Houghton & Mifflin, 1907.

Sears, Stephen W. *Landscape Turned Red: The Battle of Antietam*. New York: Warner Books, 1983.

Smith, Jean Edward. *Grant*. New York: Simon & Schuster, 2001.

Tinker, George E. *Missionary Conquest: The Gospel and Native American Cultural Genocide*. Minneapolis: Fortress Press, 1993.

Vidal, Gore. *Lincoln*. Random House, New York, 1984.

Whipple, Henry Benjamin. *Lights & Shadows of a Long Episcopate*. New York: Macmillan, 1902.

Wills, Gary. *Lincoln at Gettysburg: The Words That Remade America*. New York: Simon & Schuster, 1992.

INDEX

Printed in the USA
CPSIA information can be obtained
at www.ICGtesting.com
LVHW091723311023
762686LV00002B/262